Dick Feagler

Is it just me?

Other books by Dick Feagler

Feagler's Cleveland

"Did You Read Feagler Today?"

I know I'm not supposed to say this . . .
But I'll say it anyway

Dick Feagler
Is it just me?

More of the Best Commentary from
Cleveland's Most Outspoken Columnist

Richard Osborne, editor

GRAY & COMPANY, PUBLISHERS
CLEVELAND

Gray & Company, Publishers
1588 E. 40th St.
Cleveland, Ohio 44113-2302
www.grayco.com

Library of Congress Cataloging-in-Publication Data

Feagler, Dick, 1938–
Is it just me? / Dick Feagler ; Richard J. Osborne, editor.
p. cm.
A collection of Plain Dealer (Cleveland) columns by journalist Dick Feagler, written immediately after Sept. 11, 2001, through July 2005.
ISBN 1-886228-97-3 (hardcover)
ISBN 1-886228-98-1 (softcover)
1. Cleveland (Ohio)—Anecdotes. 2. United States—Social conditions—1980—Anecdotes. 3. September 11 Terrorist Attacks, 2001—Anecdotes. 4. War on Terrorism, 2001—Anecdotes.
I. Osborne, Richard J. II. Title.
F499.C65F44 2005
977.1'32—dc22   2005022435

ISBN 1-886228-97-3 hc
ISBN 1-886228-98-1 sc

Printed in the United States of America
First Printing

For Richard Osborne,
for his talent and friendship.

Contents

REQUIEM

Preface

This is my fourth collection of newspaper columns, and it may be my last. I'm 67, but I don't say this in the somber tones of someone preparing to meet his maker. I'm in no hurry to meet my maker, and I assume He's in no hurry to meet me.

But the odometer on these columns has run pretty high. I've been writing newspaper columns for 35 years. Three columns each week for most of those years. You do the math; I can't face it. 5460

Somewhere, in one of the first three books, I described a columnist this way: He writes opinions nobody has asked to hear, under a picture of himself nobody has asked to see.

What kind of strange egomaniac would presume to do such a thing? For six months, let alone 35 years?

Well, we columnists are strange egomaniacs all right. On the one hand, we bluff ourselves through a column of type pretending we have the answers to all the world's problems at our fingertips.

But silently, inside ourselves, we are cringing, paranoid jellyfish, hoping that the world won't catch on to how little we know or how inept we are at what we do. And what about the things we think? Is it just us? Or are we simply stating the obvious?

I never knew a columnist worth his salt who didn't go through this kind of schizophrenia. And, after more than three decades of it, sanity whispers or bellows it's time to hang it up.

I was thinking that way a year ago when two things resuscitated me. The first was the war in Iraq. The second was the war against gays.

The war in Iraq incensed me. Having covered (and visited) Vietnam, it seemed like another example of Washington suits blundering into a conflict they were too dopey to have planned for and had no idea of a goal or a way out.

I had written about such a war once before as a young man. I was sure we had learned a lesson. But we hadn't. So I kept writing because I thought the bloody tuition we had paid in the sixties must be remembered.

And then there was the gay-rights issue. The same hard-shelled crabs who sent us to this war refused civil rights to gay people who asked only to be let alone to lovingly share each other's lives with the same rights that heterosexuals have.

My columns about these subjects caused much mail and resentment. Old-time fans who had thought I was a lock-on, right-wing Republican were at first confused and then furious at my opinions. The lefties wrote to tell me they were glad I had at long last found salvation and came back to the fold.

But I hadn't moved. I had just done what a columnist does. What I had done for 35 years. Write my opinion—an opinion nobody had asked to hear, under a picture of myself nobody had asked to see.

I said at the top that this may be my last book of columns. My wife, Julie, who has the wisdom in the family, argued against such a statement.

Well, maybe she's right. You should never say never. You don't know what's coming around the corner at you. Or what may inspire you, armed only with a pen, to chase new demons up new streets.

Events overtook me, and they caused this book.

Is it just me?

9/11

A promise to keep for terror victims

We will win and they will pay.

We don't know what "win" means yet. And we don't know who "they" are yet. But we'll find out. And when we do, we will win and they will pay.

Under a rock somewhere, in a country many of us couldn't find on a map, they are congratulating themselves. They think their act of terror has terrorized us.

That's because they don't know us. They misunderstand us, as other homicidal maniacs have misunderstood us before—and always to their peril.

Our tears are not a sign of weakness. We cry for our dead buried beneath tons of rubble. But our ears are open to the sound of the dead crying out to us for justice.

On the smoky stairwells of the Trade Center, workers fleeing down passed New York firemen, struggling upward to try to save lives. Hundreds of those firemen were lost.

What made them climb into that inferno? It wasn't blind, insane loyalty to a warped idea of a bloodthirsty, treacherous god. It was guts and goodness and great moral resolve.

Does whoever did this think that we will turn our backs on such sacrifice? If so, our enemies have much to learn.

As schoolchildren, we are taught the lines of a speech delivered on another field of carnage. The man who made the speech called upon his countrymen to resolve that the dead around him shall not have died in vain.

Behind our tears and beneath our shock, such a resolve is hardening in all of us.

We have a promise to keep to Jeremy Glick, who spent his last minutes talking to his wife on a cell phone from a hijacked plane high above Pennsylvania.

"Jeremy and the people around him found out about the flights into the World Trade Center and decided that if their fate was to die, they should fight," a family spokesman said.

And it appears they did fight. For that hijacked plane crashed near Pittsburgh, the only plane that didn't make it to its target.

Does whoever did this think that we will allow Jeremy Glick and his comrades to have died in vain? Maybe they looked at us and mistook our freedom for softness. Maybe we looked like a pushover to whoever did this.

We bicker with each other. We are loud and harsh as we pursue our separate agendas. We elected a president who lacked a majority of the vote. We can be mistaken for a country that is vulnerable and in disarray.

The people who did this will be amazed to see how quickly our separate agendas become a common resolve. Today we are Americans without a hyphen. Arab-Americans, black-Americans, gay-Americans, gray-Americans, Americans in all their ethnic and ideological flavors have shelved the *pluribus* and become *unum.*

This is a new kind of war. But every war is a new kind of war. Once before, a harborside lay in smoldering ruins after a sneak attack. The spirits of men still entombed in the battleship Arizona are kindred today with the spirits of those entombed beneath the wreckage in New York.

Flags fly above both tombs. Rescue workers in New York found an American flag in the rubble. Somehow it had escaped the flames. A guy in a hard hat carried it gently, like a living thing, and tied it to a pole. The pole was a portion of an antenna which had fallen from the top of the Trade Center.

On this sober Sunday, flags are flying all over our wounded country. They fly from front porches and from the rearview mirrors of fire trucks and car aerials. I saw one painted on the hood of a car. The flag which inspires us should terrorize the terrorists. It will fly proudly, long after they meet their god in hell.

—September 16, 2001

Demand is up—for God's help

Suddenly, God is popular again. Calamity often rescues God's career. In one of the most fearful and uncertain weeks in America's history, God made a comeback. He has celebrity status once more.

The churches are crowded with people eager for a God experience. In Queens, New York, home to many firefighters, a pastor rang his church bell on the evening of Sept. 11. There was no scheduled service, but 500 people assembled in the church. The next night, the pastor rang his bell again. This time, 1,000 people showed up.

A few days ago, God was a controversial figure. Many considered him a troublemaker. Mention of him was banned from commencement speeches and halftime ceremonies at football games. Even moments of silence were prohibited for fear somebody might be thinking about God. He had become politically incorrect.

Despite the cold shoulder, God didn't go anywhere. He was on call when needed. Last week, people needed him.

Last Sunday, in a flag-decked band shell at a local park, a brass band led us in the singing of "God Bless America." Then we sang "America the Beautiful."

A guy standing next to me said he was a combat veteran of Leyte and Okinawa. He had called on God before, way back in a distant season of bloodshed. When the band played, we both serenaded God awkwardly in voices distinctly off key.

The veteran and I are not theologians. Neither of us understands God. Anybody who claims he thoroughly understands God is somebody to beware of.

Pat Robertson and Jerry Falwell made fools of themselves last week by claiming they understood why God allowed innocent people to be slaughtered. God, they implied, had been listening to their sermons on sinfulness in America and had been murderously inspired by their rant.

Presumably it bothers God to be misquoted. It happens all the time, but I can't imagine he ever gets used to it. Now, homicidal maniacs are claiming that God told them to hijack planes full of blameless travelers and crash them into buildings, thereby killing thousands of innocent people. Obviously God never said any such thing. Who would hang around with a God who issued such instructions and thought such thoughts?

I've said a lot of prayers in my life. Most have been attempts to hire God as if he were a handyman. "Please, God, help me pass the algebra test," or "Please, God, make Betty let me take her to the prom." That kind of stuff.

Over the years I whittled my prayers down to two. One is a prayer I stole from a friend. I think it's an especially good prayer for the kind of trouble we're in now.

My friend was battling cancer. She was full of fear, despair and a chilling uncertainty about the future. Somebody wise advised her to get up each morning and simply try to do the next right thing. She got through life a day at a time. Doing the next right thing gave her strength and comfort.

Our country, in its fear and chilling uncertainty, doesn't need the God of Wrath or the God of Vengeance. We need the God of the Next Right Thing.

If we pray for help to do the next right thing, everything will turn out the way it should. That's my other prayer, a very simple one. The prayer that everything turns out the way it should.

Neither of these is a big, loud-voiced, thundering prayer. They are humble and quiet. But I hope they are prayers that will persuade God, now that he's back, to shed his grace on thee. And me. And all of us.

—September 23, 2001

Blab shows find foreign policy sells

The radio said we bombed Iraq again.

It wasn't much of a news item. It lasted maybe 10 seconds. It was buried at the bottom of the newscast because the news producer figured nobody cared. And he was right.

The big story leading the news was about a congressman named Gary Condit. Remember him? The burning question of the day was whether Condit was connected with the disappearance of a Washington intern named Chandra Levy. Remember her?

Before Sept. 11, the cable talk shows kept the Condit–Levy saga going 24/7. The blab media was obsessed with it. I was obsessed with their obsession.

I kept watching, figuring I might get lucky and tune in at the exact moment when all the blabbers were struck suddenly mute, their talking heads hanging limply from their necks, exhausted because they had said all there was to say about a story that was getting nowhere.

But that never happened. It was all Condit, all the time. Several of the hosts justified the Condit binge in a way that would make the Society of Professional Journalists feel like members of the world's oldest profession.

"Let's face it," a Fox host told a visiting congressman, "Condit gets ratings. If we put on a discussion about Social Security or foreign policy, who would watch?"

That explains why the bombing of Iraq, just days before the Trade Center tragedy, got 10 seconds at the bottom of the newscast. Today it would interrupt programming and send newspaper makeup editors scurrying to find the great big type.

Sept. 11 has been described as the day America lost her innocence. But what we lost was our ignorance. We like our ignorance here, and we don't part with it willingly. Its loss is usually accompanied by flame and death.

There is a story that when Japanese planes were bombing Pearl Harbor, a sailor looked up at the markings on their wings and said, "Hell, I didn't even know they were sore at us."

Now, in the aftermath of calamity, most of us are finding out how many people in the world are sore at us. A month ago, the average person might have thought the Taliban was a rock group. Now we've been forced into a crash course about strange evils that exist in strange places.

Our tutors are the same media talking heads who were force-feeding us Condit. But now foreign policy does get ratings. The blab shows have gone to war, 24/7. They've left their old frivolous lives behind for a while. They have marched off to the recruiting station like jesters eager to put on new uniforms.

Having been caught unaware, we are trying like mad to gain awareness. And the awareness is broader than just noticing who is sitting on the airplane next to us.

Video stores report rentals of violent films are down. People think renting films that entertain with gratuitous violence is gruesome and tasteless. It always was. But now we are aware.

The word "crusade," once part of the name of a local hockey team, has been deemed too offensive to utter. Billy Graham announced he will no longer call his revival meetings "crusades." They have become "missions."

For years we've heard about the "global village." I, for one, disliked the term and always ignored it. I was happy to be snuggled between two broad oceans, handing out foreign aid to wretched populations in remote countries whose bloody quarrels seemed to have nothing to do with us.

That luxury is gone. Such blissful ignorance died a horrible death, and murder is our next-door neighbor. And it looks like it's going to stay that way, 24/7.

—September 30, 2001

One nasty instant, and the table turns

Two weeks ago, Imam Fawaz Damra, spiritual leader of Cleveland's largest mosque, was a guest on my television show. Booking him was no coup. By the time I got him, Imam Damra had appeared on most TV stations in town.

He was presented as a victim of religious intolerance. Shortly after Sept. 11, a drunk drove a car through the front door of the mosque. Imam Damra received civic apologies and became a symbol of the need for brotherhood and understanding.

I found him affable and polite. He spoke of the attempts he had made to build understanding among Clevelanders of various religions. Leaders of all faiths enthusiastically endorsed his credentials. I asked him to return the next week on a panel with the bishop, a prominent rabbi and the Rev. Marvin McMickle. All expressed interest. But things changed in a hurry.

A TV station aired a 10-year-old tape of Imam Damra at a fundraiser for radical Islamic groups. Damra, a Palestinian by birth, praised Palestinians who attacked Israeli citizens, and called Jews pigs and monkeys. His words might have come out of a Nazi propaganda film.

Suddenly Imam Damra wasn't a sympathetic victim anymore but a symbol of religious intolerance, this time as a perpetrator. He should have prayed for advice from a public-relations adviser.

Imam Damra gave an interview to the *Plain Dealer* in which he defended his comments. It didn't take a crystal ball for us at WVIZ to figure our panel show devoted to brotherhood was in trouble.

Around noon on taping day, I got a call from a tipster.

"It doesn't look like you are going to have much of a television show tonight," he said. "Neither the bishop or the rabbi are going to show up." About the same time, McMickle got a call: "If you're going to be on that television show tonight, you ought to know what you're walking into."

McMickle came to the studio anyway. No bishop, no rabbi. The imam, at last awakened to reality, cranked out a news release abjectly apologizing for his remarks. He telephoned with a voice full of woe, asking to still be on the TV show.

Since there was no panel anymore, no brotherhood visible and no ecumenical quorum of religious tolerance, we declined. We told him we hoped we could reconvene a panel in the near future. Left unspoken were our doubts that he would be on it.

Leaders of our Jewish community regarded the imam's apology as too little too late. Members of the imam's mosque voted to accept his apology and said they considered the matter closed.

But it isn't closed. Days passed and rhetoric escalated. A Jewish Defense League spokesman called for a boycott of businesses that support the imam's mosque. The president of the Cleveland Arab American Business Association called the Jewish Defense League "more radical than the Taliban." "Our business will probably triple," he said.

McMickle and other clergymen said they were willing to forgive and forget the imam's decade-old hate speech. The bishop's office issued a firm "no comment." The president of the Jewish Community Foundation said that more responsible Islamic leadership should "step up to the plate."

But the imam is still at bat. Will he eventually be accepted again as a bridge-builder? Will he be the good, new imam? Or the bad, old imam? I don't know.

All I know is that brotherhood and religious tolerance remain elusive goals, now that we need them more than ever. And that isn't just true in remote regions. It's true right here in our own town. We are the world.

—October 7, 2001

A monument to political correctness

Political correctness may do what political terrorists couldn't—haul down the Star-Spangled Banner.

Forest City Enterprises is reconsidering plans to subsidize a statue in New York that would have depicted three firemen raising an American flag in the rubble of the World Trade Center. The idea is on hold because the firemen raising the flag were all white.

Now, this statue was no artistic pipe dream. It was modeled on a photograph that has become world-famous since the Sept. 11 tragedy. It was snapped by Thomas Franklin of the Hackensack, N.J., *Record* and will live on in history books. When we saw it for the first time, most of us were probably reminded of the photo of the flag-raising on Iwo Jima.

With a snap of his shutter, photographer Franklin preserved a monumental moment in American history. If he had known about the controversy that was coming, he might have hesitated long enough to think things over and produced a photo more statue-worthy.

"Hey, you white guys!" he might have called to the firemen. "Don't put that flag up yet! In order for me to get a statue made out of this, I need an African-American and a Hispanic-American in the picture. Find some to put down their stretchers or hoses and get over here. I don't want an exclusive. I want an exclusive that's inclusive."

But, in the intensity of the moment, Franklin's diversity awareness failed him. So the committee assigned to approve the statue tried to make up for his lapse.

The memorial was to honor all the firemen killed at the WTC, including the black and Hispanic ones. So Forest City and the Fire Department proposed altering the statue faces to make one black and another Hispanic. This seemed a happy solution until somebody pointed out that it wouldn't be true. Everybody knew who the three white firemen in the photo were. Their names—McWilliams, Johnson and Eisengrein—had been in the newspaper.

It would have been a little awkward for any of them to take their kids down to view the statue. "Which one are you, Daddy?"

"I'm the Hispanic guy, Junior."

Photographer Franklin was understandably dismayed at the idea that the reality he had captured might be turned into fantasy. The whole issue became too hot to handle. So everybody let it go.

Forest City and the New York Fire Department agreed to "consider other options for a memorial." So the most famous image of one of the nation's most infamous calamities may not be preserved in bronze in front of Fire Department headquarters.

Danny McWilliams, one of the firemen who raised the flag, told the *New York Post* he was disgusted by the controversy because the whole idea of the flag-raising was to promote harmony.

"It's just disgraceful that the country should be focusing on this," he said. "Guys are dying in Afghanistan, and this is what we're fighting over."

He's right, of course. When he raised the flag in the wreckage, it was a symbol that America would never surrender to mad terrorism from abroad. Now a committee of suits is thinking about surrendering the flag to domestic political insanity.

Forest City was going to pay $180,000 for the flag statue. That amount could be raised in a heartbeat by Americans of all ethnicities who understand that when truth is sacrificed to propaganda, chaos and tyranny smile. But then again, what does that Iwo Jima statue mean to me? I wasn't a Marine.

—January 20, 2002

Colorful warnings maintain illusion

You are yellow, I am yellow, the whole Homeland is yellow and will stay yellow for quite some time. That's the unbleached advisory of Homeland Security Director Tom Ridge.

Last week, Ridge announced a color-coded terrorism warning system. It assigns a color for each level of terrorism risk. For example: Yellow is an elevated risk of terrorist attacks. High alert for violence is red, and guarded is blue.

Tom Ridge is a fellow without much to do.

It's unclear what meaningful guidelines—if any—the proposed alert system would have for the public, was the jaundiced view of the news story accompanying the color chart.

But at a time of national crisis, meaningful isn't important. What's important is a sense of participation, even if it's meaningless.

During my first national crisis, World War II, my mother saved bacon fat in a coffee can. Just about everybody's mother saved bacon fat in a coffee can. The idea was that our bacon fat could be used to make high explosives that would punish the Nazis.

Sometime during the war, scientists discovered that you couldn't kill Nazis with bacon fat. The scientists didn't have the heart to tell my mother this. So she proudly and meaninglessly saved bacon fat until V-J Day, when her frying pan was honorably discharged from military service.

In the next national crisis, the Russians had the big bomb and were capable of blowing up America with little warning. There didn't seem to be much we could do except blow Russia up in return. Since we couldn't do anything meaningful, we turned to something meaningless and pretended it was meaningful.

The kids in my class were taught to duck and cover. They showed us a movie in which Johnny and Susie were walking down a street when suddenly there was a blinding flash of light. Uh-oh! What should they do now?

"Duck and cover!" we all screamed.

And that was the right answer. In the movie, Johnny shoved

Susie down and threw himself on top of her. This was before chivalry turned into chauvinism. Presumably he helped her up and they went on their way, unscathed, through the wasteland around them. I don't know. They didn't show that part.

We were told that if the blinding flash of light came while we were in the classroom, we should immediately duck under our desks. A drawerful of Campus tablets, manila paper, watercolor paint and chamois pen-wipers would shelter us from lethal Russian technology. Meaningless? Probably. But at least we would be doing SOMETHING.

This new national crisis is the most baffling of all. Our enemies live in caves like Barney Rubble. Super technology has given way to that character right out of a Road Runner cartoon who tried to light his Acme Exploding Shoe Co. shoe with a match while riding on an airliner.

Solution: random shoe checks at airports in case another shoe drops. Meaningless? Probably. But at least we're doing SOMETHING.

Now the Office of Homeland Therapy has opened a Crayola box to give us a color scheme for our peril. You are yellow; I am yellow. That means we share a significant risk of attacks. If the risk diminishes, the code will be blue, which is strange, because we won't be.

It's a wistful spring for those of us who remember when crises came in black and white. In our corner of the world, it is all shades of gray.

—March 17, 2002

Bush should have told us . . . what?

After a week of grotesque media turmoil about what President Bush knew before Sept. 11, I decided to write the speech he should have given on Sept. 10.

Copies are free to the White House. The rest of you have to pay the usual buck-fifty.

* * *

"My fella 'merikins.

"I come before you tonight to tell you that our nation may or may not be in immediate or eventual danger.

"Intelligence reports indicate that a group of terrorists may be plotting harm to this nation. That harm may involve airplanes. But I'm just guessing. Maybe it don't.

"While you've been busy watching *Jerry Springer* or *Millionaire*, dribs and drabs of information have come in that a bunch of religious nuts who live in caves hate us and want to do us wrong.

"The Clinton administration knew about this. But they didn't tell you because they didn't want to alarm you. Tonight, for purely political reasons, I have decided to alarm you.

"You see, my fella 'merikins, the Democrats have never forgiven me for winning that weird election. So, if I don't tell you what I know, sure as hell, if anything bad happens, some Democrat is going to get in front of a microphone on Capitol Hill and say, 'What did the president know and when did he know it?'

"I'll answer that question now. I don't know much, and I haven't known it long.

"The FBI has been a shambles ever since Waco, and the CIA ain't much better. We gutted their funding after Rooshia collapsed. But there are some good agents out there, and they send in reports. I've seen some of those reports, but it doesn't strike me there's much I can do about them.

"For example, I got a report that some terrorist is going to flying school to learn how to fly a big plane. But he told his instructor to skip the lessons about landing.

"Now, that's worrisome. We also hear that some of these terrorists are thinking about crashing a plane into a low-rise building like the Pentagon or the White House.

"But there are so many nuts in the world that you never know whether to take this stuff seriously or not. And even if you take it seriously, you don't know what to do about it.

"So I've decided to just dump it all out on you. That way, nobody can say there was a cover-up or a conspiracy. I feel a little bit like I'm shouting 'fire' in a crowded theater, but here goes:

"If there are some nuts who are thinking about crashing some airplanes into something somewhere at some time, one thing I could do is shut down all air traffic all over the country. But if I do that, I don't know how long to keep it shut down. A week? A month? Forever?

"The way the airline bidness is, they'd all go broke. We'd be riding around on ox carts. So I'm not gonna do that.

"Instead, I'm just gonna tell you that we may have a big problem on our hands here. Or maybe not. If you want to fly, fly. If you don't, don't. I guess it's up to you.

"I guess mebbe I'd stay away from low-rise buildings, too. If you want to go to work, go to work. If you don't, don't.

"Just to summarize, some nuts may or may not be planning to attack America somewhere at sometime. The attack may involve airplanes and buildings. We don't know when or where or how. God bless you and good luck, and don't say I didn't warn you."

* * *

The way I read the news last week, that's what his critics think the president should have said. You can sure tell an election is coming. In America, cheap politics can be more terrifying than terrorists.

—May 19, 2002

New kinds of heroes in a new kind of war

There's a special gated community in heaven for all who died young in wars. That's what I think, anyway. You think what you want to.

This year the rules changed. A kid wandered in through the heavenly mists with a fire helmet under his arm.

"Am I in the right place?" he asked. "They sent me here, but you guys are all soldiers."

And they were. When the kid fireman looked around him he saw a fashion show of military uniforms. From cocked hats to Union blue to khaki to camouflage. The only constant was the faces. All 20-somethings. Nobody looked old enough to run for Congress. They were kids. So was he. But he was the new kid on the block.

They all stared at him for a while. Then one of the kids walked toward him. The kid was starched and all spit and polish. He was dressed like Vietnam and was immaculate but for the small hole above his heart.

"What's your story?" the Vietnam kid asked.

"Throw him out, Lenny," said a grizzled old Navy chief. "He doesn't belong with us."

Lenny held up his hand for silence.

"Tell me about your last day," he said.

"It was a normal day," said the fireman. "I was working the day shift and my wife liked that. She made me eggs. She poured me coffee. My kids went to school and I went to work."

"And then?"

"We got a call to the World Trade Center," the fireman said. "When we got there we knew it was bad—worse than bad. We had to go up the stairwell. I was with my guys. We looked at each other and we thought maybe we were dead. But we went up. That's all I remember."

"No it isn't," said Lenny. "What did you think about on the way up, in your last minutes?"

"I thought about how good those eggs smelled," the fireman said. "I thought about the coffee and how good it tasted and how shiny the pot was. And I thought about my wife in her robe and how good she looked when she bent over to pour it. And then I thought, 'I don't know why I'm doing this. But the other guys are. I can't let them down.'"

"Yeah," said the Vietnam kid.

"I wanted to leave though," the fireman said. "I was scared and I wanted to run home and see Michelle. But I just kept climbing. I was scared as hell. So maybe I don't belong here."

The Vietnam kid turned to the chief. "OK, what do you think," he said. "Does he belong here?"

The chief spat out the end of his cigar and grinned.

"Two eggs, sunny-side up," he said. "And a nice cup of Joe. On the way."

From far away a bugle blew. They all stopped to listen.

"That's taps at Arlington," said the Vietnam kid. "I got here in '67, so this is the 35th time I heard it. They think they're blowing for us, but they're blowing for themselves. They're trying to say thanks because it makes them feel better. The worst part is the speeches, but we don't listen to those."

"Why not?" said the fireman.

"Buncha politicians," said the Vietnam kid. "They bow their heads and pretend we died for them. You died for a bunch of guys in a stairwell and I died because a buddy of mine was wounded. He was only 15 feet beyond the wire and I thought I could make it."

"Eggs is up," said the chief.

"It's a new kind of war," said the Vietnam kid. "You belong all right."

Before the fireman could answer, a new guy stumbled in through the mists.

He blinked at the group. "I'm not sure I'm in the right place," he said. "I was on a plane over Pennsylvania. The last thing I remember is saying, 'Let's roll!'"

—May 26, 2002

Dec. 7 and Sept. 11 are worlds apart

On 12/7/42, the one-year anniversary of Pearl Harbor, Americans awoke to the news that their gasoline was about to be rationed.

"No Joy in Autoland," read the headline. The story beneath it said that car owners would be limited to four gallons of gasoline each week. If that gave motorists coffee nerves, the government had an answer: Coffee was about to be rationed, too.

Those who complained were greeted by the grocer or the gas station attendant with a line that shut them up: "What's the matter, lady? Don't you know there's a war on?"

A year after 12/7, everybody knew there was a war on. Service flags hung in the front windows of most homes. Each flag bore a white star for a family member who had gone off to war. Some flags had four stars. Some had gold stars for sons or husbands killed in action.

The country was in no mood to pause somberly over the bloody events of Pearl Harbor. The challenge ahead was too great to waste emotion looking backward. There was a song called "Remember Pearl Harbor," which urged us to march on to victory. We knew that 12/7 was a day that would live in infamy. The days we were marching toward were V-J Day and V-E Day. Our national purpose was to put an end to the war.

During that week of 12/7/42, a headline held a clue to how we might do that. "Atomic Fission Succeeds" it said. Scientists had produced a chain reaction that might lead to an atomic bomb. But most of us had no clue what an atomic bomb was or what it would do for us and to us.

All we knew was that Congress had declared a war. That the war would affect all of us. And that the president had pledged that, in our righteous might, we would win victory.

And we did.

I'm a grandpa. There's nobody left except grandpas and grandmas who remember when war, for all its abomination and grief, was at least explainable. We remember when you'd elect a congressman and he'd have the backbone to stand on the House floor and vote life and death in the name of the hometown folks who had sent him there.

It never happened again after 12/7. Korea, Vietnam, various excursions in Africa and the Middle East killed kids without service flags in their windows. Except for the grief of the families, such wars have seemed remote to Americans and their congressmen. And that's wrong.

For weeks now, the 24/7 television networks have been hyping their forthcoming specials, geared to the anniversary of 9/11/01. Their ratings war seems a lot hotter than the so-called war on terrorism. The promos I've seen are a tacky cross between a dirge and a celebration—a tawdry mix of a funeral Mass and Woodstock.

A year after Pearl Harbor, we were a united people sure of our goals. We knew our enemy and were ready to do whatever it took to defeat him.

A year after 9/11, we can't find our enemy, are confused by a wimpy and divided Congress and, unless we live in New York, most of us have felt no impact of this war other than taking our shoes off in an airport.

Pearl Harbor was so far away a lot of people had never heard of it. This war came so close we are numbed by it. I don't want to see planes crashing into the Twin Towers again. I don't want to see the deaths of thousands of human beings turned into mere theater, like reruns of King Kong climbing the Empire State Building.

I want to know what we're going to do now. Is there a war on or not?

—September 1, 2002

Saddam's a stand-in for Osama and Co.

The new flag I bought is still flying in front of my house. I finally gave up on the little flags that flew, a year ago, from my car windows. They kept breaking off and flying away on the freeway.

So I'm down to one flag. It's there because I still want to kick somebody in the rear end for what happened on 9/11/01. I'm mad. But I'm not mad at Iraq.

The guy I wanted to kick in the pants was Osama bin Laden. When the president promised to find him and zap him, I growled appreciatively and threw him an emotional high-five. The president didn't mention Iraq. Saddam was his father's villain in his father's war.

It seemed a sure thing that we'd find Osama. After all, we've got spy satellites that can read a license plate from outer space. I figured they ought to be able to spot a guy with a long beard who lived in a cave. If you live in a cave, you've got to go outside once in a while for a breath of air or to go to the outhouse.

My Bay Village neighbors were equally bloodthirsty and optimistic. We boldly pushed our shopping carts around Heinens and listened to Kate Smith sing "God Bless America" on the Muzak and assumed it was just a matter of time before we captured the Darth Vader of destruction. But he got away.

Then came a flat period. They took Kate Smith off the Muzak and substituted the 101 Strings playing the Beatles. So many car flags got lost on freeways that we stopped buying them. The economy went in the tank and that was a diversion. The Army was off shooting up Afghanistan for no reason we understood because the press that might have explained it was muzzled.

All presidents are box office impresarios who hate to lose their audiences. So this president stepped on stage and made an announcement:

"Ladies and gentlemen, unfortunately Osama bin Laden cannot be with us tonight. But appearing in the role of villain is Saddam Hussein. The show must go on. So we are going to go to war against Iraq."

But Iraq doesn't play. The administration has supplied no proof that Iraq had a hand in what happened on 9/11. And the people behind 9/11 are the people we want to kick in the pants.

The Iraq war plans baffle many of us. Suppose, after Pearl Harbor, FDR had said that, having been suddenly and treacherously attacked by the empire of Japan, we were going to go to war against Peru. Huh?

That's what a lot of us are thinking now: Huh?

And so is the rest of the world. The night of 9/11, 3,000 Brits turned up in London to demonstrate their sorrow at what had befallen us. And the French (who have warm feelings for nobody but the French) ran a headline in a major paper that read, "We are all Americans."

Saddam Hussein is a bad apple, but the world is full of bad apples. It's not our mission to go freelancing around the world tidying up dictatorships like Merry Maids with smart bombs.

The newspapers have told us for months that we are going to go to war with Iraq. It's inevitable, they say. And Congress seems to have swallowed that, because there has been no debate about the wisdom of such a course.

There ought to be, and soon. Our friends around the world who supported us on the bloody sunset of 9/11 are nervous about us now. I don't blame them, because so am I.

The new flag I bought is still flying in front of my house. Last week, on vacation, I took a trip around Ground Zero—a giant grave with flowers surrounding it. When you're in New York you realize what a punch in the gut we took. How about a plane wiping out the Terminal Tower?

I still want to kick somebody in the pants. But I want to make sure I get the right pants. Otherwise, it's compounding a felony.

—September 29, 2002

Put bin Laden back in U.S. crosshairs

The press, which loves clichés, says we are playing a cat-and-mouse game with Saddam Hussein. That's the right game but the wrong mouse. We're in a lethal *Tom and Jerry* cartoon with Osama bin Laden. He's Jerry, the mouse that always gets away. We're Tom, the cat that never can catch him.

Last week, Osama released another home video of himself. He pops them out on schedule like the "coming soon" list at Blockbuster's. He knows his audience. The fact that he's still alive is a morale boost to bloody Islamic extremists. If they wish, they can turn him into a miracle. He seems unkillable. We seem inept.

The White House is doing its best to sell the idea that Osama doesn't count. But he does count. He was the mastermind behind the World Trade Center atrocity. Americans, correctly, want vengeance. But we want vengeance on the right guy. That's Osama, dead or alive. Saddam is a weak understudy for our bloodlust.

We know what Osama did to us. He engineered the murder of thousands of our fellow citizens. When we couldn't find his bones, President George W. Bush offered us a war against Iraq instead. But the sudden change in menu confused many of us. That's why a thousand people met on Public Square last weekend to protest the war against Iraq. It would be hard to find five people willing to stand in the cold and chant against the killing of Osama.

So why don't we invade Yemen instead of Iraq? News accounts say Osama is alive and living in Yemen, where tribesmen "are said to be fiercely loyal to the bin Laden clan as well as extremely hostile to Westerners."

After 9-11, the president warned the world that we would take fierce action against any state that harbored terrorists. So why no talk of invading Yemen, which, it seems, had much to do with the attack on the USS *Cole* and now is harboring the most bloodthirsty terrorist ever to leave his fingerprints on our shores?

That's a good question for the press to ask the White House. But the press has let the public down during this march toward war with Iraq. Few hard questions are asked, and those are batted away by sarcastic administration spokesmen. End runs around such spokesmen to other sources are few and far between, and are scarcely reported at all.

Saddam Hussein was our good buddy 20 years ago. We backed him in his war against Iran. When he used poison gas, we turned away. The gas (obscenely) was supplied by Germany. But the weapons used for bloodletting in the Middle East were supplied largely by us.

Now we are told that this is a new day and the president has secured a U.N. resolution to inspect Iraq for "weapons of mass destruction" furnished in large part by our allies. A U.N. team has entered Iraq to begin the impossible task of searching a dictatorship as large as France to see if somewhere there is a car trunk full of smallpox cultures.

We're ready to pounce on Iraq for the slightest violation of the U.N. agreement. But as an American who has flown the flag since the World Trade Center, I don't think pouncing on Iraq is our mission at all.

If, to get the U.N. resolution, we cut a deal with the other U.N. nations for oil rights, we ought to say so. We won't, though. The press won't ask the questions, and the Beltway suits won't answer them. Whatever deal we made, let's put it to work. Let the other nations of the world search through Iraq while we try to find the guy we're after.

We're still after Osama. If he's in Yemen, let's look for him there. We can't police the world. Our allies can handle Iraq. Over here, we have a score to settle. Our war is with Osama. So let's roll.

—November 20, 2002

Before there was 9/11, there was 11/22

The 9/11 of my youth was 11/22. That's the infamous date, 39 years ago, when John F. Kennedy was murdered.

Little was made of the anniversary when it rolled around again last Friday. The blab shows revealed the smorgasbord of drugs Kennedy took to relieve his pain, ailments and anxiety. After he had been dead a seemly length of time, we were told he was a womanizer. Now we hear he was a junkie.

His pharmacology did not seem to affect his work. What is important about Kennedy is not what he swallowed before he went to bed or what he did when he got there. What we ought to think about, especially now, is how one day—the day he died—changed history and changed the lives of millions.

If Lee Harvey Oswald had missed, would Kennedy have pulled us out of Vietnam? A famous interview with Walter Cronkite shortly before Kennedy's death suggested he would have. "It is, after all, their war," he said.

His crafty millionaire father, Joe, was a businessman who knew the wisdom of cutting his losses. Lyndon Johnson, who came from a dirt-poor Texas plain, knew only tenacity and rode the war like a bronco until it threw him off and broke him.

That resurrected Nixon who, with his own mouth, had proclaimed his political career dead. Nixon kept the war going and expanded it into Cambodia. I met a guy the other night who fought there.

"It was all secret operations," he said. "We got jumped and I got wounded in the face and the hand. Because we weren't supposed to be there it was tough getting a Medevac chopper. When one finally came, my sergeant pushed me on it. I didn't think I was hurt that bad and I wanted to stay. But he said I had to go. And I went."

"What happened to him?" I said. But the way he was telling the story, I already knew.

"He was killed the next day," he said.

We didn't need to say anymore. That guy will carry a certain amount of guilt, unfounded or not, until he dies.

If Oswald had missed in Dallas, our troops might not have been in Cambodia. Nixon surely wouldn't have been president. There wouldn't have been a Watergate or the distrust of government that followed in its wake—fanned by the gotcha journalism the Watergate coverage produced.

I have lived through three dates of infamy. First 12/7, then 11/22 and then 9/11. After each, there was a congressional inquiry into why the infamy happened. The inquiries put nothing to rest. There are still people who believe that FDR knew about Pearl Harbor but did nothing as an excuse to get us into war. Movie director Oliver Stone, who has made a strumpet out of history, argues that Oswald was a patsy and Kennedy was killed by the CIA. And, in the wake of 9/11, there are conspiracy-theorist nuts who claim our government was in on the atrocity.

But sometimes history just vomits. It breaks down like a computer malfunction and gives us a terrible surprise we can't handle. Unsettling anguish comes into our lives like a bolt from the blue. The auto wreck where the kid is killed. The wife who dies too young of cancer. In our individual lives, there is no explanation for these things. They shatter us, and then we have to decide what to do next.

We all remember where we were and what we were doing on these single days of infamy. But the day is not as important as what grows out of the day. After the shock wears off, we have to think beyond the day and out into the long term.

If Lyndon Johnson had done that, perhaps my friend wouldn't mourn the death of his sergeant to his grave. If our leaders are wise, they will not change tomorrow's history by reacting to a single yesterday. The massive changes in history haven't been the result of a single event. It is the reaction to that event that makes some people die and others grieve. If there was ever a time to realize that, this is it.

—November 24, 2002

Can we recover our frayed unity?

What a difference a year makes.

A year ago, we were a united country, brought together by tragedy. We hated the tragedy, but we loved the unity.

A calamity had made us all Americans again. Not hyphenated Americans—not liberal-, conservative-, black- or white-Americans. All Americans, all in the same boat.

We flew flags from our houses and the windows of our cars and shopped in supermarkets where the Muzak played "God Bless America." In our common resolve to punish the people who had hurt us, we fell in love with one another again. But it was a brief infatuation; it did not last.

Flags still fly, but not as many. The supermarkets have gone back to playing elevator music. The people who hurt us seem to have disappeared into the mist. And we are a divided country once again.

We are on the brink of a war with Iraq. A year ago, such a bloody adventure wasn't on our vengeance agenda. For many of us, it still isn't. We wanted Osama bin Laden and his evil cadre of imps. The president, having given us no real justification, offered a war with Iraq instead. Half of us buy into that. Half of us—my half—don't. United against Osama, we are divided about Saddam. Under the cover of the terrorist threat, it looks as if we're going to whack Saddam for our oil interests. But he is no consolation prize for the World Trade Center.

Listen to the blab shows, both on radio and TV, and you'll see that we've got our hyphens back. The liberal-Americans bash the conservative-Americans every day, and vice versa. Having come face-to-face with death and carnage in New York, we have forgotten, in the space of a year, that death and carnage is a sad and serious proposition. Vietnam should have taught us never to send our kids out to kill and die in our name unless we were united and resolved to see them through. But Vietnam, so close to many of us, apparently taught us nothing.

These days, with no draft, we get to send kids who aren't ours to bomb people who have not harmed us. That gives us the license to babble on the talk shows as if war were a game played in a video arcade in a corner of a mall by kids we don't know.

Then there was the Trent Lott fiasco. It fanned the embers of the smoldering divide between black-Americans and white-Americans—a racial cold war that continues to attack America like a cancer, gnawing away within.

Lott was a dummy sitting on a powder keg. As a white boy growing up in Mississippi, he never fully understood the humiliation of blacks. He thought segregation was about politics. He didn't understand it was about the torture of human beings, physically and spiritually.

Dummy that he was, he praised Strom Thurmond for his 1948 segregationist stand. Lott just didn't get it. And his dumbness brought him down.

But in this horrid racial cold war we fight, a lot of people don't get it, black and white. A lot of black-Americans think racism is about politics, just as Lott did.

And so the blab shows are full of liberal-Americans calling conservative-Americans racists. And Democrats calling all Republicans racists. And black-Americans calling the whole society racist. The hyphens were out again, flapping like flags. And, by the end of the year, they trumped the flag that flew over the rubble of the World Trade Center.

I still believe in that flag. In Civil War days, the bravest man in the company carried it. He had to be brave because he knew that the flag made him a prime target for the enemy. But he also knew that, if he fell, someone else would snatch up the flag and carry it on as a symbol to rally his comrades.

It looks like a tough year coming up. The economy is lousy and war looms on the horizon. My New Year's prayer is that we can reach back and find the courage to overlook pettiness and demand righteousness. And do the flag proud, like they did one short year ago. Let's strain to remember when all of us, hyphenated or not, resolved to lift the banner of unity and fly it for one another.

—December 29, 2002

Stop Uncle Sam if you've heard this one

The Homeland Security Czar has given us permission to put away our duct tape and the plastic sheets we're supposed to use to cover our windows.

Duct and cover. It's déjà-vu propaganda to my ears.

When I was a kid, the catch phrase was "duck and cover." In grade school, we saw a black-and-white cartoon starring Bert the Turtle. Bert was the Homeland Security Czar of his day. The present Czar, though human, is also a cartoon, but he strikes me as far less convincing.

Back then, we lived under the threat of instant annihilation from Russian bombs. Bert the Turtle was the government's way of trying to ease anxiety. He was cuter than the current Homeland Security Czar. But he was just as full of it.

As I recall those flickering classroom movies, we saw Bert cautioning a couple of kids about what to do if an atomic bomb landed on their heads. I can't quote the text exactly, but it went very much like this:

"Here are Betty and Billy walking to school. Suddenly, there's a blinding light in the sky! Betty and Billy know just what to do: DUCK AND COVER!"

Then, in that day of bygone male chauvinism, we saw Billy shove Betty to the ground and throw himself on top of her. A great flash filled the screen, and when it abated, the two moppets scrambled to their feet and went on to geometry class—picking their way, presumably (we didn't see this), over the bodies of heedless people who hadn't ducked and covered.

Looking back on it now, it's all so absurd. The notion that anyone could survive a thermonuclear attack by simply ducking the bomb is ludicrous. But those were frightening times, and we were hungry for any assurance we could get that we might live to see the next dawn.

Bad as those times were, these are worse.

I was in the Army during the Cuban missile crisis. That was as close as we ever came to joining hands with the Soviets in a joint suicide pact of mutually assured destruction. Cool heads on both sides averted a cataclysm at the last moment.

Bad as that moment was, this moment is worse.

In those perilous days, branded into our history, we were never the aggressor nation. We had enemies around the world, but we all understood and agreed that we would not be the nation that struck first. This vow lent us a nobility that helped sustain us through those lethal times.

Now, we are about to strike first. The war against Iraq is no payback for the World Trade Center, because we have no proof that Iraq had anything to do with the World Trade Center. In our prosecution of this war, we are profaning ideals that we once subscribed to and are prostituting the language we speak.

We talk of "liberating" Iraq. Liberating Iraq from whom? In World War II, we liberated countries that had been taken over by other countries. No outsider has taken over Iraq. We just don't like the government there. If Iraq seeks liberation, let Iraq liberate itself.

We devised the United Nations in San Francisco and built its headquarters in New York. It was our hope and prayer that this body would end the barbarism of war for all time. But now, because the U.N. does not enthusiastically support our mad wish to invade a sovereign country at our pleasure, we are calling the U.N. irrelevant and talking about scrapping it and setting up a different body that would rubber-stamp our political whims.

We lived through mutually assured destruction and the Cuban deal. We lived through Vietnam and, even though I think it was a horrendous mistake, I understood why we thought we had to be there.

This new war defies understanding. It's a first for us, at least in my lifetime. I read my Orwell in college, but I never believed my country could call war peace or call domination liberation.

Duct tape and plastic sheets won't save us from the havoc we are about to unleash. A feeling of doing the right thing will. In 64 years of life, I prized my country because of her righteousness. I don't want to duck and cover to squirm away from that.

—February 23, 2003

Kucinich holds up a necessary mirror

When I urged Dennis Kucinich to run for president, my voice mail snarled back at me with the kind of scorn I expected.

"What are you smoking?"

"What are you, around the bend?"

"Your memory is going. Don't you remember what kind of mayor he was?"

"The guy's a fruitcake and so are you. I'll never read your column again."

And so on and so forth.

None of it changed my mind. People who don't like Dennis can take comfort in the fact that he can't possibly win. People like me are glad he's in the race. I don't like his chances, but I like his mouth.

An honest mouth is hard to find. Dennis speaks from conviction. He always has. In a nation that has been deceived, swindled and lied to, Dennis doesn't turn in the political winds like a weather vane. He says what he thinks, even if what he thinks may sink him.

Contrast him with our current president: George W. Bush has deceived America, swindled us and lied to us. When you see him speak, you get the impression that he has been kindergarten-taught with little, Dick-and-Jane words and long-s words, like "terrisssts." That's his favorite word. Dennis' favorite word is "peace."

Like most people in this racket, I've spent most of my career as a cynic. Ten years ago, I would have sneered at Dennis' call to create a Cabinet-level Department of Peace and Nonviolence. I would have called it a Froot Loop, Shirley MacLaine kind of pipedream.

Suddenly, it makes a great deal of sense. We are (according to us) the greatest nation on earth. In that role, why shouldn't we work hard for peace and use our leverage for the cessation of violence?

We haven't done that. We are the biggest arms suppliers to the world. We sell our weapons of mass destruction to anybody who will buy them, including our current enemy. Until 9/11, our unofficial motto was, "Who cares who kills anybody, as long as there is something in it for us." This is not a philosophy of peace. This is a lethal flea market.

But if we are the greatest nation on earth, don't we have a chance to be the greatest force for peace in the world? The best way to lead would be by example. But the current president, with some help from his puppeteers, has chosen the wrong example. He is waging war and calling it peace.

The world was with him after 9/11. All of us knew we had turned a page in the history of strife. The slaughter of Americans united our country, and there were no party lines. We wanted to find and punish the guilty. We wanted to cleanse the world to avoid a repeat of this massacre.

It could have been a new day for us and the world. But, in the hands of this president, it reverted back to the Stone Age. He was the tribal chief and he turned a rallying point into a cheap, opportunistic chance for more bloodshed. Would I have liked Dennis' Department of Peace to speak out just then? You bet I would have.

Dennis is more of a pacifist than I am. I'm not a dove. After the Twin Towers, I wanted to kick somebody hard. But I cared who. And Saddam, for all his evil, didn't seem to be the guy.

But this president lied about that. Maybe in a court of law he would not be convicted of perjury. But his implication, and that of his coaches, was clear: Saddam and 9/11 were all tied together.

Now they are trying to put a spin on it.

The president's men are saying, "We never said Saddam was an immediate danger. We're saying that, unless we strike now, he may become one."

I didn't hear it that way, did you? The way I heard it, the Texan stood on the dusty street and, provoked, had to be the quickest on the draw. Now it turns out that the bad guy had no gun in his holster. That makes it a setup.

Our wounded and dead are trickling back from this setup.

The casualties mount every day. In the back of our paper we see pictures of our troops getting used to wearing the artificial legs they will walk on for the rest of their lives.

Dennis can't win. He knows that. But what he can do is shame the other candidates into a clear and frank view of their convictions on this war.

If he can do that, he will have served his country. He'll get scant credit for it. But he'll get it here.

—October 15, 2003

Dark demanded that we see the light

The neighbors were cutting down a tall tree. So, when the electricity went off, we figured one of the tree trimmers had sliced through a power line.

Some of us held a little meeting on the sidewalk. We deputized a retired guy to go call the power company and report what we thought was a neighborhood outage.

I went home and turned on a portable radio. I couldn't get WCLV, and I couldn't get WCPN. I thought maybe the batteries in the radio were low. Then I pulled in the Kent NPR station. The announcer tersely reported that power had gone off in New York City, Toronto, Cleveland and Detroit. And hearing that, I thought what almost everybody else in America thought.

Terrorists.

In our house we did what you probably did. We rounded up all the flashlights we could find. This wasn't easy.

"Where's that big Mag-Lite I bought at Home Depot?" I asked my wife. "I thought it was right next to my bed."

"Where's my flashlight?" she countered. "It ought to be in the kitchen, but I can't find it now." Flashlights, like ballpoint pens, have the knack of wandering away from where they ought to be. Finally, we found enough flashlights to see us through the night—or nights—because this promised to be a long ordeal.

We went back to the radio and found WTAM. The on-air crew was doing the best it could. The traffic helicopter guy was reporting total gridlock downtown. Cell phones were overloaded and the reporters couldn't get through to public officials, who didn't know anything anyway.

A report came in from the Department of Homeland Security. This wasn't terrorism, the government said. We were not under attack.

Oh, but we were under attack. What was attacking us was our own too-trusting reliance on electric power, which dictates how we live our lives. When it suddenly goes away, we are forced to travel back in time. When darkness set in, my wife and I fled the heat of our unairconditioned house to sit on the patio. A candle burned between us. It was a good night for telling ghost stories, so I invoked the ghosts of the past.

Fifty years ago, my family vacationed at a cottage on a river in Illinois. The cottage had no electricity or indoor plumbing. We burned kerosene lamps until it was time to go to bed. Then we visited the outhouse (I can still smell it) and took chamber pots up to our lamp-lit bedrooms.

The drinking water came from a pump in the yard. We drank water from a dipper in a pail and the refrigerator had a lump of ice in it to keep the fish we caught cool.

We thought this was fun! We were city people and it was a novelty. But back then, many rural people lived that way. It was no novelty for them. It was just life.

Lord knows, I don't want to go back there. But it was interesting to remember, Thursday night, how far the genie of electronics has taken us into a state of dependence.

We sat in the cooling air, listening to the reports coming in from New York City. Reports like this:

People stranded in the city are being turned away from hotels. With the power gone, hotel keepers can't access their computers to find out which rooms are already reserved. And, without power, the electronic key cards that have replaced hotel keys cannot function.

A 78-year-old woman on the street contributed this gem:

A lot of people are penniless. They rely on money from the ATM machines and the ATM machines aren't working.

The traffic lights went out and created total gridlock. So much for all those well-crafted "evacuation plans." At 4:30 on Thursday, you couldn't have evacuated Cleveland with a strong enema.

I listened until . . .

" . . . Look at the stars," my wife said.

Without the glow of the city, they were as bright as any Clevelander had ever seen them. As bright as they were on those old vacations when the family sat on the porch and listened to the crickets and talked about the used-to-be for entertainment.

We Americans have a strong pioneer spirit. It showed itself the other day. We improvised and got through our troubles.

We also have a strong spirit of independence. In the autopsy following the Big Blackout, let's rethink our whole reliance on energy. If terrorists didn't do this to us, we did it to ourselves. And, as Pogo almost said, we are the toughest enemy we know.

—August 17, 2003

All God's Children

Giving thanks with spirit

Out in Chester Township they've waited long enough. The Chesterfields are going to stick logos on their police cars that feature, among other local landmarks, a picture of the Chesterland Baptist Church.

They would have done this a year ago but feared the wrath of the American Civil Liberties Union. This was more worrisome than the wrath of God, who, when slighted, doesn't file lawsuits and take you to court.

Every town likes to brag about what it's got in the way of tourist attractions. And with no disrespect meant to the Chesterfields, they haven't got all that much—an old red barn, a gazebo, and the 132-year-old church.

The ACLU didn't mind the gazebo or the barn. But the sight of the church on a piece of official stationery drove them predictably berserk, especially after the police chief said it stood for the community's spiritual strength.

I guess if the chief had said the barn stood for spiritual strength all would have been well. A barn is nondenominational, unless you're a horse or a cow.

Anyway, the Chesterfields are going to sneak the church onto the logo. They craftily chose a time when the ACLU was otherwise occupied, preparing for their seasonal raids on manger scenes and menorahs erected on city hall steps.

All this got me thinking about something that has always puzzled me. I wonder why the ACLU has never laid a glove on Thanksgiving, which in many respects is the most spiritual holiday.

Every kid has heard the story about how, after a harsh winter, the pilgrims and the Indians got together to give thanks for their survival. Who were they thanking? Not just each other. They were thanking a higher power.

So was George Washington when he proclaimed that Thanksgiving ought to be a national holiday for "favors bestowed on America" during the Revolutionary War. Who did he think bestowed the favors? He didn't say. He didn't have to.

In most homes on Thursday, when families gather around the dinner table, somebody will be asked to "say the blessing." Whose blessing? Not the turkey's.

This Thanksgiving is an extra special time to give thanks for spiritual strength. The tragedy of the terrorist attacks taught us lessons about how many of our citizens can go "above and beyond" the call of duty to find resources they never thought they had. Where did they get them? By whom were they granted? Where exactly is "above and beyond"?

We had gotten to the point that even thinking about God during a moment of silence was branded offensive. But all that changed after Sept. 11. Now, God is discussed more than Britney Spears. And getting better reviews, too.

If the police chief of Chester Township talked about spiritual strength today, he'd be part off a chorus praising it and being thankful for it. Pre-calamity, many scoffed at the notion. Post-calamity, almost nobody does.

Nobody escapes calamity. Life deals plenty of it to all of us. Some is of our own making, and some isn't. If we're lucky, we have friends who help to see us through it. And we thank them. And we give thanks for them. That's two kinds of thanks.

All of us have something to be grateful for. The nice thing about gratitude is, if you think about it hard enough, it can chase away a lot of gloom. This Thursday, after a year that hasn't been my favorite, I'm going to count the blessings I didn't earn and give thanks for them.

And pray that spiritual strength will be the landmark on my logo of life.

—November 18, 2001

Even the right man is only one man

A decade ago, when John Demjanjuk was sitting in an Israeli cell in the shadow of a hangman's noose, I wrote that it would be a bad idea to execute him if he was the wrong man.

A local rabbi responded with an article in his congregation's newspaper. It contained the following sentence: "Feagler has revealed himself as a dyed-in-the-wool anti-Semite."

Battle-hardened as I was by reader reaction, I was, nevertheless, rather shaken by the rabbi's indictment. A few weeks later, I was in New York and raised the matter with Al Cohn, my old college roommate and a reporter for *Newsday*.

I explained that Demjanjuk had been convicted of being a sadistic concentration camp guard nicknamed "Ivan the Terrible." I said that conflicting evidence and the fading and traumatized memories of some of the witnesses left this identification in some reasonable doubt.

Cohn stared at me and shook his head. "You're either crazy or you've got guts," he said.

These two responses, both unexpected, made me understand that musing about John Demjanjuk was like handling emotional nitroglycerin. As a man, Demjanjuk casts a small shadow. As a symbol, he is gigantic, and his shadow creeps into the nightmares of millions who survived the Holocaust.

It was Demjanjuk, the symbol, who was nearly put to death in Israel. But justice insists that a man be tried as a man, and when new evidence indicated that Demjanjuk was not "Ivan the Terrible," the Israeli court set him free, or so the press reported.

But Demjanjuk was not free. He returned to Seven Hills and lived as a recluse. His rare sightings were a subject of conversation. "Guess who was in here the other day," a Kmart clerk once told me. Then people began to forget what he looked like or who he was.

The U.S. Justice Department did not forget. Officials assembled a case that Demjanjuk, a Ukrainian soldier captured by the Nazis in 1941, worked as a guard in three concentration camps and assisted in the slaughter of Jews. If he wasn't Ivan the Terrible, prosecutors said, he was terrible enough to be deported for lying about his activities in order to get into America.

Demjanjuk, now 81, insists that the charges are untrue. But U.S. District Court Judge Paul Matia took away his citizenship Thursday and paved the way for his deportation.

You've got to be almost 70 to remember the years when almost all Europe was a killing field—a cauldron of blood and chaos—the World Trade Center multiplied by tens of thousands.

Civilian deaths were in the millions. Today, a single U.S. battle death is a front-page headline. Fifteen million soldiers on all sides died during World War II. The Red Army lost one soldier for every 22 people in its vast population.

After the war, Europe was filled with refugees. Many lied about their pasts and ended up living in America. Some, like the German rocket scientists, didn't have to lie. They were welcomed.

All this was 60 years ago. The ranks of war criminals and their victims are thinning. But the victims who are left remember with searing clarity. And the criminals who are caught, even the minor ones, have inherited the legacy of the great evil.

Demjanjuk may be one of them. But he cannot be judged as a symbol of all of them. He should be punished if guilty, but it seems such hollow homage to the millions of dead to offer them one old man who told one old lie.

—February 24, 2002

Church's joyous day has somber tone

I've got a friend I'll call Peter. I always thought he should have been a priest. I didn't know how right I was until recently.

Peter has made a great success of his business. He paid his dues in the grunt work of his profession. Now he's a consultant. People go to him for wisdom and insight and he's good at both. He's the kind of guy you feel like turning to if you've got a problem.

Such people are rare. I'd like to think I'm one, but I know better. Ask my advice, you get a lecture. Ask Peter's and he kindly tries to walk in your shoes.

Peter is an intensely believing Catholic. I'm a lapsed Baptist. Behind his back I used to say that Peter was born for the priesthood. The other day I said it to his face.

"I wanted to," he said. "I thought about it. But what stopped me was celibacy. I couldn't have chosen that."

Peter has a nice wife and a great family. His sister is a nun. I can tell that there is a part of Peter that remembers his call to the priesthood. That part of him, I think, will be with him until he dies.

I will confess that I've always been rather envious of my Catholic friends. I love the majesty and mystery of their faith. Catholic weddings can be a bit tedious, but Catholic funerals are marvelous celebrations of good lives well lived on their way to the Lord.

Today, the Christian church celebrates the ultimate triumph over death. All Christians are supposed to believe that Jesus Christ died for our sins. He walked the earth in human form but resisted all human failings. Except one—doubt. In the garden of his suffering, Christ had doubt. He asked God the question many of us ask when goodness seems to come with a price tag that is just too high: "Do I really have to do this? Do I really have to choose the pain?"

That is the millennia-old human question. It is a major question in psychiatry as well as religion. Only the wisest among us know when it's time to choose pain. Pain is often the door to salvation, which means healing. Christ reluctantly chose it. And today's celebration is really about the triumph over that reluctance.

As an outsider—as a non-Catholic—I feel there is a shadow over today's Easter celebration for my Catholic friends. The rules and traditions of the church, assumed to be divinely inspired, seem to have failed them. Their church leaders have practiced pain avoidance. Sins have been systematically covered up. Only in the face of newspaper headlines have the princes of the church admitted their mistakes.

I can only imagine what a blow this is to my Catholic friends as they sit in the pews this morning. Many of them have told me about their mothers who lived for the church, who donated money they could ill afford to the church's ministry. And died with a priest in the room who assured them they had given their lives to a holy cause.

But now Catholics are facing the trial that Christ faced. They are facing doubt. And they are wondering whether or not they can live and die in their faith in the face of such doubt.

One of them is my friend Peter. I know he is in a pew this morning trying to reach beyond the well-documented sins of his fathers.

As an outsider, with no standing in this argument, I think the priesthood needs more people like Peter in it. It seems to me that it is time to let a man who has a calling to marriage and to the priesthood follow both calls. There is no argument against it except stale and unexamined tradition. Such tradition has made this a somber Easter.

—March 31, 2002

Trust lawyers to get it wrong

It is the Angel Gabriel's task to break the bad news to God. He's learned to handle it deftly.

"I got some good news and some bad news for You," Gabriel said to God last week.

"Give Me the bad news first," God said.

"Well," said Gabriel, " a federal court in San Francisco ruled that the phrase 'one nation, under You' should be taken out of the Pledge of Allegiance."

"Ah, yes, San Francisco," God said. "Leave it to them."

"Aren't you wrathful?" Gabriel asked, timidly.

God smiled. And immediately 10 days of sunny weather descended on the Midwest.

"No, Gabriel," He said. "If anything I'm relieved. I keep trying to tell them that it ain't how you talk the talk, it's how you walk the walk. I don't want lip service. After all the lip service I've gotten through the millennia, I've learned I get better service at a Wendy's."

Gabriel stared at God, perplexed. He had known God for eons but he knew he'd never really get to know Him.

"The good news was supposed to be that one of the judges who ruled against you has had second thoughts," Gabriel said.

"They always have second thoughts," God said. "If they think they're in trouble, they like Me. Otherwise they ignore Me. That judge must have thought he was in trouble. What else is new?"

This was the moment Gabriel had been waiting for.

"Here's something that should please You," he said. "The U.S. Supreme Court ruled that it's OK for poor parents in Cleveland to use tax money to send their kids to religious schools if they think the kids will get a better education there."

"So?" God said, "What has that got to do with Me?"

"Why, it looks like a real victory for You," said Gabriel.

"It doesn't look that way to Me," said God. "To Me it looks like a victory for poor parents in Cleveland who want their kids to get a better education."

"But the people who opposed it said it would ruin the public school system," Gabriel said. "And they said it violated the Constitution to use tax money to fund religious schools where they talk about You."

"Their lawyers said that, right?" God said.

"Yes, Sir," said Gabriel.

God sighed and a windstorm hit North Carolina.

"If I had it to do all over again, I might not have created lawyers," God said. "I gave people a sense of right and wrong and then the lawyers came along and complicated it. Do you know what ruined the public school system, Gabriel?"

"What?"

"The public school system ruined itself. Once it was the envy of the world. Then it got corrupt. It lost its mission. It forgot it was about teaching kids. It became about power and unions and political hacks.

"It's the oldest story in history. I've told it over and over. Take your eye off the ball and the next thing you know you're out of the Garden of Eden. I don't care what they say about Me. I just care about those children—the way the voucher parents do."

Gabriel felt a great sense of relief.

"Anything much else new?" God asked.

Gabriel consulted his notebook.

"Nothing major," he said. "Oh, the Indians traded Bartolo Colon."

God put His head in His hands.

"Leave Me, will you?" He said. "I want to be alone."

—June 30, 2002

Lott's apologizing has just begun

Trent Lott will be apologizing for weeks.

Friday's *USA Today* headline read, "Lott makes 2nd round of apologies." But this is like the NBA playoffs. The second round is just the beginning.

Lott needs an apology coach. His first attempt at apology was a bungled mess.

He got into his mess innocuously enough. He attended the 100th birthday party for Sen. Strom Thurmond. He wanted to say something nice to Thurmond. Whether Thurmond, propped in corner, ever heard what he said is a matter for gerontologists.

Lott said he was proud that his state of Mississippi voted for Thurmond in his 1948 presidential bid. He added that, had Thurmond won, the country would be better off today.

Then somebody brought in a leaf-blower to extinguish the candles on Thurmond's birthday cake and Lott went home. But the omnipresent eye of C-Span had been upon him. And the next day, his aides presumably pointed out that Lott, had he fallen into the cake, would have emerged with less butter on his nose.

It took the media a couple of days to rev up for this story. That's because the media are run by young people to whom 1948 is as distant as 1776, a date some of them have heard of.

But a trip to the research libraries informed them that, in 1948, Thurmond ran on the Dixiecrat ticket. The point of his candidacy was to keep blacks in the South in a permanent state of subhumanism.

We hear, these days, about "institutional racism." Sometimes that term just seems like hot air. But in the 1948 South, it wasn't hot air at all. By law, a black man couldn't drink from a water fountain or relieve himself in a gas station restroom next to a white man. Thurmond ran to preserve the rights of whites to treat blacks as pets.

So Trent Lott might as well have been speaking at a birthday testimonial to Hitler. He might as well have said, "If everybody had listened to you, Adolf, the nation would be better off today."

I don't know whether Lott is a racist. What I do know is that he is dumb. I shudder to think how many of the people who govern us are dumb. Don't make me guess; I don't want to dwell on it.

Here's how dumb he is. When his aides pointed out that Lott was in the soup for his remarks, he issued the following apology:

"The words were terrible and I regret this," he said. "This was a mistake of the head, not the heart."

Now what the hell is that supposed to mean? In his head, Lott thought that 1948 apartheid was good for America, but in his heart he didn't? If anything, it has to be the other way around. If Lott's head is some kind of wild card, who wants him deciding the issues of the day. Like whether we go off to Iraq and kill some people with no proof that they've shot at us.

Lott reworked his apology and now he's on his second round. There are, of course, other dynamics to this story. The morally bankrupt Democratic Party smells some blood in the water here and finally has an issue to talk about. And the relentless 24/7 talk shows, whose producers yell "Feed me, feed me!" will keep the story alive.

But politics aside, Lott was a dummy. He is, however, the duly elected dummy of the voters of Mississippi, a large number of whom are black.

Thurmond kept winning elections too. Talk about pets! The U.S. Senate treated him like a pet long after he could function. His able staff ran him and made sure enough pork came home to his state that he had something to brag about. His colleagues regarded him as a sort of role model. Most senators plan to live forever and look ahead to the next fund-raiser and not backward to old sins and old sinners.

Lott may survive this. My question is, how come Thurmond did? How was he able to thrive so long? Our kids don't know history, but maybe it's the Senate that needs a proficiency test.

—December 15, 2002

Perfume can't mask the stench of racism

"Racism" is an ugly word. "Affirmative action" is a noble phrase. But the kind of affirmative action they practice at the University of Michigan is racism with perfume on it.

They've got a point system up there. If you apply as an undergraduate and have a perfect score on your SAT test, you get 12 points.

If you are black, Hispanic or American Indian, you get an automatic 20 points. Isn't that racism?

"No!" its defenders shout. "It's merely a quest for diversity."

Ugly racism is racism. Endorsed racism is "diversity." You have to learn to speak the language.

For example, you can't say "quotas" around the U of M law school. The law school says it is firmly against quotas.

The law school insists it is firmly against quotas. But what it's for is making sure a certain "percentage" of its students are minorities.

They teach English at Michigan, but they fracture it in their law school. Making sure you have a certain percentage of the right kind of students means you have set a quota.

But, in the interest of sensitivity, nobody can call a quota a quota. "Percentage" is supposed to be (for some reason that escapes me) a better word.

The Supreme Court will soon rule on whether the U of M policy is constitutional. The president, stepping very gingerly, weighed in on the subject the other day. He said the U of M policy was fundamentally flawed and unconstitutional.

A lot of the media that reported this said the president had come out against Michigan's affirmative-action policy. But he hadn't at all. He had objected to Michigan practicing racism with perfume on it.

"Quota" is a sharp word, and so is "racism." But the phrase "affirmative action" is mushy. It can mean anything anybody wants it to mean. I, for example, am all for affirmative action. But I'm entirely against the kind of racism Michigan practices in its name.

When I first broke into the newspaper business in 1963, the *Cleveland Press* had maybe one black reporter on its staff of more than 100. The people who ran the place didn't want any more. In those days, there was "black news" and "white news." The black news, what little we gathered of it, was confined to one page in one edition of the paper called the Community Page. The thinking, as I recall it, was that blacks don't advertise, so to hell with them.

But that was before Martin Luther King and the civil rights movement and fires in all the cities, including two in this one. These events shook the white editors (reluctantly) out of their comas. They began to reach out and recruit black reporters who would make their reporting staff look like the city.

That kind of affirmative action was called for and needed and successful. The newspaper you hold in your hands was a forerunner for that kind of affirmative action. It meant that editors had to try harder to go out and recruit talented black journalists. And they reached out and they found them.

But nobody got hired with a 20-point handicap. Through the eyes of an old white man, that would be demeaning and racist. If you give a runner a 20-yard start, what you're saying is, he ain't equal. Far better to hire him and say, "Welcome aboard. We're all on a level playing field here. Good luck."

The evils of racism cannot be overstated. I was in the Army in the South during the Jim Crow era, and I remember separate drinking fountains and movies where, if you were black, you sat in the balcony.

The problem we've been fooling with for at least 30 years is how to remedy our past sins. Busing was supposed to be a remedy, but it wasn't. And the Michigan affirmative-action program isn't either.

Martin Luther King, in perhaps *the* speech of the last century, looked forward to the day when people would be judged not on the color of their skin but on the content of their character.

That day hasn't arrived. But giving minorities a condescending break isn't going to get us there.

It's not as bad as the old racism. But, in a subtle way, it's equally divisive and corrosive.

—January 19, 2003

Quota system keeps good people down

I'm for affirmative action because I think it's right. I'm against reverse discrimination and racial quotas because I think they are wrong. Apparently, the University of Michigan can't tell right from wrong.

Now it's up to the U.S. Supreme Court to give the U of M guidance. Yesterday, the court heard arguments in a lawsuit that will test whether two wrongs make a right—a civil right.

Here's what's not in dispute:

In the interest of diversity, the U of M has a policy that awards minority students an automatic extra 20 points on their entrance exam. This 20-point boost is based solely on skin color or ethnic origin.

The U of M law school has a system that is not quite as blatant. The law school has decided it would like to have about a 17 percent minority enrollment. So law school screeners look at applicants with this number in their heads. They can't call it a racial quota because racial quotas are illegal. So they say it's affirmative action.

A couple of white students called the U of M policy by its proper name, which is racism. They filed lawsuits alleging that they had been unfairly barred from entering the university because they were white. And, from what I can tell, nobody denies their claim.

The issue is whether it's OK to discriminate against white students in order to make up for past discrimination against blacks and other minorities. It's a question of penance. All affirmative action is about penance. Nobody who reads history can deny that horrible injustices were committed against some of our citizens because of their skin color. Having admitted that, the hard question is what to do about it.

Many of our acts of penance have been botched. Maybe the biggest example was busing. In order to right the wrongs of de facto school segregation, cities across the nation bused children across town to try to achieve a level playing field. It didn't work. Thirty years after it began, busing was discarded. It was no remedy at all. It left poor and minority students in worse shape than they were in before their shot of penance.

I'm not a Catholic, but I do buy the spirit of the confessional. I believe in the admission of sin and the priest's adjuration to "go and sin no more."

That's why I believe in affirmative action. The way to sin no more is to reach out to blacks and minorities and give them a break—not a 20-point break because of skin color, but a break based on talent and ability. White racism once turned a color-clouded eye to minority talent and ability. The way to sin no more is to ignore racial differences and judge one another on merit.

Is there racism left in America? Sure there is. But we have come a great distance. And it's time to cut loose some of the divisive policies that keep us apart.

The quota rule at the University of Michigan is one of those policies. It's a limousine-liberal policy and the limousine liberals don't know it. If you give a black student a 20-point handicap, what you are saying is, he couldn't make the grade without it. You're saying he's inferior.

Pandering policies of this ilk have to end sometime. Once, the righteous and just demand made by blacks was to be treated equally. Now, many black activists are rallying around a cause that preaches that they are 20 points less than whites and let's leave it that way.

Skin color remains our greatest domestic problem. But class discrimination is worse, and the real poison today is between the inner city and the suburbs. The University of Michigan is not Oxford. I have black friends in Shaker who would scoff at the notion that their daughters would need a 20-point boost to enroll there.

But they'll take it. Who wouldn't? I would. There's a word for that, though, and the word is demeaning. It keeps a lock on the invisible chains of second-class citizenship.

—April 2, 2003

Somewhere, Joe McCarthy is smiling

History is our salvation but we shun it. We have always been a nation living in today's fads and tomorrow's pipe dreams.

The lessons of history are, to us, as cold and dead as a stiff in a morgue. We are bored by yesterday. A recent poll proved that.

A canvass of high school seniors revealed that 50 percent of them had no idea who our enemies were in World War II. Sixteen percent of the kids polled thought that Germany was on our side.

This is bad news for democracy. If we don't know where we've been or what we've done, we have no compass to guide us into the future. That's obvious. But we've lost our grip on the obvious.

Stick around long enough and you learn that history is a carousel. The same kind of tyrants and events keep circling back around to greet us once more.

Last week, the transcripts of Sen. Joe McCarthy's inquisition were made public. McCarthy was a Wisconsin senator who, in the '50s, became famous for accusing people he didn't like of being communist sympathizers.

We were all afraid of communists back then. Russia had the bomb and we had the bomb and this hair-trigger balance gave McCarthy the clout he needed to summon people before his "permanent committee on investigations" and grill them on their political beliefs.

We lacked the guts to remember that in America everyone is entitled to hold any political belief he or she cares to hold. But a paranoia was loose in the land, and McCarthy, an affable lightweight lush, knew he was on to something. He played off the national fear for his own personal aggrandizement. Sniffing a climate of panic, he ruined many people.

There was a famous cartoon that showed a rabbit running away from a squirrel.

"Why are you running?" the squirrel said.

"McCarthy says I'm a rabbit," the rabbit said.

"But you are a rabbit," the squirrel said.

"Yes," said the rabbit, "but can I prove it?"

One guy who was ruined was an organizer for a union. The McCarthy era branded the union communist, and this guy got out. He took a job at a factory that made paper bags for small pies. He didn't have that job very long before the FBI showed up.

"We're just here on a routine visit," an FBI agent told the foreman. "Just checking up on a guy who is working for you who used to be a member of a commie union."

The foreman fired the guy that very day, with an apology. "I hate to do this," he said. "But you got to understand that if I don't, I'm in trouble. I'm not sure exactly why I'm in trouble. But I guess I am."

So the fired guy got a job hustling baggage at the Greyhound station, midnight to six a.m. He needed the job because he was sending his kid to college. That was my father, and the kid was me.

Maybe this should have made me a left-wing radical. It didn't. It didn't make my father one, either. He voted for Goldwater in 1964. That's how much of a threat he was to jingoistic national security.

What the experience did was to teach me how fear, if packaged correctly, can be an excuse for terrible repression. How fear can be a crowbar to strip away civil rights and allow one group of Americans to brand another group as un-American.

McCarthy and his era are long gone. But the carousel has turned. A whole new battle against a whole new enemy is wrapped in the same old rhetoric.

Now that we have won this war, I am free again to say I don't like it. My distaste is not because I'm un-American. I think the war was un-American.

Nobody wants to hear that now. We have built, from the president on down, a group of people who are delighted about what we have done. Many of them have connections with the companies that will make fortunes rebuilding what we've bombed.

But where do we go from here? I have yet to hear anyone talk about Palestinian territories and the bloodletting we have abetted there. What I hear coming around the carousel is a stark choice: Am I for America or against it?

For! But can I prove it?

—May 7, 2003

International hatred is only one variety

You hear the question all the time: Why does the world hate us?

But that's not my big question. My big nosy question is, why do so many of us hate each other?

I'm so sick of the liberal-conservative thing I want to vomit on my radio and pull the roots out of my cable TV. I've lived almost 65 years and I've never seen so many Americans so spitefully at each other's throats.

I covered the Vietnam War. We called it the most divisive period in American history since the Civil War. Blood ran in the gutters, and cops swung their nightsticks at protesters. But there was a great issue at stake that cut across party lines. Johnson, a Democrat, had fanned the embers of the war into a bright, searing flame. Nixon, a Republican, had continued it. The protests in the streets swirled around the morality of American foreign policy. The debates in Congress were about whether we were right or wrong.

At present, we have no debates in this eerily mute Congress. We are engaged in one of the most adventurous acts of foreign intervention in our history. It seems to be open-ended, which means in English that we have no idea where we go from here. If ever there were a time for reasoned and rational debate, it is now.

But we hate each other too much to talk to each other. We're like a dysfunctional family, too set in our wooden-headed ways to hear and respect another's point of view.

We have become a government of radio talk shows and cable-TV polemics. Our leaders—the people who send our kids to war—are playing for cheap sound bites in the media. And the media, who were elected to nothing, have turned the most vital issues of our day into a version of the *Jerry Springer* show.

In today's media, every question boils down to shirts against skins, them against us, liberals against conservatives. Americans against Americans.

The hot media story this week is Hillary's book. It's a good media story because it gives the conservative Hillary-haters a chance to call in and bash the liberal Hillary-lovers. And vice versa.

The off-play story this week is that we haven't found any weapons of mass destruction in Iraq. This gives the liberal, anti-Bush faction a chance to call in and knock the conservative, pro-Bush faction, and vice versa. Everybody has a chance to blab, including the talk-show host who gets paid to listen to it all and put his thumb on the cutoff lever.

But government by Show Biz is not good government. A discussion of Hillary's book isn't even a good book discussion. She is not William Faulkner. The only thing anybody really wants to know about Hillary's book is what she says about Bill and Monica. She should have said nothing. I wouldn't have, would you? But she wants to be president so she has to go into Show Biz.

She wrote that she believed Bill up until the last minute. Given his track record, one might wonder weather this naiveté is a proper credential for the presidency. But it doesn't matter. She got her publicity, and if you are a "liberal" you are for her, and if you are a "conservative" you are against her.

The same holds true with Bush's weapons of mass destruction. If you are a "liberal" you think he lied about them. If you are a "conservative" you think it doesn't matter if they were there or not. The big deal is that we threw out Saddam.

I've worked in the TV media for 34 years, and I know there is nothing easier to do than start a fight between two opposing camps. Do it right and there's good money in it, and the squabbling guests are pleased with their notoriety.

But now that we obviously are the greatest superpower in the world, it seems to me that we all have a little more responsibility than we used to have. As the song says, this is our country "to have and to hold."

Maybe it's time we started caressing with some manners and class. The questions that confront us now are not Jerry Springer questions. They are Thomas Jefferson questions. Jefferson could never have invented Springer. In the age of Springer, our task is to reinvent Jefferson.

—June 11, 2003

Flagpole proliferation won't create unity

Here's an answer to Lakewood Mayor Madeline Cain's dilemma. Fly only one flag on the flagpole in front of City Hall. And make that one the American flag—the flag that belongs to all of us.

Mayor Cain, nudged by a vote of Lakewood City Council, decided to use the civic flagpole as a symbol of the suburb's diversity. So, in honor of Gay Pride Week, a gay pride flag was scheduled for hoisting on the city's pole.

But it was not a flag for all of us. And after the decision was made, Lakewood city hall was flooded with calls of protest.

The official flagpole already had three flags dangling from it: The U.S. flag, the Ohio flag (if somebody remembered to put it up) and a flag commemorating American prisoners of war. Adding a gay-rights flag to the bottom of these three stirred up a lot of anti-gay people in marvelously diverse Lakewood.

Most notably stirred up was a Lakewood resident named Pete McGrew, an ex-Marine who is to diversity what salmonella is to an old egg yolk.

"We did not like [homosexuals]," McGrew told V. David Sartin of this newspaper. "We lived off of 'em. We rolled them. We just beat the heck out of them."

Now there's an honest man. How about him! If you lived in Lakewood, who would you rather have as your neighbor? Pete McGrew, who loves to brag about hating? Or a homosexual couple? In my experience, as a former Lakewood resident, there's no contest.

Anyway, the mayor's flagpole decision caused enough of a flap that Mayor Cain mistakenly decided to defuse it with compromise. I can't blame her. That's what elected officials do. They strain to bring together the idiots in their constituencies.

Her idea was to erect a second flagpole in front of City Hall. The gay-pride banner could flutter from that. And it would be an "open" flagpole so that any Betsy Ross with a cause could stitch something up, in favor of free-range chickens, say, and run it up the flagpole to see who would salute it.

But there Mayor Cain made the mistake that is often made when dealing with fanatics and extremists. It's the pink-cloud illusion that you can negotiate with people intent on an agenda. You're fooling yourself if you think you can.

Gay activist Byranna Fish called Mayor Cain gutless, saying that Cain gave the gay community only partial support. So nobody was happy with Mayor Cain's "second flagpole" decision. And nobody should have been.

If America is going to live up to her promise, we are going to have to do it under one flag. Only one flag on top of the pole.

We don't need an Ohio flag flapping beneath it. Who really cares about an Ohio flag? When you pass an Ohio flag, do you tear up? Do you feel like coming to attention? Ours is a great state, full of astronauts and tomato juice, but it's part of a better country.

We don't even need a POW flag (a cause close to my heart). If there are POWs out there whom we need to get home, the American flag is enough to lead the way.

We don't need gay-rights flags, either. Or black nationalist flags or women's-rights flags. To make this country work, we all have to learn how to fit beneath the one flag at the top of the pole.

And if we feel we are left out—as black Americans have been and Irish and Jewish and gay Americans have been and women have been—the answer is not to fly a separate flag on a separate pole. The answer has always been to grab a piece of America's flag and wrap it around us. And claim it for our own.

I believe that's possible because I've lived long enough to see it happen. One flag, one pole, one dream.

Pull the others down, Mayor Cain, and raise the only one that counts. And let's all snuggle under that one.

—June 18, 2003

Let gays go their way; it's no affair of mine

This is the summer of gay love. Gay people dominate the news. Gayness, or is it gaiety, is hip.

The hottest show on cable is Bravo's *Queer Eye for the Straight Guy*. I never miss it.

Its premise is that a lot of dorky straight guys need help from a quintet of fashion-conscious fairy godfathers. The godfathers swarm into the dork's house, rescue him from his slovenliness, take him out and buy him clothes, get him exfoliated, mousse his hair, bring him back to a totally redecorated apartment, teach him how to cook coq au vin and ride off into a properly lit sunset.

Queer Eye raises all the gay stereotypes and flies them gleefully like banners. Carson Kressley, the fashion-conscious godfather, positively flounces through the hour. All the old wink-and-nudge gags about gays being better hairdressers and decorators and couturiers come home to roost and crow. "You're right," the show says. "We ARE better. So? . . ."

So this:

I'm an old dog who doesn't like to learn new tricks. When gays began coming out of the closet some years ago, I figured the closet was about the size of a gym locker. It soon became a walk-in closet. Now I realize that the closet was vast, its dimensions measured only by prejudice and disdain and ignorance.

I've written before that one of my friends in high school was a gay kid. I didn't know it then and, back then, there was no way he could have told us. All I knew was that he was a nice kid who a lot of other kids picked on. They nicknamed him "Bubbles." That didn't register with me.

One day he went home and hanged himself in his closet. In his closet! And even then I didn't get it. To be honest, I didn't get it for years.

Twenty years later (and this is almost 30 years ago) the brother of a girl I knew told me in a saloon one night that he was gay. He was crying when he said it. He said he didn't want to be gay. He was a good-looking Irish kid and he had tried dating girls. The girls were crazy about him. But it didn't work for him. He wanted to know what I thought he ought to do.

He couldn't have asked a worse guy. I had no bleeping idea what he was talking about. But I gave him the best advice I could.

"Change," I said.

One of the boundaries of that great, big closet was ignorance. And I was a well-meaning ignoramus. Back in that era, when people were smoking anything but tobacco and painting their bodies, I thought this kid really had a choice—that he was indulging in a fad. I thought my job was to straighten him out, the way his father had already tried to. So I told him to pull his socks up and change.

I don't know where he is now. I don't know what happened to him. But now, too late, because I come to everything late, I know he had no choice.

This is the summer of gay love and gay backlash. The news cycle is slow now because we don't know what to say about Iraq. We're stuck. That's it. How many times can an anchor-bunny say that?

So the news has turned to gays, a nice, controversial, ratings-grabbing issue that attracts all kind of yapping. Should gays be allowed to be married? Should gays be allowed to get some kind of license short of a marriage license? Should an openly gay Episcopal priest be elected bishop? Will the already-ruined marriage sacrament, which too few take seriously anymore, be profaned if a gay couple walks down a church aisle?

I'll tell you this: A part of me wishes the gays had stayed in the closet, because it would have given me one less issue to fret over. We're already on fret overload.

But then I think of the kid they called Bubbles. He couldn't choose his sexual orientation. The only choice he saw open to him, he made.

Yes, gay people should be able to pledge their vows. Yes, they should be considered next of kin and allowed to visit each other in the hospital. How the hell does any of that hurt me?

I'm too straight for the queer guys on TV. I haven't got enough hair left to get it moussed. I'm too straight ever to be hip. But I'm one guy with a straight eye for the queer guy. Leave him in peace.

—August 6, 2003

Racism comes in more than one color

Let's talk about black racism. It's never discussed.

It is not politically correct to report that black people commit racist acts against white people. The PC songbook says this can't be true.

Once, years ago, I asked a prominent black leader—a local minister—if there was such a thing as black racism. He said no. I caved, and that ended that conversation. Let's open it up again.

Surely Melissa King, who is white, believes in black racism. She is the 13-year-old girl who was beaten last May by a group of black students on her way home from Wilbur Wright Middle School.

She took her case to juvenile court. Judge Joseph Russo acquitted the black kids she claimed had assaulted her. She couldn't prove they were the right ones.

But then Judge Russo issued the following statement:

"I think the evidence was overwhelming that this was an attack based on May Day and that the victim was chosen because she is white," he said.

The story in this newspaper interpreted his ruling this way:

"White students in Cleveland's integrated public schools have reason to fear assaults by minorities in so-called May Day attacks every May 1."

That's a flawed analysis. In the Cleveland school system, black students are not the minority. They are the overwhelming majority. To call the Cleveland school system "integrated" is a joke. If Melissa had a fear, she was afraid of the majority who culturally despised her for her color.

"The lore of May Day as an excuse for minorities to attack whites is more than mythology," Judge Russo said.

Well, how does such lore get started?

And before you answer that question, spare me the discussion of slavery and how black people were dragged over here against their will. I know that. I acknowledge that. Even though my relatives came here from Germany long after the slave trade ended, I'm sorry, I'm sorry, I'm sorry.

The black kids at Wilbur Wright were not slaves. They weren't the children of slaves. Or even the great-grandchildren of slaves. The whips or the chains were not bred in their bones. The lore implanted there was "get Whitey."

Who put it there?

That's a very good question. Many movies have been made about white folks sitting around the dinner table saying nasty things about blacks. And it's true; that happens.

I haven't seen a Hollywood movie yet about black people sitting around a dinner table saying nasty bad stuff about whites. But that must happen, too. Otherwise there would have been no May Day and no Melissa.

Thirty years ago, I covered a piece of the civil rights movement. I had been down South in the Army and I understood, as best as I could, the terrible inhumanity of being treated like a lesser human being because of skin color.

Naive as I am, I thought back then that we'd be over it by now. But we're not over it at all.

If I were Melissa's father, I know what I'd do. I'd beg, borrow or steal the money to put her in a private school and rescue her from the black racism of May Day.

And that, of course, would make the so-called "integrated schools" even less integrated. Jim Crow has been gone for 40 years. But racial strife is still with us. I know I will never see it end. But when it ends, if it does, it will end because the "white culture" and the "black culture" merge as one.

And blacks have to do their share to make it happen. They have to dig themselves out of a culture of whining and hate. If Melissa had been a black student beaten by white students because of a "get-blackie day," we would have had Jesse Jackson on our doorstep in the Ritz-Carlton.

I have yet to hear any local minister speak out against the black racism that battered Melissa. Why is that? No gain in it, I suppose.

—October 5, 2003

God's day in court? We should be so lucky

The Supreme Court, which begins its sessions with the incantation "God save this honorable court," will decide whether God ought to be kicked out of the Pledge of Allegiance. What's up with that?

God's gotta be confused. I know I am.

And so, I'll bet, is the little 9-year-old "atheist" whose father pushed a lawsuit all the way from a California classroom to the high court on her behalf.

Let's talk sense. In the first place, there is no such thing as a 9-year-old atheist. I mean, really, is there? Kids aren't that sophisticated, even these days, when 13-year-olds are on cultural steroids striving to become pouty sex-symbols in the Calvin Klein ads.

This 9-year-old's father is claiming that the words "under God" in the middle of the Pledge violate his daughter's right to a separation of church and state.

But God belongs to no particular church or state. God is not a joiner. He's just God. He's there for anybody who wants Him. And, if nobody wants Him, He's there anyway.

God doesn't care whether He's in the Pledge or not. Perhaps He was pleased when, in 1954, His name was added to the Pledge. But, looking back on the decades since, it didn't do Him a hell of a lot of good, did it?

The Supreme Court has already ruled that a kid doesn't have to say the Pledge of Allegiance. A 9-year-old child, somehow opposed to God, can merely stand there mute.

But that's not good enough for the God-haters. The God-haters think that, even if a kid doesn't mention God's name, the kid is subjected to secondhand God fumes from the utterances of her classmates. Secondhand God, like secondhand smoke, offends anybody in the vicinity.

And, God knows, we are a nation easily offended. There are perils to the right and left of us. Perils that didn't used to be there at all.

I'm indebted to an anonymous e-mailer who sent me a list of things we never used to worry about. Part of it goes like this:

"People over 40 should be dead! According to today's regulators, we never should have survived.

"Our baby cribs were covered with bright-colored lead-based paint. We had no childproof lids on medicine bottles, doors or cabinets. When we rode our bikes, we had no helmets.

"We drank water from the garden hose and not from a plastic bottle. Horrors!

"We fell out of trees, got cut and broke bones and teeth. And there were no lawsuits from these accidents. They were just accidents. Remember accidents?

"Little League had tryouts and not everybody made the team. Those who didn't had to learn to deal with disappointment.

He continued, "We would leave home in the morning and play all day, as long as we were back when the streetlights came on. No one was able to reach us all day. No cell phones. Unthinkable!

"Some students weren't as smart as others, so they failed a grade and were held back to repeat the same grade. Horrors! Tests were not adjusted for any reason. Our actions were our own. Consequences were expected. The idea of a parent bailing us out if we broke a law was unheard of. They actually sided with the law. Imagine that!

"Please pass this on to others who had the luck to grow up as kids. Before lawyers and government regulated our lives for our own good. Kind of makes you want to run through the house with scissors."

The anonymous e-mailer is right. God and our parents kept a stern (but detached) eye on us.

We had real swings then, and diving boards in swimming pools and teeter-totters on the playground. We got in fights and learned real soon which kids to hate and which kids to like.

"That generation produced some of the best risk-takers and problem-solvers and inventors ever," my e-mail correspondent wrote.

Now, in this generation of the easily offended and the fancied slight, our Supreme Court is going to rule on God. Is He legal or illegal?

Well, whatever the ruling, He'll be around.

God is all the blessings of the past and all the hopes of the future. He's snubbed only in the present, but the present is an illusion. I intend to step out of it for a small vacation. See you in two weeks, God willing.

—October 19, 2003

Sweating the illegals, but not the details

What part of "illegal" does President George W. Bush not understand? Illegal is such a simple word. Certainly he heard it at Yale. It means and has always meant, "not legal." Either you're legal or you ain't.

Yet, quoting from news reports, the president plans to offer legal status to millions of illegal immigrants working in the U.S.A. This, the reports say, "might mean a steadier labor supply for businesses that rely heavily on such employees."

A *USA Today* headline summed it up beautifully:

Employers praise Bush's "guest worker" plan

They see lots of cheap labor; "migrant advocates skeptical."

There are upwards of 7 million illegal immigrants in this country and 40,000 in Ohio. In our state, a lot of them toil as migrant workers. The part of the headline that says "migrant advocates skeptical" is a skepticism I can buy.

Years ago, I was assigned to do some stories on a migrant-worker camp in the tomato fields on the west side of the state.

I went with a *Cleveland Press* photographer. Guards kept us from going in. So we sneaked in, with the photographer's camera hidden at the bottom of a bag of groceries.

The photo we got of the squalid hovel these workers lived in was so stark and searing it was printed on the entire top half of Page One—the biggest and most prominently displayed photo I've seen in 40 years of journalism.

No wonder the migrant advocates are skeptical of a president's plan that might wink at such living conditions. "They see lots of cheap labor," the headline says. But that's not what it should have said.

What it should have said was, "Employers applaud Bush's plan for second-class citizens." Because that's what the legalized illegals would become. And, in fact, they wouldn't even be second-class citizens. They'd be a bunch of disenfranchised drones, working cheap, almost a new slave class.

A Florida farmer put it honestly and well: "The jobs these people come and take are the jobs Americans don't want."

"These people." The black civil rights movement taught me that there is a sting in those words. Legalizing the illegals will make them sharecroppers, whether they are picking tomatoes in a field or swabbing out toilets in a motel.

Ours is a nation of immigrants. Some fled here and some were brought here in chains. "Give me your tired, your poor," says the poem on the base of the Statue of Liberty.

The president wants to rewrite that. He wants it to be a sentiment dedicated to employers. "Give me lots of cheap labor," it ought to say.

I lived for a while in Lakeside, Ohio. We had a handyman named Willie. Willie had fled Haiti, and when he got to Lakeside somebody gave him an old broken-down lawn mower to push.

He pushed the mower for a time and then he got a better one. He kept cutting grass for people, and eventually he bought a truck. He painted "Willie Worry-Not" on the side of his truck and honed his skills and became a general handyman. He got a tutor and took English classes at night. His dream was to bring his kids over from Haiti.

The government, in its wisdom, decided to deport Willie. A bunch of old fogies like me stormed the federal courthouse to lobby for him. It was a troublesome day at the courthouse, because the hip-replacements of Willie's advocates kept tripping the metal detectors. But we got his deportation stopped. Now, I hear, he has his kids over here from Haiti. Every Christmas we get a card from him.

I talked to an immigration lawyer at the time, and she told me what a mare's nest the system is. Willie is the kind of American we want here. But that didn't count. "For every Willie," she said, "there are four more we have to ship back."

Willie didn't want to be a legal-illegal American. He wanted to be an all-American. In his own way, he lives the American dream a century after some of the rest of us lived it.

It was the dream of the great melting pot—a dream so faded now that only the aged among us can remember it.

If we are the beacon of the world, let those who are drawn here enter the way our ancestors did. Let's not turn the clock back to the sweatshop days. Don't they teach American history at Yale?

—January 11, 2004

Gay marriage threatens nothing that matters

With everything else we've got to worry about, why are we worried about gay marriage? Why do we view gay unions as cupid's weapons of mass destruction aimed at American morality?

All the records show the biggest threat to marriage is the heterosexual union. Half of all male-female slip knots end in divorce. If the wedding vow had a perjury penalty attached, most of straight America would be behind bars.

Straight America walks down the aisle, accompanied by sonorous organ music. The straight couple is solemnly pledged to each other, under oath, for better or worse, then they dash out of the church into a face-full of rice or bird seed and embark upon an actuarially short future in which (statistically) half of them will be divorced.

How many of these divorces happen because some gay person breaks them up? How many people do you know who have been divorced? Lots, right? And how many people do you know who got divorced because of the corrosive influence of gays? None, right?

So why are all the hack politicians taking a stand against gay marriage and saying it's a threat to the marriage institution? Well, the answer is obvious. The polls show it's really easy to be against gays.

It's pure homo-electra. Our dazed country, which sees its old standards eroding away, has to make a stand somewhere. And gays are a perfect target.

There is an old country-western song (I can't remember who wrote it) that talked about a guy who brought his dog into a saloon. "The reason I keep him here," he told the barkeep, "is that when things get real tough, I can spit on him."

What passes for American culture is in turmoil these days. The Janet Jackson Super Bowl flap is just one thing in a string of things that makes people of taste and culture wring their hands and ask, "Where are we going?"

The only reason we have a "culture" is because everybody has one, even the aborigines. The front-burner question is, is our culture going downhill? Maybe. But not because of the gays.

What have gays done that offends me? Nothing. What have the ratings-hungry, money-mad, conscience-zero moguls in TV done to me? Plenty.

They have taught my grandkids it's OK to say a dirty word. They present sex without responsibility and put it on the front burner of all the shows they produce.

Many Americans claim they read the Bible, and maybe some do. It's a big book. Look hard enough and you'll find any preconceived notion in it that you want to find.

The preconceived notion about gays is that they are all perverse and unnatural. And that "homos" prey on our sons and molest them and try to convert them to the gay way of life. None of that has been my experience, talking to the gay people I've known. The headlines are full of perverse straight people who prey on children. I would guess that the amount of sick crime committed by heterosexuals far exceeds the homosexual police blotter. In other words, creeps are creeps and the queer population has a cleaner record than the straights have.

My bottom line is this: How about we let gay people get married? Fifty years from now, they'll be able to do it anyway. The Tafts of the world, who oppose it, ought to revisit the part of the Bible that instructs us on love and hate.

—February 8, 2004

Not gay, but just as proud to march

Guess who's going to be the celebrity grand marshal in the Gay Pride Parade on Saturday . . .

Me.

When they called and asked me to do it, I stalled as long as I could. You should have seen me standing there going "humma-humma-humma" on the phone and trying to figure out a way to say no.

"Hold on and let me check my calendar," I said.

What calendar? I've got a malnourished calendar and I don't want a fatter one. But the fib gave me a couple of minutes to think fast.

I knew why they were calling me. I had written some columns in favor of gay rights. And, judging from the response, those columns had caused a ripple in the gay community.

The gays had previously thought of me, if they thought of me at all, as a right-wing, stuck-in-my-tracks fuddy-duddy—a guy with calcified brain cells who couldn't possibly change his opinion on anything that had happened since 1956.

That was a pretty accurate assessment. There are a lot of things in the old days I like better than things in the new days. But human rights are human rights. And, if we stand for anything in America, we stand for the idea that all people are equal and should be treated that way. That includes gays.

I'm an old guy who was raised to think that gays were perverts. But I'm also an old newspaper reporter who, in my time, covered some hideous stories of perversion. And the vast number of those dealt with sicko heterosexual males preying on little girls. Once in a hundred, you'd get a gay-rape story. I've gone behind police lines and seen the bodies of children left in fields. And when the cops finally hunted down the beasts who had left them there, they were never gay men.

I've also sat in courtrooms, watching custody battles. I've seen heterosexual couples play tug-of-war over their kids.

Some people are saying that gay couples will ruin the sanctity of marriage. The sanctity of marriage is already in tatters. We all know that, and we say a proper "alas." But how can we possibly think that if a gay couple moves in next door, their presence will somehow weaken our marriages? It makes no sense.

If you had told me five years ago that I would be a grand marshal in a gay-rights parade, I would have said you were nuts. But gays coming out of the closet changed me.

When that closet opened up about 20 years ago, I thought it was a broom closet. Then it became a walk-in. Now I realize it was a warehouse. A lot of good people were sealed away, afraid to come out and tell us how they felt and who they were.

Let me tell you what happened to me after I wrote two little columns that merely said rights are rights and gay people deserve them.

I now have at least 30 gay people who are friends of mine. Some of them are in my own family. One of them, a woman I prize like a jewel, told me her only two sons had died of AIDS. We had suspected that but had never discussed it until I told her I was going to be the grand marshal in the Gay Pride Parade.

"You went through all that pain," I said. "Why didn't you tell anybody?"

"Who in your family could I talk to about it?" she asked.

And she was right. In the world I grew up in, nobody talked about that kind of thing. You hid it. And if a kid got sick, you invented a disease to cover him.

Trust me that all these things went through my mind before I said I'd be in the parade. But, if you talk the talk, you have to walk the walk.

Some of the best friends I treasure are the gay friends I've made since they came out to me. Gays aren't all great. But they deserve all the rights the rest of us get. I wish I'd figured that out earlier. I'm glad I've figured it out now.

—June 16, 2004

Marching in step with changing times

Here is a tiny portion of the e-mail I got after you learned I was a grand marshal in yesterday's Gay Pride parade:

"So, you've finally come out of that creaky, dusty closet. I asked my friend if the parade were to take place in Parma. He said, 'You'd see how much fire power we'd have if it did.'" —Anon

Dear Anon: Just a tip: If you want to stay Anon, don't send e-mails. We can trace you back. The Parma cops may not share your views, dummy.

"Can't believe that you have shifted so, so far to the left. This is an extreme disappointment. Thought you were one of us. However, we must now ask you to leave our beloved Bay Village and move over to Lakewood's 'Land of the Gays.'" —Jim, Bay Village

Dear Jim: Since there is no Heinens in Lakewood, I am reluctant to leave our beloved Bay Village. But I might consider a buyout. Whoever your "we" is, have them talk to my people.

"If you are so wild about Gay rights, perhaps you should marry a man, maybe Sam (Fulwood) and that would let every reader of the *Plain Dealer* know your true colors." —Spencer

Dear Spencer: I am greatly attracted to Sam but I believe he is spoken for, and so am I. Timing is everything. Try buying a calendar.

"I'm sure you'll take a lot of heat over your participation in the parade. Hope you've got your asbestos suit pressed. God bless you for helping to set a new tone." —Jim M

Dear Jim: When I got into the column-writing racket 33 years ago, I bought a tux and an asbestos suit. Due to righteous living, neither fits me any more. But thanks for your good wishes.

"I wanted to congratulate you and hereafter I will read your whole column." —Amanda

Dear Amanda: Hey, I take that as a plus. But you got to do it four times in a row.

"Dick, I think you've gone the way of Andy Rooney. It's time to retire." —Pete

Dear Pete: You may have a point there. When he does, I will.

"I can't say that I'm usually among your fans, but I appreciate your honesty and compassion. Thank you again." —Laura

Dear Laura: Thank you for the kind note. But, as a style tip, let me warn you against an effect we columnists often see. It goes like this: "Dear Columnist. Normally I don't read your columns. As a matter of fact, I think they suck. I read you years ago when I thought you had some brains. But then I gave up on you until this morning . . . etc."

Laura, that is not a flattering note. I know it seems like it is to you. But, speaking for the brotherhood and sisterhood of columnists, we just don't take it that way. Anyway, thanks for writing.

"Any chance of backing out of your agreement to be there on Saturday? I am sure many of your readers will respect you for that much more than going through with a sick demonstration of what is morally wrong under all circumstances. Are you one of 'them' also?" —Bill

Dear Bill: Nope, no chance of backing out. I nearly said no, I admit it. But it was people like you who made me say yes.

Your note was soft and polite so I suppose you and I have a lot of things in common.

You said in your note that you've often agreed with me but "will never do so again for the rest of my life." That's a mouthful, Bill. I don't care if you ever agree with me for the rest of your life. It's your life, not mine. But if you are going to live your life fully, you have to be open to change. And change is hard.

My guess, and it's just a guess, is that you don't know much about gay people outside of a handful of Bible verses and some dirty jokes about anatomical plumbing.

If you can, get to know some gays. Then write me back in a year.

The letters I've quoted above have been mostly negative. I picked them on purpose. For every negative letter, I've received 40 positive ones. I'll save them and turn them over to my kids. And 30 years from now, they will say, "Why was this ever an issue at all?"

—June 20, 2004

Senate takes time out for election nonsense

I've got a friend, I'll call him Joe, who married into a deadbeat-dad family.

Joe's new wife already had a couple of kids. The ex-husband took a walk on his child support.

The story I get from Joe is that the ex is some kind of nut case. Very bright, but doesn't work. Doesn't work, but hired a lawyer. Hired a lawyer to keep him from paying what he owes. Still demands visitation rights.

"That sounds fishy to me," I told Joe. "How does he pay his lawyer? I thought deadbeat dads went right to jail. I remember a lot of newspaper stories about that a couple of years ago."

"Naw," said Joe. "This guy keeps getting his hearing postponed. He owes us, but now we may have to hire a lawyer to get him to pay. He's living with the kids' grandparents. But they don't want to pay support, either. It's just all mixed up."

Let's call this a modern-day heterosexual love story. There are hundreds like it in this county. The institution of marriage is harshly threatened by heterosexuals with drive-by marriages—walk in, plant a couple of seeds, walk out, go to court and shirk responsibility.

I mention this because the plight of modern marriage has come to the attention of the U.S. Senate. With everything else on its plate, the Senate has paused to debate a constitutional amendment that would ban same-sex marriage.

That amendment has no possible chance of passing, and all the party hacks know it. I doubt it will even get to the floor today for an up-or-down vote. All it is, this amendment, is a transparent political ploy on the part of Bushies to make their right-wing constituency love them more.

The Bushies keep saying that if gays are allowed to marry, the institution of marriage will suffer. I can't imagine the institution of marriage suffering more than it already has. That's why I dropped that little tale in at the top of the column.

I have a good friend—a heterosexual female—who told me that

if anything killed her or her husband, she would like her kids to be raised by her best friends, a gay male couple.

She knows that gay parents don't try to "convert" their children. A loving gay couple is like any other loving couple. They want the best for their kid. And, if they argue, they argue about whose turn it is to take out the garbage.

But the Bushies, and their base of target voters, think gays are perverts. So they want to perversely tamper with the Constitution to deny civil rights to gays.

America has always been an experiment. The way the experiment has run so far, we broaden civil rights. We don't cut them off.

Screwing around with the Constitution is like playing with a well-timed clock or a well-tuned motor. You don't go in there unless you know what you're doing. And this administration has a track record of not knowing what it's doing.

All that aside, the U.S. Senate is one of the finest deliberative bodies in the history of the world. It has in front of it decisions to make about health care, the minimum wage, Social Security and the terrorist threat to America.

Into the middle of these vital arguments, the Bushies, for election reasons, have injected a blather, led by their stooges, about whether two guys can move in together as man and wife.

If they do—if they move in a block away from you and have a wedding with orange blossoms and a nice reception—how will that affect you adversely? Compared to your kid going to Iraq and getting maimed? Compared to your other kid not finding a job and moving away? Compared to your wife or husband not affording the pills that keep illness in check?

Compared to all that, when was the last time a gay did you any damage? I know the answer.

—July 14, 2004

Which decade defines your values?

The buzz is that wrong "values" lost my side of the election. If my side had the right values, we would have won. That's what the pundits say.

So I've made a list of my wrong values with the idea of changing them. Some of them will be easier to change than others. But urged on by the gloating right, I'm willing to rethink them all. Here's my new list:

Gays: I have to reconsider my position on gays. Having known many, I thought that gays were just human beings like you and me. But if I want to be a loyal, right-thinking American, I have to trash that. Gays are strange people, unlike us. They should be called nasty names because they somehow threaten us. I haven't figured out just how, but I'm working at it.

Abortion: I never was crazy about it, but I always thought it was up to the woman to decide. Now I understand that staunch men like Karl Rove should rule on these matters. What does a woman know about possession of her uterus that Karl Rove doesn't know? (I'm working on that one, too.)

Flag-burning: I was never for flag-burning, but I thought it was a First Amendment right. Now I understand that the First Amendment should be reserved for cheerleaders. What a relief!

Welfare: Hey, that just sucks. Nobody I know was ever on welfare, so it ought to be abolished. Let the deadbeats all find jobs—and in a hurry. This is America. If illegal immigrants can find a good minimum-wage job, why can't Americans?

Church: I go every Sunday. You should, too. Everybody should. There ought to be a tax credit for everybody who goes to church, assuming it's the right church.

Right churches: Those that preach against gays, abortion and flag-burning. I like a church where the preacher heals people and talks in tongues. None of this namby-pamby confusion about what Jesus meant. I want a guy who knows what Jesus meant. Even if it's not in the Bible.

Jews: Suppose you are Jewish? Well the religious right lets you in, too, according to the "Judeo-Christian Ethic." If I were you, I wouldn't trust those guys. I remember when the "Judeo" wasn't in the hyphen. But trust them if you want to. I'm trying to change my values.

How about a ban on loud rock music? How about a ban on rap? As long as I'm asserting my values, I assert that I don't want stuff going into our children's ears talking about the "ho's" and the "bitches." That sure bothers me. And in this new day of values, let's get rid of it.

Hey, now I'm on a roll. Let's get rid of Howard Stern and Jerry Springer, too. Let's get rid of everything we can't stand that comes over the airwaves. And if the kids like it, let's get rid of the kids. I don't mean that literally. I mean let's brainwash them. Get them back to the fox trot and the soda shop and being home by 10.

Oh, my, now I'm breathing hard. I want the old values back. Let's go way back to the days when women wore skirts so long that if they stepped onto a streetcar and showed an ankle, it was lascivious. Let's go back to the days when women couldn't vote, because why should they? Let's go back to those marvelous, old-time values that made us all feel so safe.

Let's go back to Cole Porter and Rogers and Hart and close dancing under a big, spangled chandelier. I voted Kerry, babe, and if you want to take me back, I'll see your nostalgia and raise you five decades.

But we can't really go back, can we?

The only way we can move is forward.

And our job, as imperfect as it is, is to try to steer forward.

What we call values change their faces with fresh makeup each decade. The so-called values of 2004 will one day be as dated as the values of 1904. So let's not worry about them. Let's just go on.

—November 10, 2004

Military lets go of gays who keep us safe

Plain Dealer headline, Feb. 25:

"Military dismisses skilled troops for being gay."

Plain Dealer headline, Feb. 22:

"Royal Navy joins program to recruit more gay sailors."

Let's turn first to Britain, the home of the enlightened.

"The British navy has joined a program to encourage recruiting homosexuals, while helping those on board to feel happier about revealing their sexuality."

And now let's turn to the bastion of the free world—the global protector of human rights—the anti-discrimination capital of the planet. Us.

"Hundreds of highly skilled troops, including translators, have been dismissed from the armed forces because of the Pentagon's rules on gays, at a cost of $200 million, the first congressional study on the impact of the 'Don't Ask, Don't Tell' policy says."

What does the British navy know that we don't know? Well, a couple of things.

First, the British navy knows that homosexuals can make good sailors. Or good doctors. Or good lawyers or good anything else you might care to mention.

And, in time of war, homosexuals can be brave and cool-headed. And patriotic, too.

In fact, homosexuals are just now fighting for something that should have been their birthright: the right to be treated as anybody else and judged by standards that apply to any other citizen.

That's really a simple concept. But in America, we've managed to tie it up like a tangle of worms.

We are supposed to be the ultimate land of the free. And now we have a president who wants to evangelize his brand of freedom all over the world. But his Army is still kicking out queers in his name.

Bill Clinton, an icon of the left, started "Don't Ask, Don't Tell" in a controversial move early in his presidency. This was considered bold at the time. But it still left a fundamental question unanswered: Are gays worthy to serve in the military?

The joker in that deck is that they always have. Gays hit the beach in Normandy and served in Vietnam. Gays fought in the first Gulf War and are serving in Iraq today. Gays have fought since Helen of Troy. And this very minute, some gay is fighting for some straight who doesn't even know it.

The worst-kept secret during the first Gulf War was the number of female pregnancies aboard our Navy's ships. If there is an issue about who goes to war, it ought to be about that. But it won't be, because the feminist movement has clout and has grabbed the gold of political correctness.

Nevertheless, it is male-female contact that causes X-rated problems for the Pentagon. A girl meets a guy and the next thing you know, she's home on compassionate leave.

This never makes headlines. Why? Because heterosexual screwing around is acceptable.

Here's who we kicked out of the Army for being gay:

"Of those discharged, 757 held critical jobs for which the Pentagon offers re-enlistment bonuses because of their specialized nature, such as data processing and translators. More than 322 spoke foreign languages such as Arabic, Farsi, Korean and Mandarin, which the Pentagon has called critical skills amid threats from terrorists."

Eventually, gays will have equal rights in America. But it's going to take a while. And that's because we are stuck in the glue of our hypocritical puritan ancestry.

Our clergy has been accused of pedophilia, but it's a news item and we turn our back. The drug war is ridiculous. Our last two presidents admitted they smoked a little weed, but we ignore that and lock up ghetto kids.

Thank God for the poor queers. They give the sinners something to hate. And yet the gays I've come to know are better than a bushel of those who hate them.

The British navy has it right. If I needed someone to watch my back, I'd take a gay friend over a bigot anytime.

—February 27, 2005

Shock and Awe

Peanut butter and a sticky situation

After a week of dropping bombs and peanut butter on Afghanistan, it's obvious this war won't be won in a Jif.

You can read allegories into anything, even peanut butter. That's why it was front-page news when an Afghan woman, having paid 70 cents for a package of American peanut butter and jelly, tasted it, disliked it, and fed it to her donkey, who liked it.

We are a nation of good-hearted people with a championship record of being generous to the world. But our generosity is often misunderstood.

We like peanut butter, so we think everybody should like peanut butter. We like democracy, so we think everybody should acquire an instant taste for it.

But sometimes people spit democracy right back in our faces, the way my kid used to spit strained spinach at me from his high chair. I'd shove a spoonful in and out it would come. Scrape it off his mouth and push it in again. Back it would come. Force-feeding nourishment was a frustrating experience for both of us.

The Afghan lady who didn't like the peanut butter paid 70 cents for a gastronomical lesson that was supposed to be tuition-free. Some of her countrymen grabbed all the peanut butter they could and sold it for a 100 percent profit.

This isn't a new development. How much of the aid we send to foreign countries gets stuck in the pockets of rulers who use it as leverage to keep the populace in check? No wonder we call it "funneling aid." Often a gush goes in on top and a trickle comes out.

Sending gifts of guns and helicopters is a far more chancy business than sending peanut butter and Spam. In this fickle world, you've got to be pretty careful who you give a gun to. Yesterday's lukewarm allies, like Saddam and Osama, can turn into today's red-hot enemies. And when the romance goes sour, they don't give the ring back. Or the rifles.

We have often been unwise or unlucky with the choice of our friends. The bitter lessons of the past are shrieking caution to us in Afghanistan. And should.

We went to Afghanistan looking for Osama bin Laden. But he may have skipped town. He could be anywhere. Perhaps he will ring your doorbell Wednesday night dressed in his Osama bin Laden Halloween costume. In which case, offer him a Reese's peanut butter cup. If he refuses it, slam the door in his face.

With Osama perhaps out of Afghanistan, the question is, what are we supposed to do now? Punish the Taliban, I gather, with the help of our anti-Taliban pals the Northern Alliance.

We could pass out guns to the Northern Alliance and let them charge the Taliban and get shot up. But discreet murmurs reach us that the Northern Alliance may be as full of thugs as the Taliban. And we don't want to go around arming thugs and letting them take over countries. Been there. Done that. Always comes back to bite us.

The last time I saw America this united, Glenn Miller was the hottest pop group. I was buying war stamps in Gracemount Elementary School, growing a victory garden and listening to Kate Smith.

Good old Kate Smith, preserved on tape for these occasions, was singing "God Bless America" over the loudspeaker in Kmart the other day where I went to buy a new flag ("Sorry, sold out.").

America is full of resolve and ready to do what it takes. What that is is far from clear. In the jittery and confusing meantime we'll look busy by dropping bombs and peanut butter.

Afghanistan's donkeys are with us!

—October 28, 2001

A not-so-seamless link to the past

Women's legs are going to war against the Axis. Excuse me, but I think this is where I came in.

The latest female fashion trend is a return to nylon stockings with seams down the back. "A leggy nod to the fact that the country is in combat," according to *USA Today*.

War nostalgia is sweeping the nation. Nobody understands what kind of war we're in or exactly where our enemies are, or even who's on our side. Not knowing how to behave, America has turned for inspiration to the "greatest generation" from "the good war." Style-wise, the war against terrorism is becoming a knockoff of World War II.

The president took us down memory lane during his State of the Union speech. He called North Korea, Iran and Iraq an "axis of evil." (I would have included Enron.)

The last time women got patriotic about their stocking seams, the Axis powers were Germany, Italy and Japan, and stocking seams were made of paint because nylons had been drafted into the war effort.

I remember my aunt and my mother smearing on leg makeup and taking turns drawing black lines down the back of their bare legs to show the boys what they were fighting for. Nobody would have put a picture of Betty Grable on the bulkhead of a destroyer if she had been wearing pantyhose under a pantsuit.

At war against the first Axis, we saved bacon grease in a coffee can on the sink, to be used to make explosives. I didn't hear the president call for fat saving last week. If he does, it will be easier during "Axis, the Sequel." We'll just eat a lot of Lean Cuisine.

For those of us who remember yesterday's war in yesterday's America, this stylistic encore was refreshing. It was good to hear a digitally remastered Kate Smith singing "God Bless America" on the supermarket P.A. system without a disclaimer from the ACLU. Or to fly a flag from your car and not be sneered at as some kind of right-wing fanatic.

Our response to 9/11 showed how parched America was to find

a reason to unite and put aside fratricidal political bickering, to be part of something big and meaningful and worthy.

But there the similarity to yesterday's war ends. In yesterday's war, we did more than mouth the words and dress the part. Houses on every street had service flags in the window to show that dads or husbands or sons were off fighting Axis One. You knew that when they got to Tokyo or Berlin, it would all be over.

I don't personally know any dads or husbands or sons (or daughters) among the troops who are off fighting the powers of Axis, the Sequel. Last September's date of infamy was a horrible hit-and-run. The murderers responsible died with their victims. Osama bin Laden vanished into the mist and is hardly mentioned now. It's like Hitler disappearing into the witness protection program in 1942.

We're holding prisoners in Cuba, but we don't even know if they are prisoners of war or what to do with them. Many are from Saudi Arabia, home of bin Laden. But Saudi Arabia isn't on our hit list. Our allies are nervous because they don't know where we are going with this war. It's small comfort that neither do we.

The spirit is willing . . . for now. Women raised on L'Eggs are ready to risk whiplash from looking over their shoulders to see if their seams are straight.

But in this war, the past has no instructions for the present. The president is using our grandfathers' rhetoric and women are wearing their grandmothers' stockings. In both cases, it's a bad fit.

—February 3, 2002

When war's just another TV show

In the coffee shop we were talking about the upcoming war against Iraq. It made us uneasy, though none of us were pacifists and all of us were veterans.

"I don't get it," said Bob. "A war ain't a wedding. You don't send announcements. But for weeks now we've been telling Iraq we're gonna' attack them."

Bill enlisted the day after Pearl Harbor.

"I think America ought to mind its own business," he said. "I don't think we ought to go looking for fights. The fights ought to come looking for us."

"The fight did come looking for us," I said. "What about the World Trade Center last September—wasn't that a kind of Pearl Harbor?"

"Not really," said Bill. "The guys who pulled that off were from Saudi Arabia and Egypt. But you don't hear us planning to attack those countries. They're our big buddies."

"And how about Iran?" said Dan. "A guy on TV said that Iran was the most friendly country toward terrorists. But we're not talking about attacking Iran."

Said Bob: "Call me a wuss if you want to. But before we go over and bomb somebody, I think we ought to know why we're doing it."

Bob was in Korea. He almost froze his feet off. He still limps when the weather's wrong.

"I'm sick of wars that nobody cares about," said Dan. "I'm sick of wars that people watch on TV like "Frontier House." If we're gonna go to war against Iraq, we ought to bring back the draft. Let everybody in on it."

"Let's see a show of hands. Who thinks we ought to bring back the draft and make everybody serve?" I said.

Everybody's hand went up.

"War is a big deal," said Dan. "War is about killing people. We ought to think real hard before we go off to kill people and get killed, in Iraq or anywhere. If the draft came back, everybody would have to stop and think."

"Besides, the military is good for people," said Bill. "It brings everybody down to the same level. It knocks the spoiled kid out of you and makes you understand how much you can take if you have to."

Everybody agreed with this.

"The trouble with war now is that it's a video game," Dan said. "We have a so-called 'all-volunteer Army.' We root for them like you root for a hometown football team. But we're not close enough to them to really care that much about what they're doing."

"You mean war isn't real anymore?" I said.

"Nothing's real anymore," said Bob. "Everybody's got 150 channels of cable with nothing on them but a massage. Everybody knows which ones the war channels are—maybe a half-dozen. We get our reality through the tube. The tube does our thinking for us. We just plug in."

"That's a bit harsh," I said.

"It's not harsh enough," said Bill. "There's the tube world, and then there's our world. In the tube world, a mush-mouthed president is talking about taking us to war. In our world, we're worried about super wrinkle cream and microwave dinners. If the people on the tube want to go someplace and bomb somebody, we let 'em. It ain't real somehow."

"Who thinks we're out of touch with reality?" I said.

There was a unanimous show of hands.

"But you know what, avoiding reality is what makes America great," said Dan.

"Yeah," said Bill. "But how long can we keep on avoiding it?

There was a show of hands. Nobody knew.

—May 5, 2002

Let's pay the Mafia to rub out Saddam

If we want to get rid of Saddam Hussein, let's do it the moral way: Let's pay the Mafia to put out a contract on him and bump him off.

This is against all the rules of polite war. The rules of polite war frown on the assassination of a nation's leader. But then, the nations' leaders made the rules.

It is considered far more honorable to kill a lot of privates, corporals, grandmothers and babies in the quest for world peace. Getting a single despot in the crosshairs is supposed to be a breach of etiquette.

If we go to war against Iraq, it will be for the sole purpose of getting rid of Saddam. Any lesser folk who die will be an oops—just so much regrettable collateral damage.

It was regrettable collateral damage that made us shoot up a wedding party in Afghanistan a couple of weeks ago. Our smart missiles weren't smart enough to tell wedding guests from terrorists. Maybe one of the partygoers fired a rifle in the air. It's a custom they have in the strange lands that we have decided to police and to Westernize. After the wedding-party incident, the propaganda honeymoon about smart weapons was over.

But at least that oops happened in Afghanistan, haven to the 9/11 terrorist who murdered our people. What does Afghanistan have to do with Iraq? What does 9/11 have to do with Saddam Hussein?

Nothing, says Brent Scowcroft, who is hardly a bleeding-heart liberal. Scowcroft, national security adviser to presidents Ford and Bush the First, said last week that a war against Saddam and Iraq "would seriously jeopardize, if not destroy, the global counterterrorist campaign we have undertaken."

He added: "There is scant evidence to tie Saddam to terrorist organizations, and even less to the Sept. 11 attacks."

So why do we keep saying and saying that we are going to wage war on Iraq? If Scowcroft doesn't know, I sure don't.

Polls show the public narrowly supports the president should he call for a "pre-emptive strike on Iraq." In English that means, "We gotta do something to him before he does something to us."

Older Americans do not support this and, as one, I know why. We were raised to believe that the Japanese attack on Pearl Harbor, unprovoked, was an act of treachery that violated all rules of civilized killing.

The Japanese have a different version of events. They learn in their schools that America forced Japan to strike the first blow. In Japan, they are teaching World War II the same way the Bush administration is sound-biting its way toward a war with Iraq.

The Bushies are telling us that the world would have been a much better place if somebody had taken Adolf Hitler out of the picture in the mid-1930s. And nobody can quarrel with that. It's patently true.

But nobody took him out, and millions died. Innocent people—privates, corporals, grandmothers and babies. And, except for one, none was named Hitler.

When we declared war on the Nazis, it was the last time Congress had the conviction or guts to declare a war. Since then, we've bloodied the world to get at a handful of people. Hitler and his gang. Ho and his gang. Mao and his gang.

Now it's Saddam and a new century. If we want him, let's get him. But let's spare the innocent and strike at the head. War is an ugly game with ridiculous rules. Give a gang of hit men a billion and let them go get him. It will be cheaper than a war. And more moral, too.

—August 18, 2002

Wise counsel from a mature Kucinich

Boy, has the Boy Mayor grown up!

Our own Dennis Kucinich is the most thoughtful and articulate spokesman in Washington against a pell-mell rush to a war against Iraq.

Dennis always marched to his own drummer. But when he was mayor of Cleveland, he followed a lot of bongo drums down a lot of blind alleys. He got mugged at the end of them.

Back then, he was a gadfly who couldn't govern. Now he holds the job he was born for. Maturity has mellowed him. He has learned to be calm and rational. And calmly, rationally, his has been the cool hand on the fevered brow of war furor.

Contrast his behavior with that of his fellow Democrats. Teddy Kennedy lumbered up to a microphone last week to deliver an anti-Bush, anti-war speech. But we expect Teddy Kennedy to be anti-anything a Republican president has in mind, including an ice cream social. He appeared and disappeared, wafting fumes of partisan politics.

Al Gore made a little speech, too, which was very tame. The eastern papers gave it front-page coverage. Ohio's greatest newspaper shoved it back where it belonged. It didn't say anything much. Gore still has hopes for political reincarnation. If he has convictions, his advisers water them down, hoping for another shot at those hanging chads in Florida.

Then there are Curly, Larry and Moe—the three Democratic congressmen who went to Iraq on our check last week and used the opportunity to call the president a liar.

Congressmen Jim McDermott, John Bonior and Mike Thompson were there on a fact-finding tour. That is Congress-ese for a free trip, good hotels and lots of limos. If they found a fact, they have not given us a peek at it. They used the Sunday blab shows to trash the president. They could have mouthed the same cant from Capitol Hill and spared us the price of an airline ticket.

The media were complicit in this. I watched five interviews with the Stooges and never heard an interviewer ask, "So what do you pick up from the people on the streets of Baghdad?" I would have liked to have known that. But the Washington media, inbred like the Jukes family, doesn't care about the buzz on the streets of Toledo, let alone Baghdad.

Dennis is a great exception. He speaks from conviction, not opportunism, and when you hear him you know and respect that. He grasps the real issue, which is not Saddam and what he may do in the future. The issue is Uncle Sam and what the future holds for us.

The Middle East is a mare's nest of problems and has been for decades. We want the oil. We fund dictators to stabilize the oil prices. We back Israel but also subsidize the rule of tyrants. We pay off leaders whose human rights policies (Saudi Arabia) would make an enlightened American gag.

This kind of crazy policy is a volatile mixture. But we've never found a solution for it.

Now, because of Sept. 11, and an election year, the solution touted by the White House is a pre-emptive strike on Iraq.

What Dennis wants to know is where such a strike will lead us. Our culture says that the bad guy draws first and the bully throws the first punch. If we change that thinking, where are we then? Who are we then?

Rep. Kucinich knows that the great matter at stake here is not a redefining of Iraq or the Middle East. What will happen next will redefine us, not them. That's what he's begging us to consider.

His mail is running 9-1 in his favor. That's 9-1 in favor of pausing to stop and think before we write the history of the next 50 years in letters of fire and blood.

Sounds reasonable. But so few in Washington value reason. Or even recognize it.

—October 2, 2002

Will U.S. kiss its assets goodbye?

"If cars ran on water, this wouldn't be happening," said Joe.

We were in the coffee shop talking about the sure-fire war against Iraq.

"But cars run on oil," Joe said. "All those suburban ladies in all those big SUVs in the Giant Eagle parking lot. What's Iraq to us? A sandbox with oil under it. But we got to defend those ladies' rights to block our view of traffic when they pull out next to us in those boxcars they drive."

Tom spoke up.

"I think that's too cynical," he said. "I heard the president's speech. He said Saddam Hussein may be close to having a nuclear bomb. He may be close to launching biological weapons our way. He's like Hitler. If we had it to do over again, wouldn't we have stopped Hitler?"

Frank chimed in then. "I don't buy the Hitler comparison," he said. "It's what comes of lousy history classes in public schools."

"Whaddya mean?" asked Tom.

"Hitler was a dictator like Saddam, that's true," said Frank. "He violated treaty agreements, that's true, too. But he built the greatest infantry in Europe and Saddam's army sucks. And we let him take Czechoslovakia. When Saddam went into Kuwait, we kicked him back out. Then we slapped sanctions on him and we've been bombing him ever since. The Hitler analogy doesn't play."

"Yeah," said Dan. "With Hitler you didn't have to guess. There were no maybes. It was all there under your nose."

"Wait a minute," I said. "These are different times. We ought to learn from our mistakes. Sen. Warner says we ought to use our assets to mount a pre-emptive strike of self-preservation."

"What does he mean by 'assets'?" asked Joe.

"He means GI's," I said.

"Ha!" said Joe. "How many around this table have ever served as 'assets'?"

We put our hands up. It was five-for-five.

"I was an asset in Vietnam," said Joe. "Fifty-thousand dead assets later, the guy who designed it is going around on book tours crying and saying he made a mistake."

"The reason we were all assets," I said, "was because back then everybody got drafted."

"It didn't work that way when I came along," said Joe. "If you could stay in college or father a kid or fake a rash or swear you wet the bed, you didn't have to go."

"When I went, everybody went," I said. "That was better because your family paid more attention to the news. Now it's somebody else's kid off someplace doing something that looks like a video game on TV."

"I heard this jerk on television," said Joe. "Guy named Ken Adelman. Never was an asset. He's in a think tank selling the war. Woman calls in and says her kid is in the Army and she's worried about Iraq. Adelman says, 'Madam, your son knew what he was risking when he enlisted.'"

"Sometimes they only enlist because they can't get another job," said Dan. "If the think-tank guys screw up, they don't come home in body bags. They go back on C-SPAN and talk about the next war."

Tom spoke up then.

"I'm with the president," he said. "We've got to hit Saddam before he hits us. He made his case."

"He left a couple of things out," said Joe. "Are we going to occupy the country? Who are we going to install as the next ruler? If Saddam attacks Israel and Israel fights back, what happens to the region. And are we now going to be in charge of the world? If that's true, your grandchildren are going to be assets before it's all over."

"We're having a better conversation in this coffee shop than they're having in Congress," said Joe. "But it's an election year and they're all covering their as-"

"Assets," said Frank, "some of which they'll cover with sod."

—October 9, 2002

Peace ends—war never seems to

I am 12 years old in 1950 and on vacation in Upper Michigan. Our rented cabin, with its outhouse, is in a huge forest. There is no electricity. My father, my uncle and I are out in the dark, fragrant pines listening to radio in my dad's '49 Chevy.

The radio says North Korea invaded South Korea and America is at war. My father and my uncle, recently returned from war, shake their heads and go back into the cabin to light the kerosene lamp and play pinochle.

I am 19 years old and sitting in an ROTC class at Ohio University. I'm wearing a recycled, ill-fitting uniform happily abandoned by a private after World War II. My teacher is an Army captain.

"Peace is a noble goal," he says. "But there is no end to war. When the crossbow was invented centuries ago, some people said it was so terrible it would bring an end to warfare. But we in the uniform know better. Now we have atomic weapons. Man cannot invent a weapon of destruction so terrible it will keep him from using it."

I am a 23-year-old lieutenant running convoys to the beaches of South Florida to prepare for an invasion of Cuba. If anything goes wrong, the world will be burned to a cinder. Washington and Moscow are playing chess, and the game ends in some kind of draw. So we all live.

I am 24 years old and in the Army Reserve. I'm assigned to a two-week summer camp at Fort Knox. One night in the Officer's Club, a major walks in. He is just back from an advisory tour in Vietnam. He is tall, lean and mean with a chest full of medals. He has a couple of drinks and says:

"It's a bitch of a war. Wrong place, wrong allies, wrong reasons. You get 50 miles outside of Saigon and they've never heard of democracy. Hell, they've never heard of Saigon!"

I am 26 years old and a reporter for the Cleveland Press when Lyndon Johnson comes to town. I cover his speech at Public Hall.

He vows never to send American boys to fight on Asian soil. Because of that vow and because of what the major said, I vote for him.

I am 29 years old aboard a chopper flying from Da Nang to Dong Ha, covering the war for my paper. The propaganda back home says that if we don't stop the North Vietnamese now, they will land in San Francisco.

A colonel talks to me above the beat of the engine. "We're winning in the field," he says. "We're winning the battles. But nobody has told us how to win the war." At Dong Ha we pick up the stateside wounded, grinning from ear to ear. And we pick up some black bags. The wounded don't want to see them. I see them even now.

I am 53 years old when we go into the Gulf War. We save the oil and stop short of Baghdad. We announce that we've won the war, and maybe we have. We remain, to this hour, Iraq's best customer for oil. Did we bury 200 Americans to keep the freeways tangled at rush hour? What else did we win when I was 53?

I am 64 years old and we are ready to attack Iraq again. We will kill more Iraqis than we will ever admit to and lose some of our own. As was the case in Vietnam, our generals know how to fight but nobody has told them how to win. There is still no endgame.

Maybe that ROTC captain was right. Maybe there's no such thing as an endgame. One war leads to the next. Every generation is bloodied by the generation that went before. Most of the politicians about to send the kids off to Iraq never served a day in the military. That's bad. But worse are the rest of us, veterans included—especially veterans—who will send them without question.

—November 13, 2002

Bush hasn't said why U.S. must go to war

Glimpses of the great peace march on Washington last weekend were nauseating. The assembly of kooks and weirdos who were handed microphones to speak against the war with Iraq almost made me pro-war. Which, indeed, I'm not. Nor is most of America.

It was a grotesque rerun of the anti-Vietnam rallies of the '60s. Any fanatic with a strange, personal, anti-American agenda got his turn at the mike. It is a sad rule of freedom of speech that people who turn up in 20-degree weather to bellow at a crowd are either half-crazed or, like Jesse Jackson, have a career riding on the line.

I had a lot of experience with such spectacles in the '60s. The people who really cared about the issue rode all night in buses and stood, frozen and sore-kneed, in the audience. The people on the podium arrived in limos, spouted their self-serving cant or twanged their soulful folk tunes and departed for the nearest Ritz or head shop. Bitter fights broke out backstage over who would get a piece of the loudspeaker. The issue at stake got lost in the anarchy. So there was always somebody who was a member of something like "Cross-dressers United Against Fascist America" who got his turn, costumed in a combat jacket and a beret, to appall Middle-America and scare away the very folks who should have been on his side but couldn't stand the thought of it.

The anti-war rally was a bust. There was nothing in it to detour the president or his advisors from the increasingly obvious madness of their Iraq adventure.

What should worry the president are the thousands of tiny anti-war rallies that occur all across the nation every day in coffee shops and saloons and around kitchen tables. The quiet, worried conversations that reach a consensus that shedding American blood to get rid of Saddam Hussein is a bad idea.

America doesn't want this war, and the polls are beginning to show it. The polls show America doesn't want us to attack Iraq alone.

Alone means even with the British. America only wants to attack if the United Nations backs us. That's code for saying "if enough other countries agree with us, maybe that means we aren't nuts."

But the rest of the world thinks we are nuts. The articulate, reasonable anti-war rallies around the world, given scant coverage here, express the overwhelming global view that Uncle Sam has lost his marbles.

I don't know how many marbles there are in the Oval Office. We know very little about this president and the way he thinks. He's had a much longer honeymoon than most presidents get. When those planes hit the twin towers, America, understandably, gave him a blank check. His credit rating got the kind of boost you get from those credit card companies that send the junk mail that tells you that suddenly you are rich.

So, suddenly, he was rich. We all flew our flags and vowed we would do whatever it took to find Osama bin Laden and his band of thugs who had murdered our own. Few presidents get that kind of unanimous emotional support.

Maybe it went to George W's head. How can I know? How can you know? Who among us can imagine the power of waving a wand and sending five carriers to the Middle East. Fathers kissing babies on the dockside. Young men hugging young women and vowing, in a wash of tears, to return. But with that kind of power comes the responsibility to explain why.

We missed bin Laden. He's still around. People who give him comfort and hide him from us are among our so-called allies. What has any of this got to do with Iraq? So far, after months and months, the president has not explained this to us.

When the Constitution was ratified, the unspoken prayer was that American people are smarter than their leaders and can lead those who govern. The kooks and nuts on the mall last weekend can be easily ignored. What the president should worry about are all the rest of us who sit here watching him and increasingly wondering if he has a clue.

—January 22, 2003

War hysteria is all around us

A maniac turned up on Fox News the other night to encourage America to torture her enemies.

His name was Jack Wheeler, and he represented something called the Freedom Research Foundation. It was one of those myriad organizations that nobody ever heard of outside of a TV talk show. I doubt we'll hear much more of Mr. Wheeler either. His message was too brutal, even for the Fox News blab hosts.

Wheeler was asked if he would torture the recently captured al-Qaida kingpin Khalid Shaikh Mohammad to pry information out of him. Without batting a beady eye, Wheeler said he would. But he would do it humanely, he said.

How do you do that? the host wanted to know.

Wheeler explained he would inject a drug into Mohammad that would paralyze his lungs so he couldn't breathe. Then he would put Mohammad on a respirator. If Mohammad didn't answer a question, he would turn the respirator off for a while, then turn it back on again. Wheeler said his method was a lot better than something low-tech like lopping off a hand with a chainsaw. Then he was dismissed with thanks and the network went to a commercial for ditech.com.

I don't call Wheeler a maniac merely because he is. He is a carrier of the present war mania, which obviously also infected the producer who booked him and the hosts who interviewed him. War mania is running high and it's coming at us from all directions—not just from warmongers but from peaceniks as well.

Toledo Congresswoman Marcy Kaptur is anti-war. So am I. But we parted company the other day when, in a newspaper interview, she compared Osama bin Laden to America's founding fathers who fought to win independence from England.

She might as well have called Abe Lincoln an imperialist tyrant for making war on the South to prevent it from gaining freedom from the union. This kind of warped and unrestrained reasoning is a product of war mania, too. It's in the air like pollution and we breathe it in daily in these tense and horrible days.

I saw some of it during the anti-war rally in London, where one protester marched down the street carrying an American flag with a big swastika painted on it.

A peace symbol? OK. Bush in a cowboy hat? OK. But a swastika on an American flag in London? Thousands of Americans died or shed their blood to help our British allies when the Nazis had them with their backs against the wall. George Bush, whatever anybody thinks of him, is no Nazi. Saddam Hussein, whatever anybody thinks of him, is no Hitler either.

The first casualty of war is truth. The first casualties of war mania are common sense and restraint. Frankly, I don't see much of either in the present war policy. War supporters see plenty of both.

They say it's only common sense to strike Iraq before Iraq strikes us. But no evidence has been presented that Iraq intends to strike us. Or that it had anything to do with 9/11.

The president says too much restraint has been showered on Saddam. That he is Hitler-lite. And that it's high time we neutralized him.

Well, we bomb him every day. We have U.N. inspectors running all over his country and troops on his borders ready to strike. Nobody was doing that to Hitler in 1938. Had they been, it surely would have prevented war.

The irony here is that the president's policy has divided a country that ought to be celebrating now. We've captured the man who masterminded the World Trade Center attacks. That's a cause for pride, hope and rejoicing. And even without Jack "the Ripper" Wheeler's humane strangulation technique, Mohammad reportedly is furnishing information that might lead to the capture of bin Laden who, all Americans agree, is our public enemy No. 1.

Jack Wheeler represents a point of view that violates all of our principles. So does a pre-emptive war against a nation that poses no immediate threat to us.

You have to be careful in war not to become the thing you hate. Are we being careful enough?

—March 9, 2003

Did we forget? War's still terrible

America learned a lot about war in a week.

There is an amnesia about warfare that requires each generation to learn its lessons from scratch. Here are the things we encountered this week that we should have remembered from the past:

Plans stop when war starts. The plan was to send the 4th Infantry Division down from the north through Turkey to put pressure on Baghdad. But no matter how hard we tried, we couldn't bribe the Turks to let us do this. So that plan fell through.

Then there was the wishful idea that we'd be greeted as liberators wherever we went. This would allow us to breeze past cities in southern Iraq on the road to Baghdad. But those southern cities did not greet our troops with flowers, kisses and open wine bottles. We were welcomed with mortars and machine gun fire. We couldn't tell the friendlies from the foe. That's an old Vietnam lesson we should have learned by heart. But if we knew it, we forgot it.

We forgot that the enemy fights dirty. Sometimes he raises a white flag just to get our troops in firing range. Sometimes he hides in clumps of civilians. Sometimes, as in Vietnam, he sends a child toward a soldier offering chewing gum—a little kid with a grenade under her little blouse.

The two-star generals who host the morning briefings call such tactics cowardly and against the rules of war. But there are only two rules of war. The first rule is, don't fight unless you have to. The second rule is, once you start fighting, there are no rules.

We're close to understanding the second rule. We are on the brink of the battle for Baghdad. When we get the sand out of our eyes, the preliminaries will be over and we'll be ready for the main event.

We've been told that our smart bombs can pick and choose between soldiers and civilians—that we can, with maximum discretion, spare the kids and kill the enemy.

But what if it doesn't work out that way? Suppose the soldiers are so blended with the civilians that we have to kill both to save American lives. What do we do then?

I know what I'd do. I'd save our troops and kill the civilians. Any conscientious military commander would do the same thing.

That's the trouble with selling a war as if it were an air freshener. A war is the dirtiest pollutant that civilization can emit. But wars always arrive in clean packages, wrapped in tissue and bows and offered by politicians as a righteous gift to the world.

When we get to Baghdad, the wrapping paper will come off. The vaunted smart bombs will retire to the wings with the vaunted smart generals. And it will all come down to somebody's kid trying to stay alive by shooting somebody else's kid.

I am on the side of our troops, but I have no illusions. Friday's front page reported that Pvt. Brandon Sloan of Bedford Heights was missing in action. I pray that he's well. But I remember that in Vietnam we used to have a rule of thumb that out of every hundred kids lost, one was from our area.

When they started dying, they died on Page One. But, after a while they died a couple of pages inside the newspaper with little five-paragraph obits and tiny half-column pictures.

These are not things we are at liberty to forget. In a week of war, our memories have been jogged and we remember war's truth: You save yourself by killing the other guy. Then you spend the rest of your life living with that.

—March 26, 2003

Savior and saved are an unlikely pair

She was a teenager from Palestine, W. Va. She wanted to be a schoolteacher but money was tight. So she joined the Army to earn her college tuition.

He was a lawyer who lived halfway around the world. The only Palestine he knew about was a place where people bleed and die for causes bewildering to the Palestine where she was raised.

They had nothing in common, the two of them.

She enlisted in the Army the same day her brother did. Her brother was sent to Fort Bragg. The Army sent her to Iraq.

He lives in Iraq, near a town called Nasiriyah. It was a town she'd never heard of—an unpronounceable town most people in West Virginia or anywhere else never heard of.

She was assigned to a maintenance unit, which is supposed to be a pretty safe assignment. They put her in a truck in a long convoy and pointed the convoy north toward Baghdad.

He watched Iraqi television and listened to shortwave radio and heard about the bombs falling on his homeland and prayed he'd survive them.

Somehow, her truck took a wrong turn, and it was ambushed by the Iraqi military. The teenager who wanted to be a kindergarten teacher picked up her rifle and kept firing until she was out of ammunition.

Many of her comrades died. She was taken prisoner and put in a hospital in Nasiriya.

His wife is a nurse in that very same hospital. By all accounts, the soldier was treated roughly. But she was still alive.

He went to the hospital to visit his wife.

While he was there, he caught a glimpse of her through a window.

He saw an Iraqi paramilitary soldier slap her in the face.

She lay in her bunk, yearning that a miracle would happen and she'd live to see Palestine, W. Va., again.

He was her miracle.

He walked six miles through what the Marines call "Ambush

Alley" to a military checkpoint. He could have been killed at any time.

He told the Marines that he'd seen an American POW in the hospital. The Marines asked him to go back to the hospital, check up on its security system and draw a map of the place showing exactly where this POW was being held.

She was lying in bed when he walked into her room.

"She think I doctor," he told reporters later. "I said, 'Good morning.' She said, 'Good morning, doctor.' I said, 'Don't worry,' and she smiled."

He made his map and took it back to the Marines. And that night, a team of joint-service commandos rushed the hospital and took her out of there.

Now she is recovering in Germany from her injuries. Her name is Pvt. Jessica Lynch. She doesn't belong to Palestine, W. Va., anymore. She belongs to all of us and to the history books.

The only name he wants to give right now is Mohammed. He doesn't want to risk the safety of his relatives now that the story of what he did is out.

His cover is good because there are lots of Mohammeds in Iraq. There are a lot of cities called Palestine, too—scattered around America and elsewhere.

But what are the odds, in this huge world of love and hate, peace and bloodshed, of Mohammed and Pvt. Lynch finding each other in a miracle moment?

Who knows what will happen to them now? Maybe she'll get that teaching job she wanted. Or maybe when Hollywood gets through with her, she'll be making music videos for MTV.

And what about him? Will he stay in his homeland to see how it fares under a new government? Or will he leave to come here and let Barbara Walters interview him?

These are unimportant questions. The profound question is how these two people, with their separate Palestines and their separate gods, found their way to each other and brought salvation from the depths of carnage.

I can't answer that. I can only call it shock and awe.

—April 6, 2003

A close-up reminder of the costs of war

The guy next to me in the barber chair had no left arm. I didn't know that right away because he had one of those barber's drop cloths pulled up to his chin.

When my turn came, I drew the chair next to his. I'm not great at chatting in barber chairs. Usually I bring a book and bury my nose in it to ward off conversation.

Barbers excel at small talk. They ask you what you think about the weather. (This year the weather is too cold. The barber and I took a vote and unanimously agreed on that.) Then the discussion tends to lull.

I closed my eyes and listened to the conversation drone on next to me. It was a conversation about Vietnam.

It turned out that both the barber and his customer had served in Vietnam in the late '60s. I opened my eyes and peeked at the guy in the next chair. He was an old guy like me—a grandpa.

So I thought about time warp. The '60s are 40 years behind us, but to many of us they seem like yesterday. Probably every generation feels that way. Forty years ago is more real than yesterday. Yesterday is hardly real at all. That's why we bore our kids and our grandkids. And in my case, maybe, the readers.

The guy in the next chair had kept most of his hair. It was gray. He had a neat fringe of a mustache, also gray. I broke my rule about chatting and spoke to him.

"When were you in Vietnam?" I asked him.

"'67 to '68," he said.

"In the Army?" I asked.

"Yep," he said.

"So was I," said his barber.

"It's funny," I said. "Young guys today think of that as an ancient war. It might as well be the Spanish-American War. But to us, it seems like it just happened."

Neither of them answered me. Then the barber spoke up. He nodded at his client beneath the sheet.

"He lost his arm there," the barber said.

"Well, not really there," said the guy in the chair. "I lost it after I got back. It was cancer. They said it was because of Agent Orange."

"You know what that was," said the barber. "That stuff we sprayed on the jungle to kill the trees so we could find the Ho Chi Minh Trail."

I knew.

"How about a trim to the nostrils and the ears?" my barber said.

"Sure," I said. "One of the hells of getting old is that you grow hair where you don't want it and don't grow it where you want it."

And then I was sorry I had said it. You can't grow back an arm.

"Let me ask you a question," I said to my neighbor. "Do you think the government knew that stuff might be toxic to you? Or do you think they never had a clue?"

"I don't know," he said. "I don't know what they knew and what they didn't know."

Then our haircuts were finished. We both got up at the same time and got the senior citizen rate, which is a buck off. When the barber pulled the sheet off my neighbor, I saw that it was his left arm that was missing. So we shook hands in the conventional way and parted. But he didn't leave me. I took him home in my head that night. And I thought about wars and how quickly we, the unblemished, get over them and how ready we are to gear ourselves up for the next one.

I also thought about a grandpa who can hug one of his grandchildren but not two at once. And I thought about the government that sends young people to war. And about how, behind the rhetoric, there are plenty of things they don't know—haven't got a clue about.

Lord knows the guy in the next chair served his country. But did his country serve him? In the present muddle, which increasingly seems to be built on half-truths and deceptions, we should demand to know if government is serving or self-serving.

The man I shook hands with has that right. So do the kids fighting today who will carry this war with them, as an ever-fresh memory, down through the decades.

—June 22, 2003

The big find is a widget of mulch destruction

It was breaking news on CNN, but it really belonged on *Saturday Night Live.*

Finally, a sort-of weapon of mass destruction had been discovered in Iraq. It was buried under a rosebush.

This horrible weapon looked pretty tame when displayed on TV. It looked like a 1950 DeSoto hubcap. It didn't appear to be the kind of thing that would make you invade a country, kill thousands of civilians, lose scores of American lives and then get bogged down for an indefinite and bloody future.

But the Bush administration was excited about it. It was the closest thing to a WMD we had found. A "senior official" made it sound like a great prize—akin to finding a solid-chocolate bunny in an Easter egg hunt.

"This is a significant find," the official told *USA Today*. "It's important because it tells us how hard the job is to uncover weapons of mass destruction in Iraq."

But exactly what was this hubcap? According to news reports, it was "a highly engineered metal component that was a sample part for a possible plan to build a gas-centrifuge plant capable of enriching uranium to weapons grade."

To the objective ear, this hardly sounds like the kind of immediate threat that would make America drop whatever else it was doing and rush over to seize Iraq. In fact, there was no immediate threat surrounding the hubcap at all. It turns out it had been buried under the rosebush for 12 years.

The guy who buried it is a nuclear scientist named Mehdi Obeidi. He said Iraqi officials told him to hide it back in 1991. The rosebush was his idea.

This kind of horticultural treachery may make the rosebush an accomplice in the war on terrorism. Perhaps, behind the scenes, the Department of Homeland Security is already on the job.

Our alert level may be raised to rosy pink. Investigators may be compiling lists of garden center customers and people who order seeds from the Burpee catalog. Patriotic Americans may be encouraged to turn against rosebushes the way we shunned French wine. A rose is not a rose is not a rose anymore. A rose is now cover for a sinister deception.

The rosebush story came at a time when it was obvious that not everything was coming up roses in Iraq. The country we "liberated" is still shooting at us and killing a couple of Americans each week. We are, to many Iraqis, an army of occupation. The troops in armies of occupation always have to watch their backs. The Bush administration was not prepared for this scenario, even though winning the peace was not nearly as sure a bet as winning the war.

The president announced a couple of weeks ago that the war was over and that we had won it. Some of his generals don't feel that way and have said so. The families of our troops who are dying every week certainly agree with these generals.

I was against this war from the beginning for both moral and practical reasons. I thought it was contrary to our tradition to wage a pre-emptive war. I thought that no case had been made that Iraq was involved in the World Trade Center attacks. And I thought, given the fact that we were bombing Iraq a couple of times each day, that Saddam and his thugs presented little immediate danger to us.

All of that aside, the practical reason was simply this: We had no exit strategy. Our generals could tell us how to go in, but they couldn't tell us how, when or why to get out.

You don't have to be a history Ph.D. to know the importance of an exit strategy. Surely, if you are president of the United States and were alive and alert during Vietnam, you ought to understand the importance of the endgame.

This president and those who advise him seem to have no endgame in mind. As the weeks drag on, more and more of us should demand to know the plan.

To many of us, this war is unjustifiable. Finding a hubcap buried under a rosebush is no justification for the bloodletting.

No war, anywhere, is ever a bed of roses. The president made his bed, but it's young Americans who have to sleep in it. And some will sleep forever.

—June 29, 2003

Bush doesn't understand Iraq

I got back from a trip to Vietnam, and I was sitting on the No. 9 bus, going to work, when the Tet offensive happened.

This, of course, is ancient history—1968. It has nothing to do with our present century, right?

Around me on the bus, commuters were reading the bold headlines about commie troops attacking Saigon. And one wing-tips-shod commuter said:

"How did they get into Saigon? I thought we had Saigon."

What I should have said was, "Brother, we haven't got squat!"

But I didn't. I said nothing. Now, 35 years later, I'll say it about Iraq and the whole cauldron of the Middle East.

Brother, we haven't got squat.

And, like Vietnam, we ain't gonna get squat.

The president doesn't seem to know this. Perhaps nobody has told him. He seems only vaguely aware of the swamp he has led us into.

If he knew his history, he'd be worried. But you get the impression that this president lives in the moment with a very limited attention span. He lacks the ability to learn from the lessons of yesterday or the imagination to plan for the problems of tomorrow. He may be our first president with attention deficit disorder.

Yesterday, when a terrorist blew up the U.N. headquarters in Baghdad, CNN told us that the president had interrupted his golf game to respond to this event.

He arrived, sweaty, in his golf shirt, and issued a statement on audiotape (because the TV sweat showed) which the entire world listened to. As usual, he spoke in platitudes. When you distilled them, what he said was laughable.

He pledged that America would continue its war of liberation in Iraq. Then, presumably, he went back to finish his 18 holes.

Our troops in Iraq are not so lucky. No golf for them. They are stuck and sweaty, and some of them are dying. They've been there longer than they were led to believe they'd be. They are wonderful kids, most of whom weren't born when the commies swarmed into

Saigon. They trusted their leaders not to put them in another impossible situation. Their leaders let them down.

Now it's new leaders, same game. Then, as now, we sent our troops into a country we knew little about. Then, as now, we asked them to win conventional battles in the field. Then, as now, they won them.

And then, having occupied the country, the troops turned to Washington and asked, "What do we do now?"

Washington has no answer.

This president strikes me as a dumb guy. Well, God bless him, it's no sin to be dumb. If you're born that way, you're born that way. There is good in all of us, even the dumbest among us. But we really don't want a dumkopf running the world. And I fear we've got one.

Now I will get 100 calls branding me a Bush-basher. For the record, I happen to be a conservative. But I can't support a president who has managed, in a couple of years, to warp my country's global mandate and stupidly plunge our troops into a quagmire that knows no bottom.

Iraq was not a threat to us. There were no weapons of mass destruction. We should not have attacked a nation that showed no signs of attacking us. We should not have freelanced such an attack and snubbed the U.N. And we should have known that many in the nation we "liberated" might greet us with bombs, not roses.

All that stuff is in the Vietnam playbook, which nobody, apparently has read. Maybe if it rains on the golf course, Bush will read it.

I'm no pacifist. I'm just old enough to have seen a few things. And I hate to see history repeat itself. I hate to see our leaders smugly sending kids to places they don't have to go.

I can't say "get out of Iraq," because we can't get out now. I'm not sure how we are going to clean up the mess we've made. But let's at least do ourselves and the world a favor: Let's let Bush and his masterminds play golf with no interruption. After the election.

—August 20, 2003

Troops used as a photo-op

On Thanksgiving Day, over a turkey, a relative told me that George W. Bush had gone to Iraq.

"Great!" I said. "That's marvelous!" But then my spirits sank. It turned out he was coming back.

To show you the miserable shape the country is in, the president's grandstand, hot-dog, two-hour photo-op in Baghdad silenced the Democrats for three whole days.

Alas, there may be no hope for the Democrats. They didn't have enough bulge in their Jockey shorts to brand Bush's visit what it was: a cheap publicity stunt.

True, it was a masterfully executed cheap publicity stunt. How can you criticize a president who flies over briefly to visit his troops in time of war? Repeatedly through the long holiday weekend we saw the president holding a great platter of turkey and trimmings, dressed up like a GI Joe doll in some kind of nonregulation Army jacket, posing for pictures, bravely facing a fusillade of flashbulbs triggered by the adoring kids he sent to risk their lives.

Then he left them and came home.

They didn't.

They are still there today. The cameras are gone but some of them are dying, out of reach of a photo-op—a quiet trickle of death, a little at a time. Bush and his turkey filled the news hole on C-SPAN. Pictures of kids in Walter Reed, without their legs, is not Thanksgiving fare. And when the kids die and come back home in flag-draped coffins, the cameras that courted George W. Bush turn their backs, by order, on the caskets.

And we—a lot of us in America—don't care.

I have lived through three wars. But I've never seen America yawn at a war before. In the past, when we sent kids off to kill and be killed, we at least paid some attention to the whys and wherefores.

In the last two wars, Korea and Vietnam, the whys and wherefores were murky. That's why neither war was a declared war. Congress, which has grown used to being gutless, and I mean gutless, sent our young people off to die for rhetoric. But at least the rhetoric seemed to have some sense to it—at least at the time it did.

This current war makes no sense at all. As bad as Vietnam was and as bad as Korea was, this war is the worst, because we have absolutely no reason to be fighting it. Even the mumbled rhetoric can't justify this.

The rhetoric of this war, as uttered by the president and his cronies, is as crooked as a three-card monte game. It's a slick con job played off suckers. And who are the suckers? The suckers are us.

Just let's ask ourselves a couple of easy questions:

Why are we in Iraq?

The only answer is, "Duh."

Did Iraq have anything to do with the Twin Towers?

No.

Does Iraq have weapons of mass destruction that were a threat to America?

No.

Had the administration planned to attack Iraq long before 9/11?

Yes.

Did America and the world support the president after 9/11 and vow to wage war against the people who did it?

Yes.

Are we now, for murky reasons, engaged in the wrong place in the wrong war for the wrong reasons, killing and being killed? And has most of the world's sentiment abandoned us?

Yes.

Once upon a time, I thought anybody in charge of my country had to be a genius. That's what happens when you're raised in a blue-collar neighborhood of plumbers and pipe fitters. You always assume that the guys in charge have to be brighter than you are.

Then, in this racket, I got to cover a lot of presidents. And I found out that many are weak and lie and connive. I was about 50 years old before I found that out.

Those kids in Baghdad, who got a sliver of turkey or the edge of a photo-op, don't know that yet.

Once I was one of them and enthusiastic. But after Vietnam, I always thought of wars as child molestation. I still do.

—December 3, 2003

Saddam's in the bag, but terrorists aren't

"We got him!" That was the front-page headline around the world.

We got him! It was translated into many languages. But, putting it in plain English, what, exactly, did we get?

What have we earned with our blood and our treasure?

What did Saddam, in his rat hole, have to do with the World Trade Center?

And how about the terrorists who planned the attack? What does the man in the hole have to say about them?

Or what about the weapons of mass destruction that we were assured were poised on our doorstep, waiting to kill us?

As evil as he was, what part did he play in any of these?

We don't know.

OK, Saddam is the mother of all muthas, we can all agree to that. And we salute our American troops who went halfway around the world to run him to earth in his badger den.

He gave up without a bite or a squeak. And, if global opinion prevails, he will not be executed for his horrible and bloodthirsty sins. He was an evil man and we got him. But we got him at the cost of a couple of hundred American troops killed and thousands more maimed.

In our celebration, let's not forget them. We got him, but he got us, too, and at such a cost.

The world is certainly better off without Saddam. But the world is also certainly far worse off without the brave, individual Americans who died in the long struggle to capture him. Is that an even trade?

Such a question hangs limp from too many Christmas trees this year. And there will be too many empty chairs at the Christmas table.

No war is an even trade. In recent wars, too many bright, marvelous kids have died in the name of some think-tank hunch—a hunch generally put forth by older men who have never seen war firsthand and have neither the stomach nor the wish to see it.

All this past weekend long, such safety-zone experts have strutted on display, trying to make us believe that the capture of Saddam was worth our dead and maimed. The anchors on the cable shows, prodding babble-meisters through at the speed of a soundbite, have asked what effect the Saddam capture will have on the next election. But the question should boil down to this: What did Saddam have to do with the World Trade Center attack? Or with the terrorists who planned that attack?

And we still don't know.

I've been against this war from the beginning. The nabbing of Saddam doesn't change my mind. Hats off to the troops who got him. But his capture hardly removes the central question. And the central question remains this: What the hell are we doing in Iraq?

I'm no pacifist. If somebody had killed my relative in the World Trade Center, I would cry for blood. After 9/11, our nation started off on a blood feud, looking for terrorists in Afghanistan. I liked that. I quickly abandoned the more tender parts of my own religion, which teaches me to turn the other cheek. I wanted anybody who bombed the World Trade Center obliterated. And I was willing to back George W. Bush in his attempt to find them all and kill them.

Now l feel used. I feel as if the president used this great, national, emotional cry for vengeance to activate a preplanned war on Iraq. It was an idea he and his advisers had on file long before 9/11. And after the World Trade Center, it was easy to artfully siphon our anger and direct it toward Iraq.

Politically, this has been a great week for Bush and all who endorse him. It's been a chaotic week for the Democrats, who have no backbone and are scrambling to sound as if they were always on the "pro" side in the war against Iraq.

I'm a Reagan Democrat, trying to get back to his old party. But right now I don't have a candidate. I guess my allegiance is to the troops. They did all that was asked of them. They gave us a good week in a bad war. They know better than us that next week the good may melt away. If it does, they'll still be the best. Let's find a candidate who can equal them.

—December 17, 2003

Bush needed time in the trenches

Of course George W. Bush wriggled his way out of Vietnam. That was a war fought mainly by poor kids who had no angles to play. The rich always have angles, and the Bushes were rich.

There were notable exceptions, and John Kerry was one of them. Kerry could have pulled some strings and stayed home too. But he felt a call of conscience, so he served.

When he came back, having won decorations for bravery, Kerry protested the war. He was 20 years ahead of Robert McNamara, who, to save his soul, is protesting it even now. But McNamara was a chart guy, blueprinting an elegant, boardroom structure of destruction. Kerry was really there, on the ground, where the blueprints turn to blood.

Anybody who sees war close up hates what he sees. It's only those people on the sidelines, like our current president, who can talk of war in righteous terms.

Kerry is now running on his war record and that's kind of a shame. If you've done something valorous, you shouldn't have to wave it. As the campaign deepens, Kerry might use his medals and his exploits to gain a political advantage. After all, he went to Nam and Bush didn't. And Vietnam, as I've often said in this space, is still very much with us.

Every war ought to be alive and instructive in the memories of those who experienced it. We thought we'd learned in the '60s that when we send our youth to kill people and be killed themselves, it ought to capture our full attention. But time passes and we forget such lessons. We forget easily.

Unlike the Europeans, we forget history. Over here, history—even recent history—goes in the trash bag with the rest of the nonessentials. We don't care enough about it to recycle it. But history recycles itself. It always comes around to bite us in the end.

The drillpress of Yale should have somehow taught the current president a bit of history. But his life experience, sheltered as it was, was his primary instructor. So, during Vietnam, he did what a lot of well-bred, well-off people did in his generation. He took a bail. He joined the National Guard, which, back in those days, was a picnic lunch. It was a refuge for kids who had pull. The kids with no pull were being daily shipped off to Saigon.

(When will we ever learn that wars are planned by people who will never fight in them? It's a lesson that echoes and re-echoes. But we never hear it.)

On Fox TV the other night, the blabbers were talking about Kerry's protest against the war he served in.

One blabber played a news clip from his testimony back then. In it, Kerry talked about atrocities committed by American servicemen. Then the blab moderator used that clip to accuse Kerry of indicting all U.S. servicemen for atrocities in Vietnam.

I watched it and got ill. The people on the panel were all too young to have seen war as Kerry did. And my bet is that if war threatened them, they would all find a way to avoid it.

Kerry knows what war is. He knows that maybe some of the kids we sent to Vietnam—on a very hot day, with underwear crawling with leaches and a buddy shot in the head by sniper fire—burned some village and killed some people who might have been innocent.

That's war. And some of those kids have been haunted by it ever since. I'd like to see the guy in charge of sending kids into combat make his decisions with the ghosts of all the lost and troubled kids who have gone before whispering in his ear.

—February 11, 2004

Everyone must have a stake in Iraq war

It's time to bring back the draft.

That way, every family in America with an eligible teenage son or daughter will have a stake in American foreign policy.

Nobody with a kid in service will be able to ignore CNN or a presidential press conference and tune to *The Apprentice* instead.

The draft would be good for Congress. With a district full of draftees and their parents and wives or husbands, Congress would have to pay more attention to the bloody messes they allow a president to get us into.

We call what's going on in Iraq a war. And in the real and violent sense, it certainly is. But it isn't a declared war. We haven't had a declared war since World War II. Korea was a "police action." Vietnam—I think they called that one a "conflict." And this thing has some kind of zippy title on it like "Operation Spread Democracy, Iraqi Freedom, Fatten Contractors, Cheaper Gas for SUVs."

It's high time we got back to the days when members of Congress would have to stand on the floor in front of God and C-Span and vote to send our kids off to kill and be killed.

John Kerry's biggest weakness in this election is going to be that he voted for war. He's going to try to say, indeed has already said, that he voted to give the president the power to wage war but that he doesn't like the way the president did it.

Sorry, but that's a cop-out. When we go to war, we ought to go from the grass roots up. Kerry, by his agreement to let George Bush blunder into Iraq, is as responsible for this mess as the president is. It will be interesting to see how he tries to worm his way out of that responsibility.

Everybody makes fun of Dennis Kucinich. They say he's on some kind of ego trip and has become a ludicrous figure by persisting in a no-chance presidential campaign this long.

But I don't agree. I live in Dennis' district and when he beat a pal of mine, Martin Hoke, I groaned. But Dennis is running on conviction. He voted against the Iraq misadventure. For that he deserves credit that Kerry cannot claim.

Those of us who shrilly opposed the war are suffering from a severe attack of cognitive dissonance. That's the marvelous phrase that means you're trying to hold two opposing ideas in your head at the same time and, while they bang into each other, make them work without an aspirin.

We never should have gone to Iraq. But, now that we are there, we can't pull out. It's hard to make logic from such thoughts. Maybe Socrates could do it. But there's no Socrates in sight.

A news report the other day reminded me that the original estimate on troop strength for Iraq was 30,000. At the moment we have 137,000 troops in Iraq, and the Pentagon is asking for more. And they'll get more. They always do. In for a penny, in for a pound. That's the great law of a war where there are no front lines, no clear objective (other than babbling about democracy) and no exit strategy. You and I have seen this drama before. Where were the guys who are running this thing? Improving their putting game?

The headline in *USA Today* read: "Fewer soldiers re-enlist. Army sees dip as war increases need."

So maybe it's draft time. In my ancient days as a Cold Warrior we all went in. I went in as an ROTC officer because I thought that was smarter than going in as a private. The guys on my block enlisted, too. We all became shareholders in what our government did.

So I say bring back the draft, and let everybody in on the action. But I want a fair draft—not like the one in Vietnam when, if you could pay your way into college you got a deferment for studying bugs. And no lottery either. Everybody goes.

If we are going to cowboy around the world and send our 20-year-olds to do it, let's send them all. Mine, yours, everybody's. A universal draft would make us feel the chill of the draft. And there would be more dishonorable discharges among the old men in charge of shortening the lives of kids they claim to represent.

—April 18, 2004

Send untrained kids to war, things go wrong

The thugs took over the prison, and they were our thugs.

Cut through the gasbag testimony of yesterday's congressional committee and what stands out is this:

Somebody sent our thugs in to violate all principles of decency. And whoever that somebody was, it was a stupid somebody.

And that's consistent with this war and the stupid people leading it.

If you heard the testimony yesterday, you heard that an untrained MP company with no experience in handling prisoners was scooped up and sent to Iraq.

They were reservists all. I won't say an unkind word in this column about reservists. Many of them are risking their necks and many have died in the name of the rest of us, who are diverted from war news by reality shows that aren't as real.

But, having had some service in the reserves myself, I know that the reserves are not so much a fighting unit as they are a Sunday picnic. They were never meant to be pitched, wholesale, into combat conditions.

I served three years as a Military Police officer. I still get ribbed for that every time I trade war stories with a veteran. When I got off active duty and served my stint as a reservist, I couldn't believe the difference.

The company I was assigned to was lax and indifferent. In the active-duty Army, I'd been a kind of hail-fellow-well-met officer. In the reserves, I was Gen. Patton.

The kids under me didn't know much and didn't want to know much more. I tried to change that, but my heart wasn't in it either. All we wanted to do was serve our time and get out.

If I'd known there was a chance that those kids were headed for a combat zone, I would have been more of an SOB But back then, we thought the reserves would be collected only for a civil rights riot or some kind of flood-control emergency.

Now we have a real war on our hands. And, because our Army is short of people, reservists and National Guard troops are being shoveled into the inferno.

That's bad. That's risky. It's made worse by the fact that this is an entirely different kind of war.

Every war is an entirely different kind of war. That's what the Pentagon visionaries never understand. Their playbook is always out of date.

An overstretched Army reached down to a reserve brigade in Appalachia and sent it overseas. No disrespect meant, but the companies in that brigade probably could not have been less trained for warfare.

When they got to Iraq, they were assigned to a military prison. That's lousy duty. You're as much locked up as the prisoners are. It takes a strong commander to maintain morale in such a situation. But the brigade commander wasn't strong. The testimony is that she hardly visited at all.

Then, after a while, the thugs took over. According to testimony, military intelligence began to run the prison. The MP brigadier was too weak to stop them. And the kids, our kids, took their cue from what these guys suggested.

I don't think America is as dirty as the testimony we've heard. Even in this lousy, dirty war, we're not that bad. My country cannot be that bad,

But maybe we're close. The world dislikes us for marching across the borders of another country. If we speak out against this war, many brand us as traitors. And if we treat our prisoners inhumanely, some say, "What's the big deal? Look how they treated us!"

We're the big deal. We're in this war now, and we have to show the world how to wage an honorable war, if there is such a thing.

But, alas, there is no such thing. All wars are dirty. The thugs take over. And, in a climate of wartime, the thugs have good reason. The dirt doesn't bother them.

—May 12, 2004

She's a disgrace—but she's not the only one

Look at her.

She's an unforgettable face in this rotten war.

Look at her and you see that destiny overtook her.

She could have been flipping burgers in some fast-food joint in West Virginia. Living in some scrabble hollow. Counting her tips at night on the bedspread.

And then the Army rescued her. Somebody told her that, if she joined the Reserves, she would get a guaranteed pay check every month. And some college too.

So she joined up for the money. Perhaps not like the money you or I would think of as money. But to her, it meant a lot.

They gave her a uniform and a beret. Once in this Army, only very special troops wore a beret. But ours has become a designer Army, and the fashion is meant to be enticing.

It's obvious she has no understanding of what the uniform means. My guess is—and it's only a guess—that she joined up for the monthly check and maybe a uniform she could wear that made her look different, at 5 feet, 1 inch, from the best dress she ever had.

Let's leave her for a moment, back in West Virginia, and go on to great, momentous things that happened far beyond her scope.

The president, for reasons still unclear, decided to go to war against Iraq. Having lied our way into the war, we had no choice but to fight it. And the question soon came, who do we fight it with?

We had a lean, mean assault team. There was never a question about whether we could beat the Iraqi army. But the problem was, how do we occupy the country we have defeated.

For that we needed reserves. So we scooped down and got some. And in that net was Pfc. Lynndie England. She never expected to have to do anything. But the fine print in her contract shipped her to Iraq.

By now you've seen her a thousand times on TV. Posing in front of a pile of naked Iraqi detainees. Holding a leash. What did she know? Iraq is a long way from a Denny's breakfast.

They shipped her over, ill-trained, and threw her in with a bunch of ill-trained louts. It was absolutely, positively the most exciting thing that had ever happened to her.

Her duty was at Abu Ghraib prison. There she met a stud, another reservist named Charles Graner. He was ill-trained too. And the two of them made sport of the Iraqi prisoners in their care. And were dumb enough to take souvenir snapshots of the fun they were having.

Which is why you've seen her.

She had a baby by the stud. He married a different woman and has been sentenced to 10 years in prison. As I write this, no sentence has been levied on Pfc. England. But she's facing 11 years.

I served three years of active duty in the Military Police Corps. Only veterans can imagine the amount of verbal abuse we got doing that. But we all wore the same uniform.

So when I see that young woman on CNN, dressed in Class A's walking toward her fate, it sickens me.

The first thing I wonder is, where are the officers who ought to be on trial with her? When they commissioned me, I was taught that I was responsible "for all my troops did or failed to do."

So where are the officers who should be on trial with Pfc. England and her cut-rate boyfriend?

This kind of thing goes up the ladder. It doesn't end with burger-flippers in West Virginia. What are we trying her for? Are we trying her because this ill-trained young woman thought she was doing what everybody else was doing? On top of everybody else was an officer. So where is he? Or she?

If I were judge and jury I would strip her of her uniform and send her home. She does disgrace the uniform. I'd put her back in a burger suit.

But then I would try to find the brass with bars or eagles on their shoulders who are hiding behind this young woman and letting her take the fall.

—May 4, 2005

Living too long; seeing too much

My father served in the Navy in World War II. He never sailed farther into the Pacific than San Diego harbor. The only scratch he returned with was a fouled anchor tattooed on his forearm. This, I suspect, was the result of an uncharacteristic night of frivolity in San Diego or Tijuana.

He was sitting in a mess hall when we dropped the bomb on Hiroshima. He was scheduled to sail in the fleet that would have invaded Japan. But the bomb disrupted all travel plans.

"We all stood up and cheered," he said, "and threw food around the mess hall. And we blessed Harry Truman and that bomb."

So everybody finally came home. We had beaten the enemy from a standing start. And then it became the American Century.

The American Century lasted less than two decades.

It was nice while it lasted. I've lived long enough to know the wonderland that was America between 1945 and the Kennedy assassination in 1963. Then things changed.

My brother-in-law bought a Toyota.

"I'll never buy a Japanese car," my father snarled. "When I was in San Diego, we used to ferry wounded Marines to the hospital. I'll never buy a Japanese anything! I want to buy an American car."

The old man lived to be 91. And, by the time he died, there was no such thing as an American car. He had been alive when the Wright Brothers pushed their motorized kite from a dune in Kitty Hawk. He had lived through a depression and a war and memories of those wounded Marines. He, like me, always wanted to put the lace in his shoe and call it tied.

But it unravels.

Yesterday, Vietnamese Prime Minister Phan Van Khai met with our president in the Oval Office of the White House.

Those fancy state meetings are reserved for people we have a special interest in. We want to sell stuff to Vietnam. What Vietnam will give us back, I'm not sure.

About 200 hundred protesters, carrying the old, red-and-yellow-striped flags, walked in circles as close to the White House as they could get.

They are the refugees of the Vietnam War. And that's a war that is sinking into the quicksand of America's memory.

Arlington Cemetery is not that far away from the White House. The white markers there mourn more than 50,000 of our dead who, if they'd known this Oval Office meeting could possibly have happened, would have spent their lives in some other useful purpose.

There is a penalty to be paid for living too long. The world turns faster than our balance can follow. We think we have a compass point, and then it's gone and we lose it.

When my father died, there was no such thing as an American car. He was raised to believe there was. But his truth had become dust.

We are all living longer. And history is flying by at a dizzying pace. Phan Van Khai in the White House? My brother-in-law buying a Toyota? These are things once thought incredible.

Now we're in a war again. Before the year is out, 2,000 of our people will have died in it.

You would think we'd bear a grudge. I'm a great grudge-bearer myself. I never bought a Japanese car because I inherited my father's anger.

I think anger is natural. Revenge feels good. I'm a booster of both.

But, in the long run, anger and revenge leave us frustrated and empty. They don't work. Life mocks our bitter resolves, and we are carried downstream on the drift of time.

All we have is a tiny oar dipped in the current. Phan Van Khai was in the Oval Office yesterday. We simply have to steer around him.

—June 22, 2005

Passing the word about Westmoreland

I try to believe in an afterlife. If there is one, the ghosts were murmuring in Arlington Cemetery last night.

The whispers went from foxhole to foxhole, grave to grave. My bet is, they sounded like this:

"Hey, Westy's dead."

That's from a marine corporal in Da Nang. Dead a while.

"Really," said an Army guy who drowned in a swamp. "How old was he?"

"He was 91," the corporal said. "He died of natural causes. He was in a retirement home."

"Well," said the Army guy, "given human nature, I guess we all died of natural causes. He just lived about 70 years longer than us."

"How old were you?" said the Marine.

"Do the math, jarhead," said the soldier. "I was 21."

"I was 20," the Marine said.

A slow, warm wind blew a newspaper across the grave. I believe the dead still get our news. It's a chilling thought. But maybe they don't care anymore. It's like watching too much CNN.

The Marine read the story to the soldier:

"Retired Gen. William Westmoreland, who commanded U.S. troops in Vietnam—the nation's longest conflict—died Monday night. He was 91."

"Did you ever see him?" the soldier asked.

"Got a glimpse," the Marine said. "He got off a chopper and we had an honor guard for him and he passed me by. That was about two weeks before I got mine."

"I got mine when he was saying he saw the light at the end of the tunnel," said the soldier. "Remember that?"

"Oh, God, yes," said the Marine. "And the body counts; remember those?"

"When we used to fudge the numbers?" said the soldier. "I sure do."

They chuckled softly in the darkness.

"You know, Westy was a great soldier," the Marine said. "He was brave and faithful. He was a semper fi kind of guy. He once said, 'They put me over there and forgot about me.' That's as close as I ever saw him to whining."

"Well," said the soldier, "they put us over there and forgot about us, too. But the difference was, he called the shots. He saw the light at the end of the tunnel."

"Ha ha," said the Marine.

"Ha, ha," said the soldier.

There was a pause then.

"You know," said the soldier. "It was pretty obvious after we got there that we weren't going to win the war. All we could win were battles."

"Yeah," said the Marine. "We ended up just fighting for each other. But the guys who were supposed to figure out what we were doing there just took a hike. Or lied about it."

"I spoke a little French," the soldier said. "And the Vietnamese I spoke to said, 'We're older than you. We've seen others come in. We'll be here when you're gone.' "

"Westy never understood that," the Marine said. "His job was to fight. And he did that. All generals do that. The public doesn't care. The politicians don't care. They are all gutless and the guys with the guts are buried . . ."

Then the night was interrupted by the noise of a machine. The machine was digging a new hole, which would be fresh and tidy in the morning.

"Iraq?" said the Marine.

"Yep," said the soldier.

And they listened through the night and heard a new foxhole being dug. Another neighbor. New midnight conversations. Somebody else to talk to.

—July 20, 2005

Back to School

For proficiency, rely on grandma

It costs a fortune to send a kid to college to get a high school education.

Another of those gloomy dumbness reports issued last week shows that more than a third of the freshmen (freshpersons) at Ohio's state schools need to learn the basic math and English courses they should have learned in high school.

The state is going to respond to this the only way it knows how: by imposing strict new standards and shipping the schools more money.

But what needs to be done is something the state can't do: Equip every home with a caring mom and grandma.

My mom took care of my basic math skills. My grandma was in charge of reading. Neither of them ever got a nickel from the state. Of course, back in those days, they didn't pay state income tax either.

Now a lot of kids learn basic math with the help of a computer. Nobody had computers when I was growing up. I learned my math with the help of a dishwasher. My mom was the dishwasher.

Every night after supper, she plunked me down at the tin-topped kitchen table and made me go through the multiplication tables while she did the dishes. I was trapped there, droning the numbers over and over until they wore a groove in my head. To this day, if you woke me from a sound sleep and asked me how much nine times nine was, the answer would leap from my brain accompanied by a faint aromatic memory of Dreft dish soap and coffee grounds.

My grandma's basic reading program was a lot more fun. We held class up in her room every afternoon for about an hour. We worked our way through the full set of the Bobbsey Twins books and then the Hardy Boys books. First, she would read a chapter aloud to me, then I would read a chapter aloud to her.

It never occurred to me that this was a reading class. I figured she was as interested as I was to learn whether Bert Bobbsey would come along in time to pull his little brother Freddie out of the creek.

When we came to the end of a book, we were gracefully conned into the next one with a sentence something like:

"The Bobbseys thought they would never have a better vacation than they'd had at Indian Hollow. But a whole new series of adventures was awaiting them as you, dear reader will learn, in the next volume of this series, *The Bobbsey Twins at Windmill Cottage*."

Neither I nor my grandma could resist rushing down to Burrows at our earliest opportunity to buy the next book. Finally one day, my grandma bought me a copy of *Robinson Crusoe* and sent me off on a solitary literary itinerary that took me through Mark Twain and Hart Crane and all the way to Henry Miller. I'm rather relieved she wasn't around when I arrived at Miller. I can't imagine trading chapters of him up in that bedroom which smelled of lavender soap.

That's how I learned my basic reading and math skills. All the state has to do is put a caring mom and grandma in each home and the education problems will be solved. Then kids could go to college and get a college education. For whatever that's worth these days.

Historian David McCullough said recently that it's possible to get a degree from a major university and never take a single history course. That might explain why a young intern at a television station once asked me earnestly, "Which came first, World War I or World War II?"

I answered her with language I had learned from Henry Miller.

—December 16, 2001

Blessed are the old and their stories

I was lucky enough to teach a couple of classes at the Cleveland School of the Arts. I felt I was one of the oldest people who had ever been propped up in front of these bright kids. They grilled me as they might have grilled Methuselah.

"Is it true there once were two riots in this city that burned down a lot of the town?" a little girl asked.

"Yes," I said, "the Hough Riot and the Glenville Riot."

"Did you ever meet Martin Luther King?" an eager boy wanted to know.

"Why, yes, once. Briefly."

"What was it like?" he asked.

I realized I had to take these questions seriously. No fast, glib answers for these alert kids. The things they were asking about were, to them, events in the olden days. I was an artifact from the past, presumably with a brain and a functioning memory. A specimen, like the fetal pig in their science class. A kind of textbook with eyes that could see their eager hands pumping the classroom air and call on them.

"What did people think of Martin Luther King?"

"Did you go to Vietnam? Did it change your life?"

"Were you scared in Vietnam? Were you scared during the riots?"

"A lot of us were scared for a lot of reasons during the whole decade of the '60s," I said. "It all got mixed up into a jumble. My main memory is of cops. Everybody was so mad at everybody else that there had to be cops all over the place. When Martin Luther King came through, I remember all the cops worrying about whether somebody would try to shoot him. And, of course, they did shoot him. But not here."

That night I thought about the day. And I wanted to go back and try again.

It's no picnic getting old. You go to bed and your bones hurt so much you can hardly get to sleep. Wake up the next day and they start hurting again. You gulp your orange juice and take your Fibercon and your multivitamin and arthritis pills and grope your way through the day.

There's not much TV for us older people. We're tight with a buck, and advertisers don't want us. In the grocery store and drugstore, we're often invisible. We've seen a lot, but our kids, burdened with the cares of the moment, have heard and forgotten all our stories. We are yesterday.

But it can be a great blessing to be yesterday. We yesterdays hold a living memory of events that will soon be handed to the care of historians who will make them dry as dust. Our last warm touch is to the kids of our kids who want to know.

Was I scared in Vietnam? The whole time I was there. Was I scared during the riots? Yeah, because I was "Whitey" and a lot of angry black guys in berets were out to get Whitey. One still night, on a street patrolled by guardsmen, a drugstore suddenly blew up in front of us with a great whooshing sound. Then silence again except for the wail of fire engines whose firemen might get sniped at.

Sitting at home thinking about my day, I thought of a story that had been in the news: the funeral of Britain's Queen Mother Elizabeth, who died at 101.

She'd been born before airplanes and automobiles, been a young woman during World War I, helped hold her nation together during the Second World War and lived to see the moon landing.

There are queen mothers (and old grandpas) scattered among all of us. They all have stories to tell. Before they go, they owe us the telling and we owe them the listening. It's a double blessing, and those are rare.

—April 21, 2002

Graduated heroes are true teachers

They are the fathers of our country, but they don't have names like Jefferson, Adams or Washington.

They are Foggio and Kucensky, Bivins and Costanzo, Zajdek and Sanchez.

Sixty years ago, they were kids in the Cleveland school system. They all became high school dropouts. Hitler was sorry they didn't stay in their classrooms. So was Tojo. They left school to enlist in the military and went off to save the world.

Thursday night, our little corner of the world said a belated thanks. On the stage of John Marshall High School, they were awarded their high school diplomas.

Columbus, which does so many things wrong, did something overwhelmingly right. Lawmakers ruled that any student who had dropped out of school to join the military during World War II and had been honorably discharged was eligible for a diploma. So a ceremony was planned. And I was honored to be the graduation speaker.

It's a role I've had before. But never with a graduation class of 70-year-olds. About 40 veterans waited nervously backstage for a tape recording of "Pomp and Circumstance" to begin. Then they filed onstage, a few walking with canes.

The audience was filled with family members. But not mothers and fathers. Children, grandchildren and great-grandchildren got to their feet and cheered when the graduates marched on stage. Nobody in this audience had to worry about grandpa staying out all night with his prom date.

I didn't make much of a speech. I told the vets that since they had waited 60 years for their diplomas, I wasn't going to keep them waiting much longer. They'd already suffered the longest detention in the history of public-school education.

I thanked them and saluted them. And, one by one, when their names were called, they proudly walked up to accept the piece of paper that proclaimed them educated men.

The detention lasted too long for some of them. Some have already left us. A young woman came forward to accept a diploma in the name of her late father. She looked around her and smiled. "I feel like you are all my fathers," she said.

At the end of the ceremony, Krystal Johnson, a senior from the Cleveland School of the Arts, stepped forward to play "God Bless America" on the trumpet. We all sang along. Everybody in this crowd knew the words.

The generation called "The Greatest Generation" is slowly leaving us. My own father, a Navy veteran, died a year ago this week. He was the last of a group of my male relatives to go. They had all served in World War II. When they came back, the war seemed to have stamped them with two qualities: humility and gratitude. They were grateful to be alive. And they enjoyed the simple pleasures of life and didn't feel they had to prove anything to anybody, ever again.

That kind of calm assurance isn't present anymore. Later generations of men and women seem frantic to prove something, though what that something is is painfully uncertain.

Foggio and Kucensky, Bivins and Constanzo, Zajdek and Sanchez wear their years with a sublime and enviable dignity. They are all our fathers on Father's Day.

It's up to us to understand what they gave us. And to make far better use of it than we have. Our generation hasn't got a diploma yet.

—June 16, 2002

Fuzzy grammar hides fuzzy ideas

My favorite sign of the times ran in Ohio's greatest newspaper on Friday.

Plain Dealer photographer Mike Levy was in Maple Heights covering the teacher strike. He shot a picture of an eighth grader brandishing a sign supporting the teachers. It read:

"Teachers is what makes school what it is. We love our teachers."

In Levy's photo, a striking teacher was giving a thumbs up to this off-key grammatical concoction. My old English teachers would have blue-penciled it. But then, my English teachers never went on strike.

But the sign raises the question: Is teachers what makes school what it is or isn't they? I think they isn't. I think what makes school what it is are the corrosive effect of popular culture.

For years, popular culture has been gnawing away at the English language. The main culprits have been the representatives of the politically correct crowd and the advertising crowd. Each one comes with their own agenda.

Once that last sentence would have been "each one comes with his own agenda." But political correctness uncoupled the singular male pronoun from the singular noun. The thinking was that male pronouns were a sign of oppressive male dominance. I've heard a lot of chauvinist guys grossly bragging about things in saloons, but I never saw a guy smugly waving his pronoun around.

English was fender-dented by the PC bunch that now insists we utter phrases like: "Stop in at Blotz Furniture and ask for Joe. Joe Blotz knows what their customers like."

That kind of English falls painfully on my ear. But at least I understand where it comes from. The infection of the language by the advertising world is harder to understand. It's been going on for years but has accelerated lately.

The beginning of the slide was the phrase "free gift." It got into the language back when banks were giving away toasters in exchange for new accounts.

"Drop in and pick up your free gift," a radio announcer would say.

This annoyed me. A gift is a gift and, by definition, free. You don't give somebody a birthday present and say, "Glad you like it—it'll cost you $29.99."

But the ad world thought it sold.

The other day I went to the eye doctor. He used to be in a doctor's office. Then a clinic. Now he's in a wellness center.

"Is that the same place he always was?" I asked the secretary.

"Yes," she said. "But now we call it a wellness center."

"Do people who are well ever come?" I asked.

"Not usually," she said.

"So it's really kind of a sickness center," I said.

She didn't much like that.

I went over and got some medication. Ten years ago I would have gotten medicine. These days you get medication. It sounds softer somehow. But it's still pills.

Why is plain English important? Here's why I think it is. We are entering one of the most confusing periods in our history. It's not a good time for fuzzy language. And our leaders have become masters at it.

If plain English was ever called for, it is now. But we must respect it. If you start respecting it in the eighth grade, maybe when you get old enough to vote or fight, you'll demand to know the difference between medication and manipulation. And between their weapons of mass destruction and ours. And between war and peace.

—September 8, 2002

John Adams High will rise again

The day they swung the wrecking ball at my high school, I went over to salvage a brick from the rubble.

I had plenty of company. Rebels, young and old, drove back to the old neighborhood to capture a souvenir of their youth. If John Adams High School had to die, we wanted to save a relic to store with our memories.

If you didn't go to Adams, you're forgiven for not reading this. But if you happen to be an Adams grad, you will share my joy on this resurrection Sunday at the news that a new John Adams High School will be built on the site of the old one at Corlett Avenue and East 116th Street.

Adams educated the famous and the infamous. Don King is a grad, and so was Ray Anthony, the band leader who got kicked out of the high school band. Nick Mileti was an Adamite, as was a notorious mob hit man whose name I will omit because his family is still in town and they've suffered enough.

Adams was always gritty and tough, even back in the warm and fuzzy '50s. One day, a kid who brought a .38 to school squared off with a guy who'd brought a knife. A teacher broke it up. If you wanted to be a teacher, you had to be tough. (You still do.)

But the teachers were phenomenal—the best I ever had. Part of the reason was sexism. In the old days, there were few career opportunities for bright young women. A lot of the best of them went into teaching and stayed. So we got, by default, the cream of the crop.

My mother graduated from Adams 30 years before me.

Neighborhoods were more stable then. People hadn't developed a yearning to follow the freeways to the suburbs. When I got to Adams, I was assigned to some of the same teachers who had educated my mom.

There was a sense of tradition and heritage that has eroded in this mobile society. I was lucky enough to get teachers who didn't think they were there to be my pal. They demanded respect and taught respect by showing it.

Mr. Burroughs, the aging geometry teacher, called me "Mr. Feagler." "Mr. Feagler," he would say, "what is the formula for finding the area of a right triangle?" He had asked my mother the same question. I was 15 years old, and nobody had ever called me Mr. before. Mr. Burroughs wasn't merely teaching geometry. He was teaching manners and decorum. Some of those lessons outlived his lessons about theorems.

I got a job on the school newspaper. Miss Follin, the faculty adviser, called me into her tiny office one day and said, "Richard, I want to tell you I think you have a flair for this." If she hadn't said that, I'm not sure where I'd be now. Maybe not on this page.

Graduation day came. We went to the Masonic Temple and trooped down the aisle in our robes. We stood on the stage and sang "The Lost Chord," an Adams graduation tradition. Then we drifted into our various lives. But we took Adams with us.

That was more than 40 years ago. But about once a month I run into somebody who says, "Hey, you went to Adams, right? I'm a Rebel, too."

"Yeah," I say, "it's a shame it was torn down. Did you get a brick?"

No, he says.

I got one, I say smugly.

And now they are going to bring our school back—football field, track and all. Who says a loss is forever? Adams was too good to die. It was asleep in all of us, but never dead.

My brick is in the garden.

I'm going to dig it up and wipe it off and give it to Barbara Byrd-Bennett. And ask her to put it back where it belongs. Somewhere in the foundation of a building that helped build so many of us.

—April 20, 2003

Brain surgery by second grade

Normally I don't share my personal mail with you. Frankly, some of it is just too obscene.

But today I'm going to make an exception. And here's why:

Yesterday, we ran a front-page story by Scott Stephens, who reported that high school and college students are really dumb when it comes to the political world around them. A battle is raging in educational circles about the best way to smarten them up.

Everybody is in a quandary about how they got so dumb. They certainly don't start school dumb. In fact, according to Ohio law, in kindergarten they are expected to be geniuses.

A friend sent a letter that described her kid's first day in kindergarten. I was fascinated by it. See if you are too. Here's what she wrote:

"I went to the open house at Danny's school, and was given the booklet *A Standards Guide for Families—What Is Expected in Grade K* by the Ohio Department of Education.

"Now, when I went to kindergarten it was show-and-tell, storytime and maybe a lesson on how to tie your shoes. Here are just some of the standards (I'm not kidding, this is word for word), for kindergarten students. When I got it home I had to reread it just to be sure I didn't dream it.

"Phonemic Awareness, Word Recognition and Fluency: Being able to read well by sounding out words, recognizing them by sight and reading out loud with ease and fluency.

"Acquisition of Vocabulary: Being able to recognize clues in reading, ask questions, listen and converse with adults and peers.

"Reading Process: Concepts of Print, Comprehension Strategies and Self-Monitoring Strategies: Through reading, students will understand the basic concepts and meanings of different types of print materials.

"Reading Applications: Informational, technical and persuasive text: Reading, understanding, explaining and critiquing different kinds of materials such as magazines, essays, maps, and on-line sites.

"Writing Processes: Using the steps of prewriting, drafting, revising and editing to publish different types of writing.

"Writing Applications: Learning about, using and choosing appropriate words for different kinds of writing, from letters to scientific reports and for different audiences.

"Research: Knowing how to gather information in all subjects using different kinds of tools (e.g. books, computers, magazines) and communicate what is found.

"Numbers, Number Sense and Operations: Using number sense and number skills, from basic counting to paper and pencil calculations, to age-appropriate use of calculators and computers.

"Geometry and Spatial Sense: Identifying, classifying and analyzing one-, two- and three-dimensional objects, understanding their properties and using that knowledge to solve problems.

"Patterns, Functions and Algebra: Representing patterns and relationships using tables, graphs and symbols and using them to solve problems.

"Data Analysis and Probability: Organizing and interpreting results through data collection to answer questions, solve problems, show relationships and make predictions.

"Physical Sciences: Understanding physical systems, concepts and properties of matter, energy, forces and motion.

"I hate to think of what First Grade is like! Love, DeeDee."

Wow! What ever happened to putting your head down on your desk for five minutes? With these criteria, Albert Einstein would have flunked out of kindergarten.

Maybe, somewhere in the middle of all this warped and grotesque committee English, there is a message for some teacher who is trying to teach little 5-year-olds to behave themselves and love learning. But if it's there it would take a code clerk to decipher it.

You can't blame the kids. Confronted with this gobbledygook they learn (and rightfully so) a distrust of education and educators. So, as they pass through school, I guess they just get dumber and dumber. By the time they graduate, they can't pass the kindergarten entrance exam as drafted by the empty suits and pantsuits in the school of jargon and nonsense.

I am of the school that says speak plain English and teach the basics. But, in the chaos of modern education, where learning is all mixed up with politics, nobody knows what the basics are anymore.

Well, at least nobody in charge knows. We know. But we don't count. Though we can. And not on our fingers, either.

—September 24, 2003

CSU leader wants sheepskins to count

My old friend Michael Schwartz is at it again. He's fighting to uphold standards of excellence in a society which insists on diluting them.

Schwartz, the president of Cleveland State University, earned a big front-page headline last week. "Tighten admissions, CSU chief urges," it read.

I first met Chief Schwartz when he was president of Kent State University some years ago. He was urging the same thing back then.

"Too many kids come in here who are just not prepared for the college experience," he told me then. "It's like a revolving door. They spin in and out in their freshman year. Then people complain about our retention rate."

Schwartz formed a partnership with Cuyahoga Community College. The idea was that Kent-bound students who were shaky on their basic skills would attend Tri-C first as a kind of basic training.

Having put this program in place, Schwartz resigned from the Kent presidency. "I just want to be a teacher," he said. "The main job of a college president is to raise money. I didn't get into this to be a fund-raiser. I got in to teach."

So he taught for a while, but then, when CSU was looking for a new president, he came back. I rib him about this and he takes it with a sense of humor.

It was only a matter of time until Schwartz the educator would triumph over Schwartz the businessman. The educator spoke out last week.

CSU has what is called an open-admissions policy. That means if you show up with a high school diploma, they have to let you in.

This approach has its drawbacks. Some years ago, Channel 3 news ran a story about a high school graduate who tried, painfully and on camera, to read his own diploma. He couldn't. A look at his tortured face was a picture worth the thousand words he could not pronounce.

Perhaps things in high school have gotten better since then. Schwartz, stuck with his open-admissions policy, might not think so.

"I think we need to send a signal that this is a university experience," he said. "When you come here, don't expect the 13th grade. This is really a very classy faculty. The student body ought to match."

So Schwartz wants prospective CSU students to prove they belong in college. Either by taking entrance exams or by showing a high school transcript with a minimum grade point average.

He says it's dishonest to collect tuition money from kids who are predestined to flunk out.

And, as he did when he was at Kent, he'd like to see borderline kids hone their skills at a community college before moving on to CSU.

The reason Schwartz is a pal of mine is that he is a bomb-thrower. So now we can sit back and see how his ideas play in the community.

I suspect we will hear talk that Schwartz is trying to turn CSU into an elitist university. And that its mandate, as an urban school, is to grant access to all.

But a university is not a soup kitchen. It ought to be a secular-sacred place of ideas—a repository of the knowledge of all mankind.

What many universities have become are branding stations. Check in, get branded with a degree, go out and try to find a job, and good luck.

College isn't for everybody. What I suspect Schwartz is worried about is that his "classy faculty," confronted with kids who just can't toe the mark, will begin to move the mark. And if that happens, the reputation of the university will erode. So that a degree from CSU, whether a student can read it or not, won't be worth much.

Education has been a hot-button issue for 50 years, ever since Sputnik. I think one of its problems is that it has been left in the hands of educators who pipe dream. They've invented things like the "new math," which raised a generation of kids who couldn't count. And then, of course, there are all of these "studies" courses—black studies, women's studies, Latino studies. Propaganda, not curriculum.

Mike Schwartz is no pipe dreamer. He wants to run a university whose degree means something. I like that. I also like the fact that if he doesn't get what he wants, he'll probably quit again. Compromise got us into this mess.

Only conviction will get us out of it.

—October 12, 2003

OU and Athens must ban sick ritual

I was the first kid in my family to go to college, and my high school English teacher recommended Ohio University in Athens.

It was a marvelous recommendation. I loved my four years at Ohio U. It is a Georgian brick campus placed like a jewel in a setting of Appalachian hills. In the fall, the hills become golden and the college below them turns russet to compliment its setting.

My wife and I went back to OU a couple of weeks ago. It was a splendid drive down I-77. The hills were painted with color, broken occasionally by a clean, white billboard announcing "Adult Videos."

"Whatever happened to Lady Bird Johnson and her highway beautification act?" I grumbled to my wife.

"That was a long time ago," she told me.

We've been together long enough that she knows the standard answer to my complaint about almost anything. It's always, "That was a long time ago." And she's always right.

Well, we had a good time at OU. A journalism buddy, Martha Towns, was there, too. Together we lectured and edified and warned and generally poisoned the minds of the next class of journalism graduates.

We walked around the campus in the clear, fall air. We saw students strolling arm-in-arm. It was a blissful sight. I felt young again, as long as I stayed away from the bathroom mirror. And then we came home. And a couple of days later, this headline hit us in the face like a cold dish rag:

"Stabbings, fires part of worst-ever Athens riot."

There is a new tradition at my old school, born after I graduated, that every Halloween is an excuse for students and their friends to get frisky. But there was nothing in the news story that qualified for such a benign word as "frisky": "A man's leg was slashed so badly in one fight that it might require amputation, police said.

A rape on Ohio University property also was reported and officers investigated several thefts.

"This event was far and away the worst event to date," Athens

Police Chief Rick Mayer said in a prepared statement. "It stretched and broke the ability of the department to respond to the needs of the public."

Ohio University depends largely on our city to ship students down to Athens. But it also has a delicious mix of students from all over the world. When I went there in the '50s, Cleveland students were the biggest bunch, followed closely by students from New York City. My roommate, Al Cohen, was from Brooklyn, and he wept in my arms when the Dodgers moved to L.A. You could order an egg cream at the student hangout. I never had heard of an egg cream. Neither have most of you.

But, as my wife continually tells me, that was a long time ago. Except for some patterns of behavior, there is no long time ago. There is only a universal now. Such as: You don't run around stabbing and raping and call it a Halloween celebration or any other kind of celebration. And if you do, you're nuts or subhuman.

To let my old school slightly off the hook, the Associated Press story says that only four of the 30 arrested were Ohio University students. But the deans of the university can't hide behind that. OU controls the town. And OU must stop these riots.

A friend of mine is taking her gifted daughter down to OU this weekend. When she asked me about the school, I was—as I have been for 40 years—enthusiastic.

But I knew she had read the story about the stabbing and the raping. It's a story that would make any parent think twice.

I'm a proud OU grad. I sat through an inspiring graduation speech. Now I'm speaking back, and in blunt terms.

OU and Athens better clean up the act. Ban Halloween celebrations. Stop this stupid ritual and stop it now.

Otherwise, no parent is going to drive down there past the "Adult Movies" sign to enroll his daughter in mayhem. Up here, we get mayhem for free.

—November 5, 2003

Riot has become a cherished OU tradition

I normally don't share my mail with you unless it astonishes me. This is one of those times.

A couple of weeks ago, I wrote a column deploring a Halloween riot that had savaged my dear old college, Ohio University.

Halloween riots have become a tradition down in Athens, but this one was especially bad (assuming there are good riots and bad riots). Scores of people were arrested. There were two reported stabbings and one reported rape. And the local chief of police lamented that he didn't have enough officers to deal with the mayhem.

Since Athens depends on Ohio U for its economy, I asked the university to put an end to this madness and ban further Halloween rioting. I pointed out that most of the thugs who rioted were not OU students. Nevertheless, I said, the university should use its leverage to stop this blot upon its name.

According to me, this was one of the most noncontroversial columns I had written in weeks. I thought it was noncontroversial to the point of blandness. And then the mail came in from pro-rioters. Here are excerpts:

"You seem, from the writing of your article, like the kind of person that would love a tradition to stop just because 'things aren't like they used to be.' Growing older is a problem you have to deal with. I can understand why you would expect these events to be canceled: you can't participate anymore and I think you miss stuff like this and would rather have them stop than to see people having a good time with their friends."

That came from Michael, a recent OU grad who works for NASA. Good luck in outer space, Michael, but I do worry about your inner-space.

"As far as the stabbing and rape, that happens on all college campuses at any time of the year. . . . That is no excuse to cancel the whole event. . . . Don't try to change what you don't understand, you should be trying to make it better. Eileen, a fellow OU grad."

As Mike said, growing older is a problem I have to deal with, but

I can't deal as nonchalantly as you do with the issues of stabbing and rape. Nor am I inclined to spend much time thinking about ways to make a riot better.

"It doesn't take a rocket scientist to predict a so-called riot every year. You have a police force of townies who hate the students, that make $27,000 per year and can't wait to line up at the end of Court St. to kick a little bit of Yuppie ass. Matt."

I have learned, Matt, that sometimes the best education a Yuppie can get is for somebody to kick a little bit of Yuppie ass. You might have learned that too, if the draft were universal.

"Yes, I feel sorry for the guy whose leg was cut up as I feel for the rape victim. But there's absolutely no sense in trying to cancel a celebration that has been going on since around 1970. It's called a tradition. James, Class of '78."

So was segregation in the South, James. Some traditions ought to end. Halloween rioting at OU is one of them.

I don't mean to imply that most of my mail was pro-riot. But an astonishing amount of it was. A good example of the other kind came from Michael, a freshman photojournalist at OU:

"On Halloween night, I ended up staying with a friend in the emergency room. He had alcohol poisoning. While I was sitting next to his bed I watched those two boys who were stabbed get carted in. I saw the paramedics cleaning the blood out of the ambulances. For my own safety and everyone who comes to Athens, I hope that there is some action taken to make the weekend a safe and fun one in years to come."

Now there's a good kid.

I got about 100 calls and letters on that bland column. And a third of them called me a fuddy-duddy for being against stabbing and raping at my old school. I was astonished, and that's why I offered some of them to you to read.

The reaction was news to me. And, at this stage of my game, anything that's news to me is news.

—November 16, 2003

New Adams High rises from the dust

On a blazing-hot day inside of a jam-packed tent, a Baptist minister prayed my old high school back to life.

Pastor General Martin of the Philippi Missionary Baptist Church blessed the ground on which the new John Adams High School will stand.

Then a backhoe took a small nibble out of the hard-baked ground of a huge, empty lot at East 116th Street and Corlett Avenue. And the school a lot of us thought was gone forever began to grow again.

Maybe I'm not objective, but I think John Adams was a very special high school. That feeling was endorsed when hundreds of people turned up to cheer its resurrection.

The folks who organized the groundbreaking were startled by the size of the crowd who came to see it. As an Adams graduate, I was happy but not surprised. John Adams was a special place.

The oldest alumnus in the crowd graduated in 1933. That's about the time my mother and my aunt were Adams students. I graduated in 1956 and was taught by some of the same teachers who taught my mother.

So many times in the years since, people have approached me at public gatherings to say, "You went to Adams, right? I was class of '42 (or '58 or '76.)"

And the next line always was, "Wasn't it a great school?"

It was.

When I graduated from Adams, I went on to Ohio University, a school I dearly love. But my first love was Adams. I learned more in my three years there than I learned at OU. Back then, the Cleveland schools were among the best in the nation. I grew up on the border of Shaker Heights, where the rich kids called their school a campus. We never called Corlett and East 116th a campus. But we knew we were not shortchanged by the education available to us there.

It was in a journalism class at Adams that Virginia Follin, the adviser to the school paper, called me aside and said, "Richard, I think you have a flair."

Nobody had ever told me I had a flair for anything before. But that word of encouragement, which I remember after almost a half century, changed my life. Adams' teachers changed our lives. That's why all those people showed up for the groundbreaking for the new school.

It was a far cry from the wake that occurred when the old Adams was torn down nine years ago. A crowd drifted in for that demolition. But nobody was happy.

The wrecking crew allowed us to come and pick up a brick from the old school. I excused myself from work and drove over to get one. I took it home and saved it and thought, "This is all I have left."

All I have left of what? Of that terrible transition from 15 to 17, guided by the wisdom of wonderful teachers? Of my first interaction with kids who were colored differently? Of football games and prom dresses and corsages and a whole lot of brand-new emotions and adventures?

The last time I saw John Adams standing wasn't pleasant. Back in the early '90s, the school looked great. And the kids were bright and bubbly and eager to learn.

But the doors had chains on them. The chains weren't to keep the kids inside. They were to keep the gang-bangers out—the dropouts who flitted around the school trying to recruit kids to the dope business.

In place of student hall guards, the school hired eight security cops with walkie-talkies to respond to any emergency. And when I asked a class of 16-year-olds how many knew a friend who had been shot, almost half raised their hands.

Shortly after that, they ripped the school down. My memories were dust and so were the memories of my mother and my aunt. I went over and got my brick and took it home and consigned Adams to the dead past.

But the people in Ward 2 weren't satisfied with that. The absence of the school had literally left a hole in their neighborhood. So they lobbied and campaigned and finally got a promise that Adams would be rebuilt.

Last Thursday was the groundbreaking. I've been gone from Adams almost 50 years now, but I wouldn't have missed it.

I brought my brick back. I gave it to Chris Smith, the principal architect of the new school. "Do me a favor and find someplace to stick it," I said.

And then, we heard the prayer. Pastor Martin gave a good, impassioned prayer. But I was praying, too.

"Let this school be as good as it was for me," I prayed. "Give these kids the same shot I got. And let the Ward 2 neighborhood watch over it and keep it strong."

Then the fallow ground turned into hallowed ground. And all of us Adamites, old and young, black and white, went home happy.

—September 26, 2004

Hall monitors weren't always professionals

I was a schoolyard cop once. I was on hall duty at John Adams High School. It was an elective period you got credit for.

My assignment was to sit at a desk outside 208-B on the second floor. The best-looking girls in the class came in and out of 208-B. My job was to challenge them for a hall pass.

Later—much later—in the Army, I would learn that the proper challenge was, "Halt! Who goes there?"

But if you had seen Doris or Rita, I'll bet you, buddy, the challenge would have stuck in your throat. It did in mine.

Those were the last days of what we used to call "sweater girls." And those girls, coming out of 208-B, were the true example of the art. They went off on their errands unhindered by me. The guys got past me all the time without the wooden spoon hall pass. I was a lousy cop.

About 30 years later, I went back to John Adams. It was still a great school full of kids who wanted to learn. But the student hall guards were gone. Now they had eight professional security guards with walkie-talkies prowling the school each day.

All the doors of the school were locked. Not locked to keep the kids in. Locked to keep the gang kids out. The day I went to the school, a child went into labor and the paramedics came to help her to deliver a baby. It was her second child.

That was, as I said, years ago. I've tried my best to keep up with the old John Adams ever since.

When it was torn down, I went and got a brick. And at the groundbreaking for the new school, I brought my brick back and asked the officials if they would plug it back into the new building.

The John Adams class of '54 and '55, just ahead of mine, had a 50th reunion over at Harlan Diamond's saloon (Landerhaven) on the East Side.

The turnout was marvelous. Adams graduates are a tight-knit and emotional breed. I was escorted by a friend who had flown in from Seattle. We ran into a guy who had come from Leeds, England. We were all there because we loved our old high school. But we loved more than that.

We loved the old neighborhood. We never heard the word "diversity," but maybe we invented it.

The old school in the old days had Jews from Kinsman, where there was a Yiddish theater. A block away was an Italian spumoni place where you could get ice cream better than I've ever tasted since. The blacks came from the Mount Pleasant neighborhood. And, of course, all of the Eastern European countries—from 55th and Broadway and Fleet Ave—heard their accordion music every Sunday morning on the car radio.

Back then, you knew better than to call a Slovenian a Slovak. You knew that the Hungarians didn't get along with the Bohemians. You knew that Russian Easter was after your Easter.

All this "diversity" before the word was invented. All this little United Nations under the roof of one school, and who was in charge of keeping the roof on? I was. In my little desk outside of 208-B.

What did we have that has gone lost now? When the John Adams reunion broke up and headed for the compass points, what did we know then that we don't know now? The answer is so obvious we ought to be embarrassed. Because we know it.

We had parents who cared. We had neighborhoods that cared. We had a universal sense of what was right and what was wrong.

Yesterday's headlines said the mayor will send a phalanx of on-duty cops to the schools. She's got to do something because it's an election year.

But she knows, as I do—as you do—that the problem is at home. The problem is with the inner-city culture. There is a culture grown from poverty that yields a smugness about failure. We all know it exists. It happens when a black kid gets an "A" and another kid mocks him for acting "white." That kind of thinking is tearing at the guts of our town. But we don't mention it. To do that would be to risk the "racist" tag.

And so, to duck that stigma, we in the suburbs, black and white, will go on our way. Mourning for the city we lost and left behind us. Me, dreaming of my seat in the hall guard's desk when motes of dust stirred in the sunbeams and all was quiet and dozy and I knew that the most exciting thing that would happen all day was when Rita and Doris came by.

—April 20, 2005

Cleveland: You Gotta Be Tough

New mayor lacks the best timing

Merry Christmas, Jane Campbell. You already got your present. You're the brand-new mayor, and you'll inherit a brand-new mess.

For new mayors in our town, the housewarming present is usually a time bomb. The welcome wagon brought George Voinovich a city digging its way out of fiscal collapse. Mike White arrived to find the baseball team on the verge of leaving and schools held hostage by a Taliban of greedy lawyers.

Now it's your turn, Jane, to greet the calamities that fate has assigned to you. The steel business, the muscle of this community, is dying. Downtown shopping is dead.

Drive past what's left of Dillard's, and avert your eyes. You don't want to look in the big show windows that once were full of holiday magic and glory.

The lights still glitter on Public Square, and the Terminal Tower glows with Christmas cheer. But the best Dillard's windows can do is display a couple of green shrubs in pots and a little red ribbon. They should have hung crepe and a funeral wreath. The last downtown department store is holding its holiday wake.

The wake-up call has been sounding for years, but we kept hitting the snooze button. Once there were six department stores between Moses Cleaveland's statue and Playhouse Square. That stretch of Euclid Ave. was the showcase of the city. Now it's a commercial slum.

Twenty years ago, we knew this would happen if we didn't get more people living downtown. It was obvious tourists wouldn't save the shopping district. But we built the Rock and Roll Hall of Fame and Museum and thumped our chest and sat back waiting for millions of pilgrims to arrive from remote regions eager to glimpse Elvis' zoot suit. Shucks! We couldn't even get the guitar-twangers to show up for their own induction ceremonies.

We need downtown housing and plenty of it, Jane. Maybe we can put it on the site of Burke Lakefront Airport, now a parking lot for the Gulfstream jets of the rich. Let the Blue Angels and the midget car racers go elsewhere to wheel and cavort.

Of course, the biggest piece of land threatening to become available is the land beneath LTV Steel. But if the steel mill closes, that land will be a no-man's land. The EPA will require a spacesuit just to walk on it. Cleaning it up will cost tens of millions of dollars. And everybody seems a little short right now, the economy being the way it is.

The steel-crisis time bomb has been sputtering and fizzing for years. But nobody paid much attention until the wick had burned down to the detonator. And that's when they handed it to you, Jane.

It looks like a grim Christmas for the thousands of steelworkers whose jobs and dreams will die along with the plant. And for the thousands of retirees whose pensions are in peril. And for thousands more whose jobs are tied to the steel industry.

What a dirty little joke it is to read that William Bricker, LTV's CEO, walked away with a $660,000 bonus as a reward for helping to kill his steel plant. Those are hit-man wages that would make a mob executioner jealous.

The days of the Comeback City are over, Jane. Your timing was a little off. You missed the fun. All those great articles the Growth Association planted in all those magazines about how Cleveland was a municipal Moses leading rust belt cities toward the promised land—that sparkling prose is yesterday's news. That champagne has gone flat in the face of today's headlines.

Merry Christmas, Mayor Campbell. And a fervent Happy New Year too . . . somehow.

—December 2, 2001

Conventioners won't revive downtown

About 25 years ago, I had a notion for a column. I decided to find a kid, about 14, who lived in Greater Cleveland but had never been downtown.

It seemed like a great idea at the time. Cleveland was climbing out of default, and our surrounding area was called the rust belt. We had such a lousy reputation on the late-night talk shows that merchants were dropping "Cleveland" from their company names in the Yellow Pages. I thought it would poignantly underline our decay to find a Cleveland kid who knew nothing of Cleveland.

But it didn't work. The Indians and the Browns were playing here. Every good suburban dad brought his kid downtown for a ball game at the old Stadium. I couldn't find a kid who had never seen downtown, even if he'd only seen it coming and going from the Stadium parking lot.

In the double decade since, nothing much has changed. Suburban kids know Cleveland because of drive-by visits to major league sports. The Flats were hot for a while, but they are cooling rapidly. Out in the soccer-mom belt, kids don't know the city as a city. Kids of my generation did.

When I was a kid, the population of Cleveland was nudging a million. Downtown was Downtown! It was the place where everything happened. I was born and raised within the city limits, so downtown Cleveland meant a lot to me. And to my parents.

If my mother needed a new dress, she came downtown to find it. Downtown had six department stores with better values and a bigger selection than you could find in the suburbs. We shopped in May's basement, where the goods were heaped in a jumble on the counter. Mom got her dress, I got a frosted malted and we hit the streetcar for home.

When I got older, downtown was where you took a big date. The hot, new movies always ran in the theaters around Playhouse Square weeks before they got out to the neighborhood theaters. If you wanted to be hip, you had to go downtown. And maybe after the show you dropped in at the Theatrical on Short Vincent

Street, which was run by a guy named Mushy Wexler. (Who is named "Mushy" anymore?) Or you drove over to the Gypsy Cellar on Buckeye Road and drank Tokay and danced to a syrupy fiddler.

Those days are almost past recall. No more department stores. No more Mushy. No more Gypsy Cellar. And no more Cleveland with a population nudging a million. The old city is below 500 grand now. And the mayor wants to boost its population.

Her problem (and how I hate to say this) is that nobody needs the old town anymore. Mom buys her dresses in malls where there is plenty of free parking—no streetcars needed. Junior borrows the SUV and drives his date to a multiplex cinema. Nobody goes downtown. Nobody needs to and nobody wants to.

The mayor is plugging two initiatives. She wants to build a new convention center and she wants more people to move back to the city and swell its population. The convention center idea, paid for by us, will enrich the pockets of the people who build it. But it will not make our chilly city a warm place to convene.

The other idea, bringing the county's diaspora back inside the city limits, is a more laudable notion, though harder to accomplish.

If people came back, stores would come back. Downtown would be a necessity again, not a pale shadow of a strip mall. The city would be alive again. You could find a drugstore in it. Or a place to buy a bra or a pair of BVDs. And if that happened, if the city came back to life, then there might be a reason for lively people from other cities to hold a convention here.

What bait can the mayor use to lure Greater Clevelanders back home? That's what we ought to be discussing. Not convention centers. If our city ain't a great place to live in, it ain't a great place to visit.

"Build it and they will come" is a backwards notion for a convention center. Let them come first, then building it makes much more sense.

—March 5, 2003

Image problems? They're old hat

How long do I have to live before I've lived through everything twice?

The Cleveland movers and shakers (an inert bunch because nothing's moving or shaking) are sore at a local cartoonist named Harvey Pekar. They think he might poison the reputation of the city.

Pekar has been in our town for a long time. I don't happen to read his cartoons, and he probably doesn't read my columns. But, because he's a fellow Clevelander, I'm happy for his hard-won fame.

Hollywood has turned his comic strips into a highly successful movie called *American Splendor*.

The movie, set in Cleveland, describes our town as a down-and-out, rust-belt city where the sky is always gray.

That's about half right. We may not be down and out, but we're surely on the ropes and reeling. And Pekar is wrong about the weather. The weather is great here for seven months of the year. We natives have steeled ourselves to block out those long, gray weeks between Thanksgiving and Easter.

There is nothing as gloomy as a dark, rainy Christmas Eve in Cleveland. It's a time to go home and pull down the shades and listen to Bing Crosby crooning about a white Christmas. We get our white—12 inches of it—in early November or late March. Irving Berlin never wrote about us.

Still, we love our city. And so does Harvey Pekar. But when *American Splendor* came out the city's image-boosters turned on Pekar as if he were some kind of civic terrorist.

"Having someone of his notoriety, an insider, portray his town like that, it's not a good thing," said Dennis Roche, interim president of the Greater Cleveland Convention and Visitor's Bureau. "This is not helpful at all."

Mayor Jane Campbell groused about it too.

"If people actually came to Cleveland, they'd find out there's a lot more things going on than Harvey Pekar seems to know," she told the press.

Reading these comments took me back to the dark days of the '70s. What our city is going through now, I've lived through before.

Back then, the town was broke and the name "Cleveland" was good for a giggle on the Johnny Carson show. I was invited to appear on the *Today* show with Tom Brokaw to defend our city. Sure enough, he asked me about the weather.

"Well, it's not really our weather, Tom," I said. "I mean, we don't make it here. It comes in from the west and goes out to the east and then it's gone."

I followed this meteorological briefing with some friendly remarks about the city I was born in. And then, feeling rather smug about my performance, I strutted off to work.

Well! The next day's paper (this one, I didn't work here at the time) ran a spate of letters eviscerating me for the comments I had made on national TV. One guy—some long-forgotten head of some long-forgotten board of some limp-rag, empty-suited, Union-Club-brunch-time, aren't-we-all-great-because-we're-here—wrote a letter to the editor calling me a clown.

The letter said something like this: "With all the marvelous things he could have talked about, this clown used his national spotlight to make fun of our weather. This is not helpful at all."

In other words, I was Harvey Pekar before Harvey was Harvey. So I ask you again: How long do I have to live before I've lived through everything twice?

Some years later, National Public Radio called me. This time the host wanted to know how it felt to be part of a comeback city.

"I dunno," I said. "I've never been away."

And maybe that's the trouble with living in this town from birth certificate to Social Security. We go with the flow. Cleveland dies and comes back and dies and comes back. But you always can tell when we're on the down slope. It's when city officials worry about people like Harvey Pekar or me.

What Interim Mr. Roche from the Convention and Visitors Bureau and many others ought to worry about is the egg on their faces after the recent convention-center fiasco.

And, if I were the mayor, I'd take a brief walk down Euclid Avenue after, say, 6 p.m., and ask myself if this was the kind of wasteland I wanted to ribbon-cut and rule.

Harvey Pekar is not our archenemy. When the city mothers and fathers start lashing out at a guy like him, all they do is pump up the balloons on the comic pages. That's a slapstick idea. And this year, the movers and shakers look silly enough.

—September 14, 2003

The goodbyes won't be easy

St. Michael Hospital used to be St. Alexis. Soon it will be St. Elsewhere.

This time, a rally won't resuscitate it. University Health Systems, which owns the hospital, plans to close it down in December.

The folks who live around E. 55th and Broadway want to save it. I understand why. A hospital is a kind of guardian angel watching over a neighborhood. A sort of passive-aggressive guardian angel. Nobody wants to go in, but everybody's glad it's there.

In the old days, most of my relatives lived around 55th and Broadway. They did their serious doctoring at St. Alexis. They didn't confuse it with the Mayo Clinic. Back then, the street name for St. Alexis was "the butcher shop." But this was said with affection. St. Alexis was where they all went when somebody thought that maybe she was pregnant. Or when the cough just didn't go away. Or when the chest pains came.

For many, it was the last stop before check out. My grandmother died in St. Alexis. So did many of my great aunts and cousins. It was a short couple of blocks to Nosek's or Eddie Kubu's Funeral Home near the old Olympia Theater.

Eddie would put the organ music on the tape machine, and the family, after a proper interval of whispered respect, would leave the departed to fend for himself and go downstairs to the knotty-pine reception room where maybe, if you were a steady customer, you could get a shot of whiskey and review the dramatic events leading up to the present gathering.

"She came home and found him on the floor," an aunt would say. "They rushed him to the hospital, but, by the time he got there it was too late."

A hospital is always a place you are rushed to. As an old rewrite man, I know all the cliches. You are never sped to a hospital or hurried to a hospital. You are always rushed to a hospital. It's in the language and in the culture. That's what worries the folks around St. Michael. If they are going to be rushed to a hospital, they don't want to lay their bets on an 82-yard run. They want a nine-yard gain. They want their hospital close at hand.

I understand that. I used to live in Lakewood, which, even though I've moved to the sylvan glades of Bay Village, is still my favorite town. It's my favorite for a lot of reasons, but one of them certainly is Lakewood Hospital.

I've had some fairly serious doctoring at Lakewood Hospital. So has my wife. One night I came home from the late shift and found her having a heart difficulty. "Come on, you're going," I said. It was nice that we had to drive only 10 blocks.

Even though I don't live in Lakewood anymore, I have made a point to tell all my friends—the ones I might keel over in front of—to tell the ambulance guy to take me to Lakewood Hospital. If you're under 40, this may sound stupid to you. If you're over 60, it won't sound stupid at all.

If somebody came along and closed Lakewood Hospital, I'd feel a little bit the way I'd feel if they took away my Social Security. The very last thing you try to plan is how and where you want to die. And if you've lived there all your life, you want to go out in your neighborhood.

Once Cleveland was crowded with strong, vibrant neighborhoods. Now they've mostly been winnowed away. Fifty-fifth and Broadway has struggled valiantly to stay alive. Because my roots are there, I've stood in the wings and given it muffled applause.

But, speaking in rewrite journalese, "the hand writing is on the wall." When Dennis Kucinich stepped in a couple of years ago to save St. Michael, everybody knew it was a stopgap measure.

I wrote a column at the time, blasting him for being a political opportunist. Then I thought twice about it and wrote another column, retracting the first one and saying he was doing what he was supposed to do: fighting for his constituents.

But the old neighborhoods are waning as the city melts. Eddie Kubu is gone, the Olympia Theater is long gone and St. Michael is going.

That neighborhood used to be so close that, when somebody died in the hospital, the church bells would sound one stroke for every year that person had lived.

No bells will toll for St. Michael/St. Alexis. The only sounds of its passing will be the scratch of a pen and the rustling of red tape.

—September 21, 2003

If we had an emperor, he'd wear "offshore"

About 30 years ago, I needed a fancy suit for some kind of swanky affair. So I went to an East Side clothing store that a friend had touted. It was one of those "mention my name" deals.

I mentioned his name, but the salesman was less than impressed. He eyeballed the clothes I'd walked in with. Back in those days, I wore a paper clip for a tie pin. (By the way, that's not a bad idea if you haven't tried it.) The salesman's eyes lasered in on the paper clip. Then he looked me straight in the forehead and said:

"Would you like to see something offshore, sir?"

I had no idea what he was talking about. Now I know. He was talking about the death of the textile industry in America. He had pegged me, accurately, as a guy who belonged in a cheap suit. He figured I would faint dead away at the price of a good American suit. And the cheap suits were all "offshore," made someplace else.

These days, you can't buy an article of clothing that was made in the USA. Our stores still wear their American names, Dillard's, Saks, Wal-Mart and so forth. But look at the labels and you'll find they are made in countries you never studied in school. The clothes on our backs are postcards from stitching hands we will never know. But our neighbors' hands didn't stitch them.

Textiles were never that big in our town, so we didn't notice their departure. It was only when the steel mills began closing that we began to wonder what was happening to us and our economy.

Those mills were the arteries of our town. They stank, but we were proud of them. They were part of what FDR called the arsenal of democracy. We thought we beat Hitler with those mills. The mills paid wages that fed thousands of people and the mills gave them something back. In lean times and good times, in peace and war, the mills were always there.

On New Year's Eve, in the old neighborhoods, Republic Steel would blow its whistle at midnight. And my Aunt Emma, who had been a scrub lady for Republic, would call us out to her side porch to hear the whistle which was for her the only official beginning of the new year.

Republic is long gone now. So is my Aunt Emma. By the time she went, I had a television show. I booked smart guys and let them talk. Often they would talk about how steel leaving wasn't really so bad.

"Well the economy is changing," they would say. "It's changing from an industrial economy to a service economy. What we really need is more education to train our people to better fit in with this new service economy."

That service economy stuff was obviously bunk. A *USA Today* poll of white-collar service workers making over $100K each year shows they have no faith in the service economy.

The menace of "offshore" has spread to the white-collar world. The people who didn't care when Jenny was laid off at the textile mill or Steve was let go from the foundry now see a reason to worry.

The mantra of education isn't the answer now. The white-collar jobs going to India and China are jobs for educated people who can figure tax forms and read X-rays. And their most important skill is, they work cheap.

We blundered our way into a screwy war in Iraq and that's going to be a hot-button issue in this election campaign. But someday that war will be over. They all end somehow.

What won't be over in our lifetimes is the impact of the global economy and the way it will change the world. America, Ohio, the Cleveland we once knew will never be the same again.

Offshore, a phrase that once confused me, is on shore now, and we are drowning in it. Who among the candidates is speaking about it?

My big fear is, none of them will dare.

—February 25, 2004

Rock Hall: Now that's an Outkast

It was obvious from the beginning that no major rockhead gave a damn that we've got the Rock and Roll Hall of Fame here in Cleveland, backed by our public money.

There it sits, on prime lakefront real estate. The only hall of fame I've ever heard of at which the inductees aren't inducted.

In the interest of full disclosure, I want to say up front that I can't stand rock 'n' roll music. I was lucky enough to be born at a time when music was more than noise, and lyrics were more than wails and moans. Mine is the Gershwin-Porter-Berlin school. When dance music had a beat you could dance to and singers sang words you could comprehend without blushing.

But that's my problem. I just wanted to get it said.

Now we're in a whole new musical era. I understand that. You park at a stoplight next to some guy in a modified pickup truck and his thermonuclear speakers punch at your eardrums. You watch a show on TV and as soon as the station goes to a commercial break, some kind of rock music comes on to back up a spiel for Viagra or bathroom deodorant spray.

"Turn it down! Hit the mute!" my wife says from her adjoining La-Z-Boy.

"Aw-right, aw-right!" I say, fumbling for the remote zapper. "I'm not as fast as Wyatt Earp, you know."

So I don't like rock 'n' roll music. But I am a civic patriot. And when (because we won it in a silly contest) we became the site of the Rock and Roll Hall of Fame, I didn't object.

The city fathers and mothers and even members of Congress were very proud of this achievement. It came along at a time when our town was down on itself. They told us that if we could become the capital of rock 'n' roll, tourists would flock here and we would glitter and shine.

So, as a civic booster, I held my fire. The rock 'n' roll industry could have built itself a hall of fame out of its pocket change. But we ponied up to build it here and hired one of those new-age architects who, when he got through, created something that looked like a storm door propped against a small silo.

The idea was that, every year, the stars of rock 'n' roll would roll into town to be inducted into our hall of fame. It would be a gala night—a night that would put Cleveland on the map.

But they don't want to come.

We are the proprietors of the only hall of fame whose inductees don't show up for their induction ceremonies. Even those willing to fly across the country to show up for random drug tests.

The Baseball Hall of Fame isn't like that. I've been there. It's in Cooperstown, N.Y., which happens to be one of the hardest places to get to east of the Mississippi River. There aren't any fancy hotels. The sight of a stretch limo would draw crowds. It ain't a happening place.

But every year, multimillion-dollar baseball players find their way to Cooperstown to be inducted into the hall of fame. For them, the honor is more important than the accommodations.

I'm not a big-time football fan, nor do I think Canton is the garden spot of the universe. But that's where the Pro Football Hall of Fame is. And that's where the players go to be inducted. There are few no-shows.

We in Cleveland run the only hall of fame that is empty of celebrities during induction ceremonies. Oh, I guess you could go over there and see a TV show beamed in from the Waldorf in New York. But what's that? Just a fancy version of TIVO. And an insult to our town.

Many of you out there are rabid rock fans. I've already told you I'm not. So this is one war I don't want to fight in.

But if you really think Cleveland is the capital of rock 'n' roll, then you ought to lobby to get the next induction ceremony held here.

Every year the rockheads stay away, it's just a big, fat snub. Or dis, if that's the word. I may be an old man, but I know when I'm being snubbed. When that happens, you either walk away or fight. You don't just sit there and take it.

—March 17, 2004

This is a fine time to let Sheppard case go

On July 4, 1954, my father packed the Chevy for a fishing trip to upper Michigan. Back then, any vacation was a big adventure. For no really good reason, we always left before sunup. The old man's goal was to reach a diner by sunrise so we could have our eggs where the truckers ate.

Our route on that now-infamous day took us right past the Sam Sheppard house. This gave us boasting rights for years to come. "You know where I was when Marilyn Sheppard was murdered?" I could say to the kids in school. "Going right past her house on Lake Road."

That matter of absolute fact is one of the few matters of absolute fact to surface in the Sam Sheppard murder case. The other facts are that Marilyn died and Sam lived on for a while.

He was convicted of murdering her in one of the most famous trials of the previous century. And then, after a retrial, he was acquitted. The second trial was granted because of an appeal.

The high court ruled that his first trial was tainted by biased news coverage. The biased news coverage came largely from my alma mater, the *Cleveland Press*.

I went to work for the *Press* as a cub reporter in 1963. I remember sitting in the lunch room with a bunch of veterans who had covered the Sheppard case. And I remember saying, "I don't know if he did it, but I never thought they had enough evidence to convict him."

They all gave me the evil eye. They would have left me eating alone if I hadn't been a rookie. I never met anybody connected with this crime who didn't think Sam had done it.

That includes the Bay Village cops. The cops were friendly to Sam because he was helpful to them. When there was an auto accident in Bay Village and somebody was hurt, the cops would call Sam. He'd show up in the middle of the night to treat the injured at no charge.

So, on that morning 50 years ago, when the cops arrived at the Sheppard house, they wanted to believe Sam's story about a "bushy-haired intruder" who had somehow broken in, killed Marilyn and assaulted Sam.

But the evidence argued against his story. One cop who was on the scene told me that when they dusted the house for fingerprints, everything was clean as a whistle—including the telephone Sam told them he used to call his neighbor Spencer Houk, Bay Village's mayor at the time.

All cops know that when a wife is murdered, the obvious suspect is the husband. And as the investigation churned on, there was no way to clear Sam. So he was convicted and sent to prison.

Then came the second trial. A young F. Lee Bailey got Sam off. I covered a piece of that trial and tried not to smirk around the lunch room. In a murder trial, what is on trial is reasonable doubt. Bailey planted enough reasonable doubt to let Sam walk.

By that time, Sam had married Arianne Tebbenjohanns, a sexy weirdo who had Nazi connections and had been a pen pal of Sam's in prison.

It doesn't take a V-2 rocket scientist to know there is something strange about a woman who courts a convicted wife-slayer. But the Sheppard murder case broke all conventional rules.

It was bigger than it should have been—attracted far more press than it should have—and never went away. Hollywood glommed onto it and fashioned a TV series and a movie, *The Fugitive,* after it. Many books were written saying that Sam didn't murder Marilyn; many were written saying he did. Somehow this small-town murder stayed alive.

Now the murder is celebrating its golden anniversary. Will we ever know whether Sam killed Marilyn? No.

The day that Ariane divorced him, my editor stashed her in a West Side motel. The idea was that the divorce story wouldn't break until the next day, and the *Cleveland Press* would break it. And we did.

I had dinner with her that night. She told me she thought Sam was nuts—that he slept with a gun under his bed. But when I asked her if he had killed Marilyn, she said she didn't know.

I don't know, either. Sam was tried twice and he batted 1-1—one conviction, one acquittal. All I know is that 50 years later there is still some fascination with that murder. I think he did it. But my opinion is no better than yours. When it comes to reasonable doubt, there's always a reason to doubt. Sometimes, you have to just bury it.

—July 4, 2004

Cleveland's problems are our problems

The six-column headline said, "Cleveland No. 1 in big-city poverty."

So I guess there's no place to go but up.

Except which way is up?

I live in Bay Village, but I call myself a Clevelander. I was born in the front bedroom of a house on Anderson Avenue near 93rd and Union. And I was born into a great town.

We used to call ourselves the "best location in the nation" and a lot of us believed it. Cleveland had almost a million people then. And it had more.

The Cleveland schools I went to were ranked among the best in the country. We were the sixth-largest city in America. You can still drive down an old street and see, where the side of a building has been scraped clean, old signs that say "Sixth City Ice Co." We may not have been a heavyweight town, but we sure were a light heavyweight.

Back then, the Clevelanders I knew lived in Cleveland. They were happy about that. We had little to do with suburbanites. I grew up a block from Shaker Heights but always viewed the Shaker kids with suspicion. Their bikes had gears on them and the kids wore white tennis shoes. Wearing white tennis shoes in a Cleveland school back then might get you a bloody nose.

My mother mothered me, to my great embarrassment. But she let me ride the Rapid downtown with a friend of mine. We'd hang out all day, peeping at the billboards on the Roxy burlesque, shopping for naughty stuff in Jean's Funny House where, for a quarter, a kid could buy a plastic shot glass with a naked lady at the bottom of it.

Christmas was great in the Cleveland of my youth. A shopping trip downtown was mandatory. We would stop at five department stores and watch the mechanical elves in the windows. Our mothers would take us down to May's basement or Higbee's and buy us bargain-basement clothing. Then we'd get a frosted malt on the way to the Rapid and lick the froth off our lips.

That was my Cleveland . . . the "best location in the nation."

Today's Cleveland is a deadbeat town with a deadbeat headline. How did this happen?

Well, it happened for a lot of reasons. When you walked around my Cleveland, you smelled the sulfur from the mills. The mills in the flats were churning out jobs. I remember when the steelworkers union guaranteed its members a six-week vacation. If you dropped out of high school back in my day, you could get a job in the mills and buy a brand-new Plymouth Fury to shame your pals who were headed for college.

The mills went. The great public schools went because of busing. This town always was segregated black and white. Busing was supposed to cure that. But all it did was chase people out of town. Both black and white people fled to avoid busing. And the ones who fled were the ones who could afford to go. So Cleveland was left without a middle class.

That's when the schools went to hell. Now, more than two-thirds of the babies born in Cleveland are born to unmarried mothers. These children are fed into the school system. What chance do they have? Will more money cure this? Of course not.

I would love to tag this column with a bright idea. But I have none. Here's the best I can do, but I don't like it:

Cleveland should disappear. It should become part of a regional government, ruled by the county. Because of the Moses Cleaveland statue, we could still call it Cleveland. But Cleveland should transcend its limits.

Bay Village and Beachwood draw their cachet from their nearness to the big city. Residents go to Playhouse Square and are proud of our world-acclaimed orchestra.

Let us pick up the tab for the city in the midst of these wonders. Let's make Cleveland a countywide city. Because without it, where would the county be?

I don't expect this to happen. But so many of us in the suburbs are willing to spend money to support Ireland or Russia or any ancestral place we hold dear.

How about here?

—August 29, 2004

Set-asides helped the rich get richer

Tax-paying Clevelanders ought to be delighted that this newspaper broke its self-imposed vow of silence and published a rape story last week.

The rapists in the story were self-styled civic leaders and their cronies. The victims were the citizens.

Plain Dealer reporter Mike Tobin, in a brilliant and well-researched set of articles, described how a tightly knit group of influence peddlers allegedly took kickbacks in a shakedown operation that went across state lines.

There are many painful parts to this story. But here is what ought to sting the most:

It was black-on-black crime.

Just about all of the principals named in the federal shakedown probe were black. And the crowbar they used to pry money from the wallets of contractors was civil rights.

Years ago, in a turbulent fight led by George Forbes, Cleveland decided that contractors who wanted to do business in the city had to employ black workers.

On the face of it, this made sense. Cleveland has a vast black population. Why should white people, who don't even live in the city, get city contracts and hang a Jim Crow sign on the construction tool shed?

Almost immediately though, this high-principled notion fell apart. Suppose there simply weren't enough black contractors. Suppose, for example, there were no black contractors who could supply bulk paper. Yeah, just paper. The avalanche of paper the city uses every day. Well, in that case, you had to deal with a black contractor fronting for a white firm. No matter what, you had to pass muster with City Hall to get the contract. Soon, the aroma of kickback was in the air.

According to an FBI memo obtained by the *Plain Dealer*, Ricardo Teamor, an African-American lawyer and friend of former Cleveland Mayor Mike White, said that in just one contract deal—the expansion of Cleveland Hopkins International Airport—he got hundreds of thousands of dollars for doing little work.

Teamor told FBI agents his involvement was a sham designed to help construction companies circumvent city rules requiring participation by businesses owned by minorities and women.

Black-on-black crime.

George Forbes and I have had our innings. But I believe his idea for making sure blacks got to share the wealth was well founded. It was also easily abused and could quickly be turned into a scam. And that, it appears, is what happened.

I've just scratched the surface here. If you read this newspaper, you saw the giant-sized mug shot of Mike White on Thursday. The headline said, "White was target of investigation."

And that is true. The feds were climbing up the ladder. They were trying to get the goods on White, who was cheek-by-jowl with people who took money.

The *Plain Dealer* has known all this for months. But because of the paper's tipster, who had violated a court secrecy order by supplying documents, the paper decided not to run the story.

Finally, after *Scene* magazine reported that the *Plain Dealer* had the documents, the paper ran it. And now a federal judge has ordered federal prosecutors to conduct a criminal investigation into the leaking of the documents.

Naturally, Mike Tobin knows the source of the leak. The guy from *Scene* magazine knows the source.

But one needn't know the source of the leak to conclude that the evidence in those documents pointing to wrongdoing is solid gold. And in our journalistic community, everybody thinks tax-paying Clevelanders should know where the shenanigans are.

This troubled town has become road kill for anybody who can work a deal to sell its vital organs. I'm glad the story finally got out. I'm just sorry it didn't get out sooner.

"I'll go to jail if it comes to that," Tobin told me.

I'd make it a double date.

—July 24, 2005

And Another Thing . . .

Dems can't stand tall without a platform

If you grew up on my block, you were a Democrat. It was unthinkable to be anything else.

My block was blue-collar. Our parents were pipe fitters, carpenters, a cop. My father had a white-collar job. It paid him less than what most of the blue-collar fathers were earning. But he was a union organizer, so he was a Democrat, too. The white collar meant he didn't have to stand over the wash tub in the basement scrubbing the grime off his fingers with Lava soap.

We lived near the border of Shaker. Sometimes we would go over there to see what Republican kids looked like. They looked a lot different. They had gears on their bicycles, which was unheard of on my block.

They wore white tennis shoes, too. Ours were all "Ball-brand" black.

Such pilgrimages confirmed what we'd heard at home: Republicans were for the rich people.

Democrats were for people like us. Our parents had come of age during the Depression. Franklin Roosevelt was a god to them—included in the Holy Trinity to make it a Holy Quartet. When people had no work, he created jobs for them. For those too old to work, he created Social Security. He steered us through an economic crisis and the crisis of the war. And when he died, our parents wept. They thought he would live and be president forever.

Under such circumstances, it was natural for me to become a Democrat. And I was for years. But I lost the faith. Now I am a Feaglerian—a disciple of neither party.

The Republicans never quite captured me, but the Democrats lost me. Last Tuesday's election shows the Democrats have lost a lot of people. All the pundits are right about why. Nobody knows what the Democrats stand for anymore.

The Democrats like to call themselves the "party of inclusion." But over time they've included too much. They stopped being Democrats and started being "liberals." Tagging the label "liberal" on Democrats is the smartest thing the Republicans ever did.

Every crack-brained notion from every liberal pressure group has been thumbtacked to the Democratic Party. Christopher Columbus was a bloodthirsty adventurer. Thomas Jefferson was a racist. Busing is a solution to segregation. Black people whose ancestors may or may not have been slaves deserve huge chunks of money from the government. A Boy Scout, unwilling to recite the scout oath because the word "God" is in it, deserves the nation's attention.

All of these issues have been hung on the Democratic Party. And the party is so paranoid about losing voters that it has disavowed none of them.

Franklin Roosevelt told the nation that the only thing we had to fear was fear itself. The last election taught us that the Democrats are afraid of being Democrats. They are afraid to take a stand on vital issues. If they continue in that vein, they face extinction, like the dodo bird or the Whigs.

The ideas that FDR pioneered are still here, worthy of discussing and defending. Social Security is still a safety belt for low-income families. The Republicans are lobbying to invest Social Security funds in the stock market. The erratic performance of the market makes this laughable. Where were the Democrats on that issue?

Our educational system is dumber than those of most industrialized countries. Our healthcare system forces seniors to eat cat food to save the money for prescription drugs. Where were the Democrats on that issue?

They are fuzzily focused and otherwise occupied. In the recent election, they had no story to tell, no case to make. If the Democrats wish to survive, they had better decide what they are for. They said nothing wrong this election. In fact, they said nothing at all.

—November 9, 2002

My father was right: E-check is a scam

My father, God rest him, hated the E-check. He thought it was a swindle, and he thought I ought to expose it.

He owned an ancient Chevy Citation that he never drove. It was 20 years old and had about 12,000 miles on it. The last trip he took in it caused us much alarm.

"Your father has gone out in the car," my mother telephoned one day. "He went out to the garage to look at it and he saw it had a flat tire. So he's driving it over to the Chevy dealer, flat tire and all."

This did not surprise me. When it came to bullheadedness, my father had no peer. I called the Chevy dealer with an all-points bulletin. Soon the dealer called back.

"He got here all right," the dealer said. "He came in riding on the rim. We've fixed the rim and fixed the tire. How about next time we find another way to get it here?"

I hung up, awash in guilt. My father had a genius for making me feel guilty about things that were beyond my control. Since all the things he did were beyond my control, my reservoir of guilt was as deep as a pond in a stone quarry.

The flat-tire trip was the last trip my 90-year-old father ever took in his car. But he wanted to keep the license plates up to date. So he needed an E-check. He left it up to me to get this done. But never without a lecture.

"It's a gyp," he told me. "You're supposed to be some hot-shot reporter. Why don't you expose it?"

"Dad," I said. "Let's just go with the flow. Let's just calm down."

"Listen," my father said. "The guys in Columbus got this E-check thing passed to reward their friends with fancy contracts. The whole thing is a con game."

"I think it's supposed to be about clean air," I said.

"Listen," he said. "What about the trucks and buses that don't have to get one? Hell, they've exempted Columbus from the E-check. That's where all the bought-off politicians register their cars. It's a sweetheart deal that's as plain as the nose on your face."

I was used to this kind of conversation. My father raised me to believe that I had to watch my back at all times because somebody was out to get me. As we grew older, I came to realize that the person out to get me was him. But there wasn't much I could do about that. So, a couple of years ago, I found myself driving his Citation down to the E-check station for a test.

I nearly killed myself on a freeway ramp. I stepped on the brakes and nothing much happened. Hitting the Citation's brakes amounted only to a suggestion that the car should consider an eventual stop. I had to stand on them to actually stop it.

At the E-check station, the Citation flunked the test. I tried my best to win over the checkers' softer sentiments.

"Look," I said. "This is my old man's car. You can't imagine the amount of grief I'm in for if I have to go back and tell him I've flunked the test."

The checkers were sympathetic. They asked me to pull into a bay that hadn't been used that day. They said that sometimes lingering fumes would make a car flunk the test. But, no matter what we tried, the Citation couldn't pass.

So I dropped it off at a garage and they did about $800 worth of work on it. That included a brake job. My father was not happy. "You let yourself get conned," he said.

"Those brakes could have killed you," I said.

"Listen," he said. "It's all a scheme."

He never drove the car again. But he never let me forget that last E-check. A year later, when he was in a nursing home, he still brought it up to me. He thought I was a patsy. I had flunked the test, not the Citation.

My dad didn't live to see E-check on its deathbed. But now that E-check seems to be going, I have to admit the evidence is in my father's favor.

What is the point of it all, other than sweetheart contracts? Why is Columbus exempt? We'll never know. But, in heaven, my old man is chortling.

"I tried to tell the kid," he is saying. "But he didn't listen." Isn't that the bottom line on what parents always say?

—March 16, 2003

That unpleasant odor is E-check surviving

My celebration was premature. It looks as if the governor is going to veto repeal of the E-check.

If he does, we may be stuck with this meaningless bureaucratic con game for a long-term ride with a short-term governor. And the masses cry out, why?

Well, Chris Jones, director of the Ohio Environmental Protection Agency, knows why. He pointed out that if we fired the E-check people, we would have to pay them $25 million to go away. I wish I'd had that kind of contract when I was anchoring the nightly news. I would have happily gone away for mere thousands. Maybe less.

The E-check arrived wrapped in noble motives. We were all supposed to breathe better because there would be less bad stuff in the air. But soon the air began to smell like old mackerel. It was the smell of a government contract gone rotten.

E-check became just a revenue-producer for the state. It brought millions of dollars in inspection fees to Columbus' coffers. It was, in other words, a hidden kind of state tax. It had less to do with fresh air than a can of Glade.

I'm no ecology expert, so I quote Jones as my guru. The quote comes from my favorite newspaper—this one:

"Jones testified earlier that exempting more cars from the inspections would throw the state's environmental plan out of compliance with federal guidelines by 15,000 tons of hydrocarbons a year . . ."

Here's my favorite part:

"He said that number does not represent actual pollution generated by cars but the number of credits the state receives for testing them."

And then he added this:

"We could have lived with it from an environmental standpoint, but it becomes a contractor issue."

When I apply a simple command of English to these paragraphs, here's the translation I get:

Some faceless suit in Washington bribed our state into holding E-checks.

The alleged idea behind the E-checks was to make our air cleaner.

A fancy contract was let to hire a company to administer these E-checks. That company had a damn good lawyer who negotiated a damn good contract.

The faceless suit in D.C. didn't bother checking the air to see if the idea had any merit. He handed out tax dollars based on the number of E-check tests performed.

This worked OK when Columbus was fat.

But when the economic crunch came, Columbus had to wheel and deal. And there was no wiggle room out of the E-check deal.

So the governor will veto the repeal of E-check even though his EPA director could breathe just as easily without it. If we keep E-check, its preservation has little to do with our lungs but much to do with government wallets.

Maybe I've got this all wrong, in which case I'll be happy to retract it. Why not? I've got egg on my face already.

When it looked as if E-check might be repealed, I wrote a column about my late father, whose favorite lecture was that E-check was a scam. I predicted it was going away and I lamented the fact that he wasn't around to see that happen.

If he were still around, he would have reminded me that no tax just goes away. Once government figures out a way to pry money out of us, it never surrenders.

I always thought he was too cynical. But now I'm beginning to wonder. We have a governor who won his last election by preaching that, though times were tough, things would be OK.

Well, things are far from OK. Companies that belly up to the public trough to make a living on sweetheart deals are still there while others suffer. If the "E" in E-check stood for ethical, we'd all be gasping for air.

—March 30, 2003

Flag raised (again) as cheap political issue

The American flag is fireproof. I don't know why some of the yahoos in Congress don't understand that. But they don't.

Every couple of years, some congressional committee, full of shallow jingoistic fervor, tries to amend the Constitution to make it a crime to burn the flag.

This always gives me the opportunity (I think this is my fourth) to point out that the flag is incombustible. It needs no fire protection. It is true that flags occasionally burn. But not The Flag. It never has.

Last week, the House Judiciary Subcommittee on the Constitution voted to make flag burning an anti-American act, punishable by law.

This vote, as usual, will go nowhere. If it ever gets out of committee, it will be gunned down in the House or the Senate by those who have read the First Amendment and understand where the real strength of our nation lies.

There are two things wrong with an anti-flag-burning law. One is practical and the other is spiritual. The practical one is the most fun to deal with, so let's deal with it first.

The subcommittee amendment reads like this:

"The Congress shall have power to prohibit the physical desecration of the flag of the United States."

Dandy. But try to enforce it.

Suppose I get out my Crayolas and draw a flag on paper. Then suppose I set it alight? Can I be charged and hauled into federal prison for that? Have I burned "the flag," or have I merely burned my representation of it?

Suppose the paper flag I burn carries 51 stars? Is it still "the flag"? Or do I beat the rap on a technicality?

How about those cocktail weenies we serve on July Fourth with tiny flag-wrapped toothpicks stuck in them. If I singe the flag on a cocktail weenie, am I looking at a term in Leavenworth?

Since very few flags are made in this country anymore, how about if I burn one made in a Third World country? Can I torch it claiming that it was not really the flag but merely a bolt of imported dry goods with a pattern on it?

Any lawyer fresh from his third try at the bar exam could get me off for any of the above reasons. A flag amendment would be virtually unenforceable. But there's a lot more wrong with it than just that.

Our flag needs no help from the chest-thumping souls on the House Judiciary Subcommittee on the Constitution.

Better people have gone before them. My Uncle Ziggy protected the flag on Okinawa. My Cousin Billy protected the flag as he lay in the mud looking across the Rhine river.

Men and women on Bataan and Corregidor watched while the flag was lowered by a ruthless enemy and trampled into the dirt. But the flag flew on in their hearts. The brave firemen and cops who ran into the World Trade Center carried the spirit of America with them. Nothing Congress could have done would have augmented their courage. And the charred flag recovered from the carnage made a mockery of our nation's enemies.

Our troops fighting in Iraq constantly see hostile demonstrations in which the flag is burned. Does it make them mad? Sure it does. But do they think America has been wounded by such antics? Of course not.

We have built such a great country that the only people on earth who can wound it is us. And the way we can ruin it is to forget the difficult principles we stand for. Among them is the First Amendment right to criticize our country in a manner that is offensive. That includes giving protection to some idiot who decides to burn a flag.

A flag. But never The Flag.

At the end of the seldom-sung second verse of our national anthem is a wish so strong, it's almost a prayer: "'Tis the star-spangled banner, O long may it wave o'er the land of the free and the home of the brave."

It is a tenuous balance that, being both free and brave. Brave men die so imbeciles can squander their freedom. But the test of our land lies in that very balancing act. If the members of the subcommittee on the Constitution don't know that, they ought to learn it.

—May 14, 2003

The genes fit snugly, but victim tag falls off

Some sharpie lawyers tried to sue the fast-food industry for making people fat. The suit got nowhere, but the sharpie lawyers vowed to try again. Put the scent of a cash settlement in the water and the lawyers swarm like sharks around a rare leg of lamb.

The lawsuit got me thinking, though: I am a chubby, portly, hefty, stocky guy. In non-PC terms, a fat guy. If I could sue somebody for my condition, my self-esteem would get an XL boost. With the right lawyer, I could become a victim.

There is nothing better to be in America than a victim. Being a victim takes the heat off you and puts it on somebody else—Ronald McDonald, say.

Since I'm a white, straight, male, Anglo-Saxon, Protestant American, the victim parade has passed me by. Given my demographics, I have always been cast as the victimizer. I and my ilk have been accused of causing everybody else's problems. We are the universal donor to society's ills.

I have pined for years to be a victim, too. But I saw no way into that charmed circle. Now there is a ray of hope. I am a fat guy, and fat guys are the newest class of victims. All that is required is to find the right lawyer and aim him at my victimizer.

I've already got the lawyer picked out. My cable TV runs a commercial for a father-and-son law firm called Elk and Elk. A rough paraphrase of the Elk and Elk commercial urges us to consider that anything bad that befalls us may be somebody else's fault and that the somebody else ought to pay. Elk and Elk are talking my language.

I even know whom to sue. The guy responsible for my fatness is a fellow named Harry Kugler. There is one slight hitch. The statute of limitations has probably run out on Harry Kugler. He is beneath the sod in Harvard Grove Cemetery, dead these 65 years.

He was my grandfather, a Cleveland police sergeant. I know him only through pictures, but the pictures look a lot like me. He had my kind of build and my kind of belly. He had the same bald spot on the back of his head that I have. If there's a reason I am fat, it's because Harry stuck me with his genes. It wasn't my fault. Do you think Elk and Elk would take my case?

Harry was on my mother's side of the family. My father, thin all his life, withheld his genes from me. Looking back, I can see that it was a clear case of gene-deprivation.

My father never exercised. He ate anything he wanted to eat. He spent the last 20 years of his life largely supine on the couch. He could knock off a box of Malley's chocolates in a day. And he never gained an ounce.

He was a nonfiltered Camel smoker from age 12. He smoked them down so small he should have had a roach clip for the last puff. When he was 85, his doctor told him he should quit. He promised my mother he would. He started stepping outside in the winter for a breath of fresh air. When the snow melted in spring, the back yard was full of Camel butts.

He died in a nursing home at 91. He never had a spare ounce of flesh on his body, and he smoked to the end.

As I victim, I can see that my father's genes gave me cruel, false hope.

I went on diet after diet—sustaining some of them for as long as two weeks. I jogged three miles each day, four times a week. Granted, I jogged slowly and smoked the occasional cigarette while running. But always a low-tar filter.

Harry was always there, though. His genes finally caught up with me. In a recent photo of me with my grandchild on my lap, I look just like him.

Everybody said he was a wonderful guy. He was just fat, that's all. Probably, he didn't want to be fat. Who does?

But I doubt he would have sued anybody because of it. Back in his day, you played the hand life had dealt you, and said, "That's how it goes."

Nobody gets a level playing field in life. We all just do the best we can, and some days our best is better than other days. Seeking victimhood just sours us.

One of my favorite quotes goes like this: "We are all happy, we just don't know it." Belly up to a Wendy's and think about that one.

—July 6, 2003

Empty stomach or full, Jerry's hard to take

I had lunch with Jerry Springer yesterday. It was a technological lunch. I was home, eating a baloney sandwich, watching Springer's noon show on Channel 43.

I'd never watched a *Jerry Springer* show. But now he has officially stated that he wants to represent our state in the U.S. Senate. So I felt a duty, as an Ohio voter, to familiarize myself with the man and his career in public life.

The show began with startling honesty.

"The *Jerry Springer Show* has been voted the worst show in the history of television," an offstage announcer crowed. Seemingly delighted with this trumpeted indictment, Springer gaily pranced on stage, took a bow and introduced his first guest. He ushered in a transsexual in a dress whose name was Bacon. Bacon's secret (all of Jerry's guests have secrets) was that she was sleeping with her pregnant sister's boyfriend.

Jerry tossed in his first quip of the day.

"Your name is Bacon, does that mean you were born a pig?" he asked. The audience loved it. "Jer-ry, Jer-ry!" they chanted. "Just a joke," Jerry said.

At that point, I noticed something about Jerry that may be unique in the history of broadcasting. When he holds his mike, he carries around a little green sign that says "Jerry Springer" on it. Murrow never did that, nor did Cronkite nor does Brokaw. But Jerry wants to make sure that, every time the camera is on him, we know the name of the man who runs the worst show in the history of television.

Anyway, getting back to Bacon, she was confronted by her sister Yolanda and Yolanda's boyfriend, Jamal. A lot of screaming and clawing and stuff went on. Jerry's bouncers, who are stars of the show, broke them up. And then we paused for a commercial.

The commercials on Springer's shows are excellent media buys because they appeal to Springer's audience. They are all of the, "if you're in financial trouble, file bankruptcy today" variety. If you can't get a credit card, call us. If you can't cash a check, call us. If you want to sue somebody, call us. Springer, a millionaire, exploits the bottom of the food chain. And he knows it. And thrives on it.

I'll skim over the details of the rest of the show. We had Co-co, whose girlfriend didn't know she was a woman. We had Kevin, the cowboy (dressed in about a 30-gallon hat) whose wife had run off with an ice cream man. Kevin, wife and ice cream man appeared on stage. The bouncers again had to intervene. But there was one poignant moment when Kevin dropped to his knees and told his ex:

"Please come back. I'll give you more baths. I'll shave your legs more than I used to."

I was out of baloney by then, but Springer wasn't. He trotted out Eboney, who had gone to bed with Will while baby-sitting her friend Lenora's kids. Eboney was forthcoming about her feelings:

"I don't care if this pisses her off or not. I can't stand the bitch and her brats any longer," she said. This resulted in another 911 call to the weary bouncers. But Eboney was the last card on the bill. After the commercial (Can't get a loan? Consolidate your bills with us.), we were into the last segment of the show. That's the segment where young women in the audience pull up their T-shirts and show their breasts, always electronically fuzzed out by canny producers who want to avoid after-peek-a-boo lawsuits.

And then Jerry gave a little homily. I paid a lot of attention to that because it probably is going to be the kind of Jerry sermon we're going to hear in the Senate primary campaign.

"We often know what we want," Jerry said. "We don't always know what's best for us. Sometimes, something you want, you're better off without it."

That's certainly true. Springer, once a fairly respected TV anchor and commentator, decided to become a million-dollar pimp to seduce the worst of American culture.

In his run for Senate, he'd be better off without that. But he's got enough money and name recognition to be a serious candidate. All he lacks are principles. Have lunch with Jerry tomorrow and ask yourself if this is the guy you want to represent you. If he is, you're a dope. And I don't think you are.

—July 16, 2003

Economic rebound should get Bush bounced

We do a lot of our Christmas shopping out of catalogs. A couple of weeks before Christmas, I called a toll-free number to order a gift for some relatives in San Francisco. The guy who answered the phone spoke in a thick Indian accent.

How thick? As thick as French fries drowned in curry. About 60 seconds into the phone call, I realized that this transaction needed an interpreter. None being handy, I hung up. Then I did what I always do when I'm frustrated. I went off to find my wife so I could rant at her.

"Why do they put people who can't speak English on telemarketing calls?" I fumed. "Weren't the cab drivers bad enough? You hail a New York cabbie and he can't speak English and you can't speak whatever he speaks. So off you go. He's up in the front seat, burning incense to some unfamiliar god and listening to twangy music on Radio Sahara, but he doesn't understand where 34th and Fifth is!"

"Calm down. I'll call," said my wife.

Twenty minutes later she came back. "I talked to an Indian person, too," she said. "But she understood me."

"Gee," I said, "isn't that a coincidence. We both called the same toll-free number and we both got Indians."

"Anyway," she said. "I ordered the Christmas present for Ed and Nina. It's on the way."

I mentioned this at a party over the weekend. My host spoke up.

"The reason you were talking to Indians," he said, "was that your call was answered in India."

I was baffled and told him so.

"Don't you know how many telemarketing jobs are outsourced?" he said.

"No," I said. "I guess I don't."

"It's not just catalog items," he said. "Some of the leading hospitals send their X-rays and MRIs over to India to have an Indian physician take a look at them. Indian doctors work a lot cheaper than American doctors. So your Indian doc takes a gander and sends back his findings right away and the American hospitals get them cheap and quick."

I guess that's when I realized how little I know about the global economy. It's not just Chinese flashlights anymore. The global economy apparently is running amok. We Americans don't have a real economy now. We just have the ghost of one.

If you play the stock market (I don't) maybe you are heartened by those chirpy little *Wall Street Journal* reports that say the economy is on the upswing. A lot of people are getting rich in America if they have money to invest. But suppose you don't have money to invest? Suppose you just want a job?

Last month, the Bush economy created 1,000 new jobs nationwide. That's 20 new jobs a state. That's 0.23 jobs for each Ohio county. This is no economic upturn. This is a crisis.

In our adopt-a-trash-can city, the heavy manufacturing jobs wandered away years ago. First they went down South, where labor was cheaper. Then they crossed the Rio Grande, where labor worked for coins in a tin cup. The slick economists told us this was a natural evolution. America was evolving from a manufacturing economy to a service economy, they said.

None of us knew exactly what that meant. But like the suckers we are, we bought it. Now, even the service jobs are being exported. The guys on top know where the cheap labor is. And nothing will stop them from using it.

I think 2004 will be a pivotal year for all of us. I think we are deep in a new kind of wilderness. All of the old precepts that made us the America we were have been warped and eroded. The middle class—the bulwark of any democracy—has been mauled by the greed of the coupon-snippers. First, we shipped out plants to Mexico in search of cheap labor. Now, this president wants to bring cheap labor up here, in the form of indentured servants, to undercut decent wages and fair rules in the workplace.

Our kids are dying in Iraq while our leaders hold business meetings and pass out contracts like party favors to those countries willing to kiss our ring. If you never voted before, this is your year. At least the guy on the phone in India can't vote. Our vote is still made in America. It's one of the last things that is really ours. Let's use it.

—January 14, 2004

Slowing gun buyers makes lots of sense

Almost 40 years ago, I covered a story about a woman shot to death downtown in a public building. Her killer bought the murder gun a couple of hours before he killed her.

In the aftermath, there was a cry for a waiting period on the purchase of handguns. The sane rationale for this argument was that nobody needs a handgun right away unless he's some kind of a nut.

George Kallas, I think I may say without fear of libel, is some kind of a nut. He allegedly bought a pistol and killed his wife of 40 years in the Lorain Public Library parking lot in front of an audience of frightened kids. The headline in our paper said:

"Man buys gun on day of murder."

Déjà vu all over again.

The American love affair with guns is a strange and quirky romance. It's like a dating relationship on a dark soap opera. Always a lot of passion, never much common sense.

In the 40 years since I covered "Woman shot to death downtown," Martin Luther King, Bobby Kennedy, Ronald Reagan, James Brady and John Lennon (to name a high-profile few) have been shot at and hit by crazies. Every tragedy brought a call for tougher gun control. And every call was answered by a bleat of opposition by the so-called gun lobby.

I guess I have to include myself in the gun lobby. I own a handgun and have no intention of surrendering it. I believe in Second Amendment rights, a confession that will probably dismay many readers of this column.

But I also believe that with such rights go great responsibilities. And some of those responsibilities fall on the shoulders of the gun dealers, who will probably fill my voice mail with anger by noon.

After Jim Brady was shot, his wife led a crusade for strict gun-sale rules. She met opposition at every turn, but she persevered. Or at least I thought she had persevered until I read last Thursday's "Man buys gun on day of murder."

That story, by *Plain Dealer* reporter Rachel Dissell, said, "In

Ohio, there is no wait to buy a gun for a person who has no criminal record . . . Before 1998, a buyer had to wait up to five days, but the requirement disappeared when the federal government enabled a gun dealer to sell in as little as 30 seconds."

George Kallas had no criminal record, so he could get a gun as fast as he could get a Wendy's burger—in and out of the gun store and then goodbye Barbara Kallas.

Some days before he shot his wife, Lorain police, responding to a domestic disturbance call, confiscated three rifles and a .38-caliber pistol from the Kallas home. But they charged him with nothing. So under current Ohio law, he was free to rearm and did.

Cops tend to be conservative. But the cops I know don't want to see guns on the street. Lorain Detective Jim Rohner was quoted as saying, "I think it's crazy someone can go in and have a background check and have a gun in a matter of an hour. When you're buying a gun, why do you need it right now?"

Well, you don't. I'll admit it's possible that George Kallas, infected with whatever mania had consumed him, might have waited for 10 or 15 days and then collected his gun and shot his wife. But it certainly is equally possible that he wouldn't have. The crazed mind goes up and down like a roller coaster, and a couple of days might have prevented a funeral and two families wounded forever.

Our governor, a human rubber stamp, has signed a bill that will allow all of us to carry guns anywhere we go. So maybe I'll carry mine around just for the heck of it. When you're built like me, what's another bulge?

The same governor is about to sign a bill banning the rights of homosexuals couples to exchange vows of love and support. His priorities are somewhat askew. If he thinks homosexual couples are a danger to heterosexual marriage, he ought to thumb through the police reports. He can start with Kallas and work backward through time.

—January 25, 2004

Trading right and wrong for ratings

When obnoxious TV things happen like the Super Bowl halftime show, I retreat to the grandmother test.

If my grandmother, who died in 1955, could come back to life long enough to view the show, how would she react?

Well, the shock would kill her.

And, if the shock didn't kill her, she would certainly look for an exit back to her world—the gentler world she knew.

I see her now as I knew her then, sitting in her high-backed wing chair, watching a baseball game or Sid Caesar or Kate Smith singing "Bless This House" on Easter.

Then in my mind's eye, I yank her forward to the present and try to picture her watching Super Bowl commercials in which horses break gale-force wind and dancers grab their crotches and shriek dirty lyrics and a star performer rips the bra off a member of a notoriously dysfunctional family.

If my grandmother were still with us, she might turn to me and say, "Richard, how did this happen? How did we get this way?"

Now there's a fair question. How did we? We spend a lot of time questioning the past. Every year, somebody's new book rips apart our founding fathers and catalogues their sins of racism and narrow-mindedness. But hasn't the past got a right to question the present, too? I think so. That's why I apply the grandmother test.

If I had time to answer her, I would say to my grandmother, "We lost four things that your generation believed in: We lost our sense of shame, responsibility, civility and conscience."

Back when William Paley ran CBS, he would never have let his network broadcast this notorious halftime show. He was in charge, and he wouldn't air anything he'd be ashamed of. If he did, he knew that he would face weekends in the Hamptons where he would mingle with his peer group and suffer criticism for polluting the air with a standard of broadcasting that was beneath him.

But William Paley doesn't run CBS anymore. It has become a conglomerate, as have all the networks. Conglomerates have no shame because their chairmen can hide from it and do so. Shame is out. The sole responsibility is to the ratings. Raunchy sex builds ratings. And conscience? Well, that's not a business thing. It only gets in the way of ratings.

Back in my grandma's day, all of the frisky young men in the family went off to war. By the time they came back, there wasn't a dirty word they hadn't heard or used. But when they came back home, they came back to a civil society. They left the crudeness behind them. They had seen terrible things, but they yearned for civility and gentleness.

Who taught them that? Well, first their families did. And then their teachers. And then, maybe their church. And then, finally, the media—films and the radio.

There was, back in those days, a kind of national standard—a consensus about the way to behave. Somehow it cut across all social and economic bounds. Maybe you had to be there to feel it, but we all knew the right way to behave.

Now it's gone. If my grandmother came back, I would have to try to explain its loss to her:

"There is no right and wrong now, grandma. There's only opinion."

"But it can't be right to let that child's bosom be exposed in front of children on television."

"Well, you have to understand, grandma, that since you left us there really are no rules anymore."

"No rules?"

"No grandma. Since you died, it's all about money."

"But isn't there a line you can't cross?"

"No grandma. We don't even know who is supposed to draw the line."

And there she leaves me.

—February 4, 2004

Now for the brain-food fight

In an election season full of hate mail, I saved this one because I thought you might get a kick out of it. Here it is, just the way it came in—capital letters and all:

DICK. I USED TO ENJOY YOUR ARTICLES WHEN YOU HAD GOOD IDEAS AND A YOUNG MIND. RECENTLY YOUR POLITICAL REASONING IS GOOFY.

WHEN I SAW YOU AT HEINENS RECENTLY I WANTED TO SHAKE THE HAND OF A CELEBRITY AND GIVE YOU A RIGHT CROSS WITH MY LEFT. WE ARE ABOUT THE SAME AGE SO I WOULD NOT BE TAKING ADVANTAGE OF YOU.

HOW YOU CAN LIKE THE THREE PRESIDENTIAL CANDIDATES YOU MENTION OVER PRESIDENT BUSH IS BEYOND BELIEF.

TRY SOME LECTIN, WHICH IS A BRAIN FOOD. ALSO TAKE SOME BOXING LESSONS IN CASE YOU'RE AT HEINENS AND I SPOT YOU AFTER READING MORE OF YOUR NONSENSE.

It was signed, "RICH."

Yo, Rich.

I've written columns now for more than 30 years. I've received bomb threats and death threats, some written in crayon and some in neat, Spenserian hand. Only once did I turn a letter over to the cops. And that was because I lived in a condo and if they bombed me, somebody else would get hurt.

But never before have I been threatened with a high-noon sucker punch at Heinen's sushi counter.

Since you've seen me there, you know I love our Bay Village Heinen's. It really is the cradle of civilization in our village. The parking lot is full of soccer moms driving gigantic SUVs, and the wide aisles are full of nice people sipping their free samples of Merlot and nibbling little cubes of French cheese and being nice to one another.

I mean, Rich, it's hardly the place for a sneaky right cross (thrown with the left hand, no less) over a handshake. A busted jar of olives and an occasional geriatric cardiac arrest is really all the excitement Heinen's is ready for.

And you know what, Rich? You shouldn't have warned me. First of all, you telegraphed your punch, which is a definite no-no. I intend now to browse the aisles of Heinen's with a nice, big can of tuna in my hand. Here's the way the mano-a-mano goes. I duck your left-handed right cross and counter with a Chicken of the Sea to your temple. How about that?

Should you survive that, I intend to battle you back to the Heinen's vegetable section, where I will draw a big fat zucchini on you and flail away until security comes.

So there, Rich. Be warned.

And now to the point of all this.

The letter you read above was a real letter. But it's only one of thousands of letters I've received about this election.

What these letters tell me is what everybody already knows: We are a nation angrily divided, well past the point of reasoned discourse. It's going to be a very grumpy year.

And that's OK. That's why the Founding Fathers invented elections: to keep us from throwing tomatoes at one another.

Rich and I certainly agree on this: We think we live in the greatest nation on earth. The argument is about how we keep ourselves great.

I think we do it by keeping an open mind. I've never heard of the brain food that Rich wanted me to take. But he's right when he says my brain isn't young anymore. It's six decades old and changing by the minute.

In the '50s, I didn't much care that a colleague like Sam Fulwood couldn't go to the same Deep South men's room as I could. In the '60s, I didn't much care about women's rights. Until recently, I didn't much care about gay rights.

My aging mind taught me to care about these things. I don't think I want any Lectin. I'm happy still learning.

But I respect your point of view, Rich. If you want to settle this your way, what do you say to zucchinis at three paces?

—March 3, 2004

No one can see it, but it sure stands out

The phone rang the other day and the guy who called had the wrong number. Somehow we got into a chat.

It was a pleasant chat. So, when we began to hang up, I said, "Nice talking to you. By the way, my name is . . ."

"Oh, I know who you are," he said. "I can tell by the voice. I watch you on TV and read your column. I don't always agree with you, though."

"I don't always agree with me, either," I said, which is my standard answer to such comments. Then we disconnected. And I was left to think about my voice.

The evidence is that I have a strange voice. It is probably my only remarkable feature. Look at me and you see your average balding, mid-60-ish, portly grandpa. But when I open my yap, heads turn and people say, "Oh, I know you."

I discovered I had a strange voice 30 years ago when I began doing television commentaries. I had no desire to launch my voice over the airwaves. But necessity was at the helm. My newspaper had locked us out and I needed work.

So I got into broadcasting. And I wasn't there very long before various people on other stations began having fun imitating my voice. They did my voice in a kind of high-pitched, nasal drawl. It is obviously impossible to recreate this in print. The best I can do is: "And nyowww, Leon, let's get back to the nyEEEws."

Toldja it was impossible.

My career in television might have been cemented by the people on radio stations who imitated the way I talked. One popular morning host did a regular feature imitating me. When I worked at Channel 3, my pal Jim Donovan was so good at sounding like me that we conspired one night to let Jim cut a promo for my show so I could go out and make a speech. I honestly don't remember if we tried it. But if we did, I'm sure we pulled it off.

When it comes to the question of voice, I know I've got a lot of company out there. Years ago, with the invention of the cassette tape recorder, we all heard ourselves as others heard us. And most of us were shocked.

A rendition, captured on tape, of "Happy Birthday to You" in which we thought we sounded like Pavarotti, came out sounding like an off-key Muppet. The first time you hear your voice on tape is always a downer. Thirty years later, I avoid the sound of my voice whenever I can.

I can't do it in banks. Sometimes, when I want to cash a check and am confronted by a new teller, she asks for identification. "Will a driver's license do?" I say. And she says, "Oh, that's all right, Mr. Feagler. I recognize the voice." If I ever took up bank robbery, I'd have to scribble a note. Even a nylon stocking over my voice would not disguise a verbal command of, "Awww-right, Leon, give me all your MONyeeee."

If you've gone this far, you may be wondering why I'm telling you all this. Well, it's because of a story in our newspaper headlined: "Next up for nip 'n tuck is your voice: Some pick surgery to sound younger."

The story said that, in their quest for eternal youth, baby-boomers, who have already had their eye jobs, their tummy jobs and their teeth jobs, are now turning to voice jobs.

If you're an old person in disguise, you don't want your voice to give you away. I mean, suppose you are a 60-year-old stud with transplanted hair, a liposuctioned belly, skin full of Botox and a pocketful of Viagra? You don't want to sit next to a 30-something on a barstool and say:

"Ssshay, sweet thing. Lessh go somewhere where the mushic is shofter."

So now the voice job may be the hot new thing in the forever-young business.

I gotta tell you, I'm intrigued.

My voice and I have been companions for years. But if I could find an operation that would give me a Broadway voice like Tommy Tune's, I'd be tempted to do it.

But I'm not sure how I'd adapt. I am, after all, what I am. And you know, it hasn't been bad having those guys imitate me. I guess I have to say, don't change voices in midstream. You find your voice and play it.

—April 21, 2004

The wailing you hear isn't from smokers

I'm all for no-smoking sections in restaurants. But how about no-baby sections?

Smoking pollutes. Our city, with all its problems, is wrestling with an ordinance that would ban tobacco-puffers from restaurants, bars and every other public place.

Right now, this idea is on the back burner. The City Council president thinks there are more important threats to the Comeback City than secondhand smoke.

But, as a smoker, I have some sympathy with the notion of smoke-free environments. I have tried to cut down—oh, Lord, have I tried!—and even with His help I haven't succeeded.

There were days when, if I had a lunch date over business, I would call ahead and say "Has my boss reserved a smoking table?" And if the answer was no, I would say, "There must have been some mistake. We want smoking."

I could get away with that one. But it got embarrassing when I was with a group of people, all sitting in nonsmoking, and I was trapped there, a pack of butts in my pocket and no graceful way out.

I have never been a salad eater. So when the salad course was delivered, I would excuse myself and go out and smoke a cigarette on the curb. There I would stand, puffing away, apart from my family and friends, saying "Hi-ya" to any strangers who passed by on the sidewalk. Peering though the window, I could see my joyously smoke-free companions engaging in entertaining conversation that I could not hear. I felt like a waif on the street.

Now I'm better.

I still smoke. I feel I have to. My lungs have built two stadiums and a basketball arena. The taxes on my cigarettes have helped bring my town back to life. But I have cut down. These days, when I walk into Bob Evans and the clerk says "Smoking or non?" I say "non."

What I wish the clerk would say is, "Baby or non?" I would say, "Non-baby, please," and be ushered to a section of the restaurant where screaming children were prohibited.

I first spelled out my "non-baby section" idea in a column some years ago. I knew I had a hit on my hands when somebody plagiarized me (the only time it ever happened) and put my idea in a big-city newspaper.

This was flattering. I thought the idea might take hold. But alas, it never did. So I repeat it now.

Secondhand smoke pollution, I can see, might be annoying to diners. But so is secondhand baby-shriek pollution.

If it's your own kid (and I've got four) you grin and bear it. You take your kids into a restaurant, put a couple of them in high chairs, and all of a sudden one of them begins to shriek like an air-raid siren.

And, by the way, if I were manufacturing air-raid sirens, I'd get a shrieking kid on tape and use that for the sound. Nothing gets and keeps your attention like a shrieking kid in a restaurant. Or at church.

Just as smokers don't smell their own smoke, most parents don't hear their own babies' shrieks. They know it's happening, but they don't know the effect it's having on the atmosphere.

If you're in the booth behind baby-shriek you say, "Oh, God. I hope this doesn't go on for the whole meal." Honestly, I've never heard anybody say that about a smoker.

So if we are going to begin to segregate our restaurants to try to make everybody comfortable, let's add a no-baby section to the no-smoking sections.

I won't go as far as to say we ought to ban babies entirely, which is what they want to do with smokers. Babies are a necessity to society. Smokers are only a necessity to the politicians who fleece them for taxes.

Is there a way we can tax shrieking babies? Naw. If there was, we would have thought it up a long, long time ago.

Probably about 3 a.m.

—June 12, 2004

If you see a left turn, it's the columnist

"Look at how fast poor Dick Feagler swung left when it was explained to him that his job was on the line."

That's part of a letter that ran on our Opinion page the other day. I thought about ignoring it. But then I thought, maybe this is a good time to share with you how journalistic sausage is made.

If the writer had said, "Feagler's a jerk, Feagler's a dunce, Feagler's a dummy," I would have left it alone.

But the writer claimed I swung left when it was explained to me that my job was on the line.

The implication of that is clear. It implies that my bosses at the paper came to me and said, "Start writing anti-Bush, anti-war and pro-gay stuff or you're out of here."

I don't know where to begin to answer this sinister fantasy. Let me begin with the job threat.

I'll be 66 years old next month. I'm drawing full Social Security, plus a pension from working on commercial television, plus an old *Cleveland Press* pension, plus a check from public TV. And plus all that, I don't have much of an ego anymore.

If an editor came to me and said, "Write some lefty stuff or you're outta here," I'd be outta there. And I wouldn't have far to go, because I work from home.

The letter writer is correct when he says I've swung to the left. But it wasn't a *Plain Dealer* editor pushing the swing. It was George W. Bush. I don't like his war and I don't like his stand on civil liberties. So I began writing what I thought about those things. If the *Plain Dealer* bosses had told me I couldn't, I would have said adios. But they didn't. And they wouldn't.

Here's what went on backstage. When I swam over to the left side of the pool, the editors were concerned that the editorial page lacked a conservative voice.

So they cajoled Deputy Editorial Director Kevin O'Brien, a staunch conservative, to begin writing regular columns. Kevin's columns are perky and provocative and they've drawn an immense amount of reader response.

It so happens, mirable dicto, that Kevin is also my editor. He edits each column I write. Does he agree with most of them? Hardly. But his job as an editor is to help me say, as cogently and sprightly as I can say it, what my point is. And he's a whiz at it.

If our roles were reversed and I were editing Kevin, I'd try for the same thing. His politics would interest me far less than his copy. My job would be, even though I disagreed with him, to help make his message come through as clearly and strongly as he could state it.

That's the wonderful thing about newsrooms. That's why I've loved working in them for 40 years. When it comes to bipartisan effort for a greater good, we are far and away ahead of the U.S. Congress. We bypass our differences and try for a quality product.

I know readers don't believe this. I've known it for years. Every newspaper man or woman has to listen to how their stories are slanted, this way or that.

Even C-SPAN, the straightest-down-the-middle news organization ever invented, takes calls from irate viewers who complain that C-SPAN is too far left or too far right.

In this year of total political polarization, such attacks are worse than ever. And we are stuck with them until November.

But the media—newspapers—when they are doing their job, are a mirror. Look into it and you see what you see. But, if you don't like your haircut, don't blame the mirror.

And please, don't blame the editors for what I write. One of the many tough jobs of being an editor is the tongue-biting that goes on when a piece of copy gets into the paper that the editor knows will cause a flood of angry calls.

Somebody wanted to make me an editor once. I thought about it and turned it down. I'd rather cause trouble than resolve it.

And when the day comes that somebody says to me that my job is on the line, I'm gone.

—June 30, 2004

Kucinich was the candidate we needed

Dennis, I'm glad you ran. I think you ran well.

Sure, you were the butt of late-night Jay Leno jokes. Cartoonists made fun of your shoe-polish hair. But your skin is thick. You are a poor kid who grew up in this town and worked the streets door-to-door and became mayor. Your problem was that you were mayor too young and not yet mellow.

On your last day as mayor, 25 years ago, I wrote a column saying good-bye. I wrote in part:

"You scorn balance. You've kept it all off balance. You rock the town like a canoe in the rapids . . .

"When people live together, they have to have harmony and co-operation. People have been telling you that all along. The people around you would blow a police whistle at a funeral. The people around you get on everybody's nerves."

I don't take back a word of that, Dennis. But I'm glad you ran for president of the United States, even though we both knew you never had a chance.

I knew you'd be back in some form. When I wrote that kiss-off column in 1979 I said: "You're young and you'll be back. You had the heart but you lacked the humility. When you come back, bring it with you."

A quarter-century later you were the congressman for my district. And you served me well in the small things that make all politics local.

You managed to get the trains rerouted so that Bay Village wasn't sealed off 15 times a day by crossing gates. You're a door-knocker, Dennis. You beat on doors and ask people for their votes. And that's because you grew up in a family that didn't expect anything unless they worked twice as hard to get it done.

But I have to say this, Dennis. I didn't think you were a very good mayor. The spirit of compromise was never in you. You were an idealist. And idealists can't govern. The concessions they have to give are too great for them to handle.

I heard your speech at the Democratic convention. I liked it. You said some things that your party was panting to hear. Things that the safe candidates were unwilling to say.

On your bed-and-breakfast campaign trail, you called for a Cabinet slot that would create a U.S. Department of Peace.

You were giggled down for that one. But why? Does it really make more sense to have a Department of Defense passing out war tools than to have another department working on peace? After the jokes are over, what's the matter with that idea?

You also talked about the weapons of mass destruction you had seen in cities like ours: poverty, bad health care, inferior education. It seems to me, Dennis, you named the destruction that erodes the soul of America. And these are things we can do something about. So why don't we start?

Dennis, you never had a chance, and you knew it. And some people are going to say that the only reason you stayed in the race was ego.

Whoever wins this election is going to win because of ego. A combination of ego and polls and fashioning speeches to pander to the voters.

I'll give you this, Dennis. I don't think a word ever came out of your mouth that you didn't mean. I frankly don't think you would have made a great president. But I think you made a great candidate. And that's why I'm glad you ran.

You tugged your party a little farther to the left. And in this jaded nation that pretends both parties are the same, that was good. You spoke up and offered a choice.

Maybe you'd revisit your mayorship. Maybe not. I know I'd take back that old column about balance. Balance can be a sellout.

You never sold out. And the older I get and the more I see, the more I realize what a virtue that is. Glad you ran, Dennis. America needs losers with tongues.

—August 4, 2004

Get out of the car, and never complain

This is a column about nothing. Unless it means something to you.

Why do we lose our wives in supermarkets?

I was in Heinen's the other day—the cultural center of Bay Village—and I lost my wife for 30 minutes.

It shouldn't have happened, because we only dropped in for a couple of items.

"We're only going to get a couple of items," my wife said. "You don't have to come in. Would you rather stay in the car?"

Now the answer I should have given was "yes." Women and their shopping habits are a far cry from the shopping habits of men.

If a man hops in the car and goes off to buy something, he's back in 10 minutes. Let's say the man wants a bag of charcoal. OK, zoom-zoom, he's off and he's back with the charcoal.

But if a woman goes out to buy a bag of charcoal, she's liable to be gone for an hour and a half. You sit and wait for her, and you begin to think about calling 911. Then finally she arrives. With a bag of charcoal.

Now what we guys don't say is something like this:

"Geez, you went out to buy a bag of charcoal. What the hell took you so long?"

We don't say that. Because we know that this is a woman who washes our dirty underwear. We know which side of the bread the butter is on. So we keep our yaps shut. But it perplexes us nevertheless.

Far worse than that is when we lose our wives in supermarkets. Here is a scenario taken from last week.

We drive up and park between two huge SUVs with blackened windows—the kind of cars that might be used by terrorists. Already I'm wondering how I'm going to back out of here without a soccer mom in a Land Rover creaming me.

"If you want to sit here and listen to the radio, that's all right," my wife says. "I'll be right back."

Now, if a guy said that to you, you'd sit there and listen to the radio, and he'd be right back. But if a woman in my generation says that to you, there is the sniff of guilt in it.

So you say, "Naw, I'll come in with you."

You walk into the supermarket together, and you pick up your cart and that's when, instantly, chaos reigns.

There are two kinds of supermarket shoppers. I am a cart-parker. My wife is a cart-stroller.

When I go into a supermarket, I park my cart near the peanut butter alley. I leave it there. Then I range around the store, hands free, to select the items I want and bring them back to the cart.

I am married to a cart-stroller. My wife regards the trip around a supermarket as a 16-day cruise to the Caribbean. Lord knows what ports of call she may make.

And she is as elusive as a spy in a James Bond novel. Suppose we go into the store for some milk. I scurry off to get my bacon, but when I come back to the cart there's no milk in sight. She has, cart and all, vanished.

But that's not the uncanny part. I prowl through the store, bacon in hand, looking for her. Looking right and left. Down the coffee aisle, down the bread aisle, back with the frozen pizzas, up front at the sushi bar (that shows you my desperation.)

But I can't find her. You lose your wife in a supermarket, and she's gone forever.

What I don't know and never will know is, where did she go? Does she have, in a supermarket, the power, like the Shadow did, to cloud men's minds so they cannot see her?

It somehow works out OK at the checkout counter. And we drive home together and never speak of our adventure.

Which is why this is a column about nothing. Unless it's about just getting along together. In which case it's about the most important thing there is.

—August 11, 2004

"Take care of yourself"

My father graduated from East Tech the year the Great Depression hit. He was a smart guy, but there was no money for college and there was no future.

He wangled a job as clerk in a peanut store on the corner of Carnegie and Ninth. The guy who owned the store smoked cigars. Once he threw his cigar butt on the floor and stomped it out with his foot and ordered my father to pick it up.

"If you don't, Roy, I got a line of people around the block looking for your job," he said. My father picked it up. He held on to his job. He was married, and he had me.

Before the war, he left that job and became a business agent for a labor union. I've got a hunch that old man Kelly's cigar butts had something to do with that.

The labor union was the ILWU. It was the chief longshoremen's union on the West Coast. The East Coast longshoremen were the ILA. The West Coast union was called commie. The East Coast union was called Mafia.

I remember when my dad left for the Navy. He left in the hubub of the old Union Terminal. I remember leaning from my mother's arms, afraid of the scowly-faced train announcer who sat on a high seat in front of a clock and bawled into a microphone:

TRAIN NUMBER 26—THE CHICAGO MERCURY—NOW BOARDING AT TRACK 26.

Everybody kissed everybody and half of them went off to war. My dad came home two years later.

He went back to his old job, but the political climate had changed. The anti-commie witch hunts had begun and my father's union was a target. My father was more right-wing than Dick Cheney, but the *Cleveland News* ran my dad's name on the front page as part of "Cleveland's Red Network."

By that time I was 12, and it was tough to go to school with my classmates' parents reading that kind of press. Now I know it was harder on my parents. My father quit the union job and got another job at a company that made little bags for little snack pies.

He had that job two weeks before the FBI came sniffing around. "You got a guy named Feagler working here?" the FBI asked.

"Yeah, why?" my father's boss answered.

"No reason. Just checking," the FBI said.

So the pie-bag guy fired my father. "You understand there's nothing personal, Roy," he said. "But I just can't have these guys hanging around."

And then my father got a job rustling baggage on the night trick at the Greyhound bus station. My mother went back to work for the first time since World War II. I was college-age then, and little Richard was going to go to college no matter what it took.

I was such a smarty pants, I was too damn dumb to realize what my parents sacrificed for me. I took so many things for granted then. When kids figure these things out, it's decades late.

My father's sweat sent me to college. I joined the ROTC and was up for a commission. One day my commanding officer called me in and said a couple of guys wanted to see me.

One of the guys was an Army intelligence captain. The other guy was FBI.

They wanted to quiz me about my father.

I have to tell you now that when this quiz took place I was engaged to be married. And I had no money. And the only future I could see was to get my gold bar and go into the Army.

They were nice, soft-spoken people, my inquisitors were.

"Did you ever talk to your father about politics?" one of them asked.

"No, sir. Not at all," I said.

That was a lie. I remembered my father, on his way to work, catching me coming in from a date in his borrowed car. We leaned against the sink at 11 o'clock. And sometimes, but not often, he poured me a shot of booze. He was not a drinker; he did it to be man-to-man.

"The lesson I want you to learn is to take care of yourself," he said. "Nobody else will take care of you. Governments promise they will, but they won't. If you want to be free from slavery, take care of yourself."

Eventually, those FBI guys who grilled me about my father's politics forgot about it and granted me a top-secret security clearance.

But all that's well doesn't always end well. I live with the fact that I lied about my father's late-night talks. I fear that labor unions today are so weak that now too many Mr. Kellys are saying, "Pick it up. I got a line of people around the block looking for your job. And some of them are in India."

I was invited to be the grand marshal of Friday's Labor Day parade. I wish my father, who is dead now, could have been there.

I had to make a speech, and this is pretty much what I said:

I know about labor. I know about unions. And I know a lot about oppression of unions from government and management. Trust me, I know.

But the American worker is the backbone of this country. He is our might, he is our strength and, when called upon, he fights our wars. Always has.

His enemy is greed. His battle cry is fairness. Shipping jobs offshore in the name of greed is not fairness. That's a swindle to American workers. And while the swindle goes on, American workers are the ones who pay the price, in blood and dollars, while the fat guys get sleek with greed.

My father voted for Barry Goldwater in 1964. He was as far away from the things he was accused of as you can get.

Maybe I got into this business to speak out against the tyrants. And maybe I got into this business because my old man worked his shift in the bus station to pay for my voice. Maybe both. But the midnight shift is what I remember. His labor brought me my dawn.

—September 5, 2004

He gave me a sob story and I bought it

Here's a time I got set up.

A guy walked into the city room and was directed to me. He had a sad story to tell.

He lived with his wife and four kids in a small house on the West Side. And, as the kids grew bigger, my guy wanted to make a room in the attic for his girls.

"But they tell me I can't," he said. "The city says that the walls of the attic are a foot too short. Otherwise, there's plenty of room up there. I can't afford to move. What will I do? Can you help?"

I went to his house and looked at his attic. It looked roomy enough to my eye. The guy showed me paperwork from the city, which said the walls were too low.

So I wrote a bleeding-heart column about him. The thrust of the column was that an oppressive government had come down hard on the heels of a poor man who was trying to keep his family together. I went home and slept the sleep of the just.

The next day, I got a call from a fellow in the city building department.

"Nice column yesterday," the building guy said. "Very touching."

I was young and dumb, but I wasn't stupid. When government calls you after you've written a story, government often has a hand full of aces.

"Was there a mistake in the story?" I asked.

"Oh, no," the building guy said, "you got it all right as far as it went. We did deny his permit to build a room in his attic."

"So?" I said.

"So," said the building guy, "why didn't you mention the other house he owns?"

"The other house?" I asked with a sinking feeling.

"Yeah," said the building guy. "Your victim lives in a small house, but he rents out another one. The house he rents out is big enough to house his kids. If he was desperate, he could move into that one. Or didn't he tell you about the other house?"

There is no worse feeling in journalism than the feeling that you have been snookered. I sat at my desk and asked myself what I'd done wrong. I'd gone to bat for a guy who had come to me with a sob story, taken me out to his attic and produced paperwork that backed up his tale of woe. I thought I had all I needed to endorse him. And he had fleeced me.

I did a slow walk to the city desk and told my editor what had happened. Trust me, that's a long walk.

"What do I do, Louie?" I asked.

"Nothing," the city editor said. "The guy in the city housing department isn't going to make a stink. Yesterday's front page is yesterday. Forget about it."

But I never did forget about it. From that day to today, if anybody hands me a hard-luck story, I demand that he comes in with what we call the doctrine of clean hands. That means I check him out thoroughly before I buy his act.

After decades in this business, you can smell the shady informants. Good journalists are a lot like good cops. When somebody comes in to spill his guts, you don't listen to what he says. You listen to what he leaves out. And what he leaves out is what trips your wire.

This is a column about Dan Rather and the CBS exposé on George W. Bush's service in the National Guard. Rather and his producers did everything wrong. They listened to what the guy had to say. They didn't listen to what he left out.

In a horrible election year when lies fly against lies, all good newsmen struggle to find a tiny piece of truth. I don't know anybody in this business who wasn't snookered like I was. But ours is a business that hates to admit it.

In this exceptional year, stark facts, accurately reported, can't speak for themselves. They are twisted through spin and ratings drive. They get lost.

Once Walter Cronkite went to Vietnam and came home and pronounced that war unwinnable. President Lyndon Johnson said, "If we've lost Cronkite, we've lost America."

This is a new generation and a new set up. Let's learn from the past and not be fleeced again.

—September 22, 2004

I demand my flu shot, by cracky

I walked into the Lakewood Urgent Care Center, strode up to the receptionist and said:

"Here I am. I'm an old man and I've got the driver's license to prove it. Lemme have a flu shot."

"Try someplace else," the receptionist said. "If you can't find a flu shot anyplace else, come back in about a month. Maybe we'll have some then."

That's when I knew that the flu news I'd read in the papers was all true.

As a senior citizen, I'm used to getting special treatment. It's a compensation for getting old. My Golden Buckeye Card peeps out of my wallet, ready for a quick draw at any ham-and-eggs restaurant that honors it. The card behind it gives me a 10 percent discount at Medic Drug any Wednesday I need a tube of toothpaste.

These cards show me that I am on the endangered species list. It's not easy to be on the endangered species list. In fact, when I turned 65 about a year ago, I railed against the whole idea.

A lot of us who are officially old and have cards to prove it still don't believe it. For me, that trip down to the Social Security office to get my Medicare card was like a ride in a tumbrel. It was the opposite end of the first day of school. I knew that when I walked out with that card, I would be certifiably old. And I didn't want to be old. Oh, I wanted the money, all right. But I didn't want to be old.

Old had been gaining on me for years. Old sneaks up on you in many ways. I guess it first got me when I didn't like pop music anymore. The musicians shrieked and pranced around the stage. I just couldn't understand it.

"Why don't they just stand there and sing, like Sinatra or Nat King Cole?" I asked anybody near me. "How the hell can the kids like this stuff? They don't know what they're missing."

The other thing that happened to me was that beautiful young women started coming on to me. This totally short-circuited my memory of those times I was such a nerd I couldn't get a date. All of a sudden, at 65, I was hot.

Thank God for my mental acuity, I figured that one out: These dames saw me as a harmless old grandpa. They liked me better than their dates. And, frankly, having seen their dates, I agreed with them.

But it did throw me for a loop. Was I young or was I old? That's a thing that all of us geriatrics really have to wrestle with.

When I was a kid, I wanted to act like a man. And, when I was a middle-aged man, I wanted to act like a middle-aged man—you know, the fount of all wisdom, cool, in command, Lauren-dressed and just superlative.

Women go through the same cycle. Middle age is hard because it's really so much of an act. Women get promoted to the head of Health and Human Resources and suddenly the Gap is behind them forever. They are off to Nordstrom with a female buddy, trying to dress for who they think they have become.

The beautiful thing about certifiable old age is, you can dress old. You just do it naturally. Winter is coming and I will wear an old Elmer Fudd cap I bought at Wal-Mart. And when I look in the mirror, that cap looks just right on me.

Well, anyway, the flu shot:

I don't like shots. Maybe, in the last 10 years, I've had five flu shots. I come from a generation that never did what was good for us, but muddled through anyway.

This year, though, I want a flu shot. The main reason I want one is because I can't get one. Tell people they can't have something and they automatically want it.

I'm going to try not to get the flu this year. I will bundle in front of my television set and watch all the drugs available to me. Erectile enhancement pills and getting-in-the-mood pills for women. Penis enlargement drugs and drugs that will pump up breasts.

It is said that we Americans have the best medical care in the world. But they're lining up in Buffalo to go to Canada to get flu shots. Maybe they don't worry as much about penis sizes and D-cups in Canada. Maybe they just worry about health.

—October 20, 2004

Giving Bush the boot is the only option

I'll vote for John Kerry next Tuesday.

My reason is simple: I think we have to fire George W. Bush.

Bush has been a terrible CEO. And when you have a terrible CEO running a company or a country, you get rid of him.

It's called damage control. First, you stop the damage. Then you figure out a way to repair it.

John Kerry may not be the perfect repairman. Like me, a lot of the people who vote for him will not be casting pro-Kerry votes. They'll be casting anti-Bush votes.

If Kerry, a largely unknown quantity, fails in his stewardship of the country, he'll be fired, too. We'll just keep trying until we put the right man at the helm.

George W. Bush is the wrong man. He not only shouldn't be at the helm; he shouldn't even be in the wheelhouse.

In the four years that he has been in office, he has:

Sent us off on an ill-advised and ill-planned war.

Used as justification for his adventure the idea that we were somehow under threat from Iraq, which we were not.

Reduced our credibility around the world by undertaking a pre-emptive strike which, understandably, makes many nations cringe.

Invented new reasons for his actions when the old ones proved bogus.

Declared, either from duplicity or stupidity, "Mission Accomplished" at a time when the "mission" had hardly begun.

Failed to explain what the "mission" is, other than to say it's a war against terror—a war he has never really defined.

Allowed his cronies who talked him into this misadventure to remain unscathed while bungling a bad war with their lack of planning.

It's time to fire him. If he goes, his cronies go with him.

Will Kerry do better? I don't know.

He will have to take office playing the hand that Bush left him. That's like starting a drive deep in your own end zone. If he gets us back to midfield, it will be an accomplishment.

On the domestic front, Bush, who talked four years ago about uniting our country, has managed to divide it in ways unprecedented in my lifetime. And my lifetime includes Vietnam.

Preaching the notion that tax cuts will allow us all to grow rich, he has spent our money fraudulently in war and in peace and left generations of our kids with an IOU that they can't hope to repay.

He has not addressed (nor, in fairness, has his opponent) the major domestic issues of health care or Social Security in any meaningful way. And these are issues that must be addressed—eventually—by somebody. Maybe Kerry won't tackle them, either. If he doesn't, he ought to be fired, too. The way I'm hoping George W. Bush is fired next Tuesday.

When I began writing columns harshly critical of Bush, a lot of you were astonished, then dismayed, then angered. The rap on me was that I had suddenly gone soft in the head. What had changed me, many wanted to know. And my answer was always the same: One man turned me against George W. Bush. And that was George W. Bush.

When somebody says that, he's called a "Bush-hater." I don't hate Bush. I'm 66 years old, and what happens over a lifespan is the hatred hormone dries up.

I've got enough left to hate the people who brought down the towers. Or to hate the scum who saw the heads off the innocent and then sell their videos to TV. Those are the guys I hate, not Bush.

I'm not a pacifist, I'm not a commie, I'm not a tree-hugger—hell, I'm not even a Democrat. I'm just an American.

I remember, when I was about 6 years old, wondering how it happened that I was an American kid. As opposed to, say, a French kid or an Italian kid. We're all accidents of birth. Rich or poor, gay or straight, black, white or brown. A roll of the dice and you could be a different person in a different place.

America, though, is really only a concept. When you hear them talk about the American Dream, they're right. We've been lucky. We've had great dreamers to lead us, and some of their dreams have actually come true.

George W. Bush has dreams, too. But they seem to be fantasy and illusion. He took one of our greatest tragedies, when everybody was united behind him, and turned it into a situation of bitter division.

The only reason this election is going to be so painfully close in the middle of a war is testimony to the failure of George W. Bush's leadership.

I'm voting for Kerry next Tuesday. It just ain't possible he can do worse.

—October 27, 2004

What's next? They left us stewing

After the bitterest campaign I've ever seen, George W. Bush and John Kerry exchanged gracious speeches last Wednesday. Both called for us to put our anger aside and come together as some sort of epoxy glue—a healing bond.

This is ridiculous.

For the entire campaign—a campaign that has lasted longer than a fractious teenager's trip through puberty—these candidates have done their best to get us to the point where we can't stand each other.

The big campaign issue this year was mutual disgust and hatred. The "despise-each-other" issue was way out front of real issues that should have been discussed, like Social Security, health care, outsourcing and the environment.

I didn't see these things on the scummy little television commercials that bombarded us in the last few weeks of the campaign. What I saw were screeds that said John Kerry, a decorated war hero, was a traitor. And that George W. Bush was a draft dodger who had somehow gone AWOL.

Naturally, these commercials got us all stirred up. That was what they were supposed to do. So it's going to be pretty hard for us to calm down just because these two accused villains have shaken hands and called for a thousand flowers to bloom.

I've already said I've seen some bitter campaigns, but there was something especially spooky about this one. Kerry voters didn't just dislike Bush voters.

Each side saw the other as almost extraterrestrial.

In my case, I had to make pacts with three of my friends that we just wouldn't discuss politics. My friends and I are gabbers. We had never had to make such a pact before, but this time we did.

If you read this column (and you've gotten this far) you know that I was on the Kerry side of this brawl.

My side lost. Bush won, and this time it was no fluke.

So, I'm going to have to get used to the idea that the majority of my fellow Americans disagree with me. And these are not evil people. They include the nice couples on either side of my house who planted Bush-Cheney signs on their lawns. And it includes my own son-in-law, who flooded me daily with pro-Bush e-mails, thinking he would—what?—change my mind.

The Democrats are now deep into the postmortem, trying to figure out how they lost and what they might have done to win. The Republicans, feathered out like peacocks on Viagra, are claiming they won because they have a lock on the moral conscience of America.

None of this musing will last more than two weeks. The simple fact is that my side lost and theirs won. They did it better than we did.

The main reason they did it better was they got out the vote. Democrats used to be famous for producing a great vote on Election Day. They did well last Tuesday. But the Republicans, astonishingly, did better.

The other thing that boosted the Republicans was the flawed calculation by the Democrats (and me) that anybody could beat Bush. Our mantra was, "Anybody but Bush." It was never, "Go, Kerry!"

So Kerry's campaign was really based on the idea that whatever Bush had done, he could do better. And, in the long run, that's not enough.

Just this last word:

I wasn't for Bush and I haven't forgotten why. But I am for the fact that however we all voted Tuesday, and whatever comes around the corner, we all have to face it together.

Four years is a long, long time. What's for sure is that the issues in front of us will require the very best of all of us. The story of our future, yet unpenned, will be better, we hope, than the story of this last election.

The future demands the best of us. This election, shamefully, did not.

—November 7, 2004

We are sick to the point of plastination

It's no news to me that I'm out of touch with modern times. Things that disgust me in today's culture are shrugged off by my fellow citizens.

The bar of decency keeps getting lower and lower. I have no idea where the bottom is. Each time I think we've found it, I'm a fathom or two too high.

Now our city is about to play host to a freak show of human bodies shrink-wrapped in plastic. The name of the show is Gunther von Hagens' "Body Worlds 2."

I quote from the press release:

"The Anatomical Exhibition of Real Human Bodies invites visitors to learn about anatomy, physiology and health by viewing real human bodies preserved through a unique method called plastination. Cleveland is only the third U.S. city to host this profound and awe-inspiring exhibition."

Cutting through the rest of the crap in the press release, what is on display in this freak show are the bodies of 20 dead people who volunteered to be "plastinized." According to the hype, this is supposed to be some kind of science-meets-art breakthrough.

According to me, what it is, is ghoulish.

I know we are a town desperate to get anybody to come here, alive or dead. So I suppose, at this low moment of civic morale, we ought to rejoice that we are only the third U.S. city to host this abomination.

After all, we have the Rock and Roll Hall of Fame and Museum. And we can't get any of those live loud-and-twitchy yowlers to show up to be canonized. So maybe playing host to a score of plastinized dead people fits our town.

The plastinized dead people work cheap, have no agents and require little from their surroundings. I would guess if you put 20 plastinized dead people down in the middle of Utah, they would have no complaints. The one nice thing about ghouls is, they don't care about room service.

A sane person might ask, "What's the point of lugging dead bodies around the country? Is there some redeeming social value in that?"

I quote again from the ghouls' press sheet:

"Guests can compare smokers' and non smokers' lungs as well as healthy and diseased hearts. Close-up studies . . . provide viewers an opportunity to re-evaluate their lifestyles and consider more healthful habits."

Every morning when I shave, I look into the mirror and consider more healthful habits. I grant you the resolve doesn't last much past the shower. But there's no way some medicine show populated with preserved dummies is going to argue me into re-evaluating my lifestyle.

Here's the biggest fraud about this whole deal: I was a kid in the Cleveland schools when the health museum invented Juno, the transparent woman. She was one of a kind in America, and we Cleveland schoolkids got bused down to see her.

I'll admit there was some prurient interest there. Few of us had seen a partially clothed woman, let alone a transparent one. But Juno was chaste. She stood there, her capillaries smoothly flowing, and gave us a peek at what was going on in our own bodies. All of this astonishing news, we promptly forgot.

That was more than 50 years ago. Since then, millions of autopsies have been performed in this country. All that we can know about the human body and how it functions is probably known.

So this Body Works show is really only vaudeville. As I said above, it is a freak show. And I think it's disgusting.

But I've learned that what I think is disgusting is merely my opinion. And the older I get, the fainter my opinion gets.

Somebody told me there's a waiting list of 6,000 people who wish to volunteer their bodies to be plastinized.

I guess we can sign up our loved ones so we can haul them out of the closet at Christmas and Easter and direct the occasional conversation toward them, not expecting an answer.

But not me. When I leave, I'm gone. And you know what? I'm beginning to think it's high time.

—April 10, 2005

Nixon blemished politics, blighted Journalism

Richard Nixon is a fading memory. The disclosure of Deep Throat's identity is interesting only to gray-hairs and old reporters.

He was the guy who squealed on Nixon. But he didn't bring Nixon down. Nixon brought Nixon down, with a lot of help from psychology. And his sycophant pals.

The Watergate story, like much of history, is a collision of the accidents of human nature. Simply put, it goes like this:

Kennedy was shot and Johnson became president. Johnson tried to prosecute the Vietnam War, which was out of control. So Johnson decided not to run again.

That left his vice president, Hubert Humphrey, as the favorite. But Humphrey couldn't figure out a way to distance himself from Johnson and the war. When he finally tried, he was too late.

Enter Nixon, who had lost the presidential race to Kennedy and then tried for the governorship in California. When he lost that one, he held a press conference and said to the media, "You won't have Nixon to kick around anymore."

He was a terrible prophet. He rose from his self-proclaimed political sepulcher and returned to mournfully stalk the D.C. graveyard. He beat poor Hubert with his "secret plan to end the war." This left the Democratic Party a shambles, and when Nixon ran again four years later, he won in a landslide.

But he was a haunted man. He haunted himself.

Every year, the president takes a physical. The results are clinically spread before the public. We hear about polyps and a trace of colon cancer and some presidents even show us their scars.

But there are no psychiatric tests for presidents. One might think that would be the most important test of all.

If anybody believed in shrinks, it should have been Nixon. But like a lot of nutty people, he didn't know anything was the matter with him. And the lapdogs around him were not about to suggest a problem. So the crazy in him ate the good.

So he left us a legacy of the bad. And we haven't recovered yet.

Journalism hasn't recovered, either. I'll tell you why I think so in a minute. But America hasn't recovered, and that's far more important.

Watergate was the beginning of the brutalization of American politics. Until then, even through the terrible years of Vietnam, Congress and both political parties struggled to find common ground. It wasn't easy. But the people in Congress thought it was their job to try to represent all of America, and to reach a consensus that would send Americans to bed each night not hating each other.

After Watergate, that all changed. We know what we have now: mud wrestling with cheering sections on both sides of the aisle. No longer do we see debates between Republicans and Democrats. Now, it's a spitting cat fight between "liberals" and "conservatives" with three cable networks goading both sides on.

No civility left. And civility, when it washes away, takes civilization with it.

Watergate eroded it. After Watergate, we were at each other's throats.

Civility is last year's dance card. A forgotten tune.

Journalism changed, too, after Watergate. When I broke in, there was no such phrase as "investigative reporter." Every reporter, whether covering an arson fire or a stickup, was supposed to investigate it.

Woodward and Bernstein changed that. Their relentless reporting on a paranoid president finally brought him down. And suddenly thousands of kids in hundreds of journalism schools wanted to practice "gotcha journalism." And they became "investigative reporters." Their goal, they said, was to "make a difference,"

When I became a newspaperman, nobody talked about making a difference. I only heard about "who, what, when, where, why and how." That's all Woodward and Bernstein were after. On the trail, they found Deep Throat. If you dig hard enough, there is always a Deep Throat or a Shallow Throat or, best of all, a Sore Throat.

Mark Felt was the Deep Throat of journalistic legend. He was also the Sore Throat of journalistic commonplace. He didn't like what was happening to his FBI, so he softly blew a whistle without a pea in it to a couple of reporters. Now he's 91 and we know who he is. And it's a bit of a letdown. We were hoping for bigger game. We got a guy we'd never heard of. The theater of his absence was more dramatic than his unmasked curtain call.

"Now I'll arrange to write a book or something and collect all the money I can," he said.

But so what. We have different problems today with new administrations that duck and lie and cheat. The questions remain the same: who, what, when, where and how.

And why.

—*June 5, 2005*

Old Glory can take the heat

When will Congress learn you can't burn the flag?

Again, a constitutional amendment prohibiting flag burning cleared the House last week. If it becomes law, which it certainly won't, it will become a crime to burn the flag.

But you can't burn the flag. That's the point these numbskulls don't seem to get.

This flag amendment comes up every year. And every year it goes down to defeat. It's like the movie *Groundhog Day*. Year after year, the jingoists in Congress wrap themselves in the flag and vote to make it fireproof.

And every year, the amendment is repeated and defeated. And every year, I write a column about why. This is really getting old, ain't it?

There are two things wrong with an anti-flag-burning amendment. The first one is a simple matter of law. So simple that the folks we send to Congress, a lot of them lawyers who learned the loopholes, ought to understand.

Suppose it was a federal crime to burn the flag. OK, what's a flag?

If I draw a picture of a flag with Crayola crayons and then set it ablaze, am I in violation of the Constitution of the United States of America?

Suppose my kid comes home from school on Flag Day with a drawing of a 12-star flag on an aqua field? Do I throw that in the garbage? Or must I give it proper burial honors?

What is the flag?

Is a flag those little toothpicks in midget weenie rolls at a picnic with tiny flags stuck on them? After the party is over, can I put them in the trash? Or am I obligated to hold a ceremony and blow "Taps" over them before I bury them in the disposal?

Would that be a crime if this stupid amendment were to pass? Which anybody with more brains than Congress knows it won't.

We send these people to Congress to run our country. We pay their salaries. We expect a full day's work for a full day's pay. And lately, we've been gypped.

With all the problems we face—this crummy war, a lack of health insurance, Social Security going bust, jobs outsourcing to India, the gas crisis and alternative energy—they have found time to debate about the burning of our flag! And they do it every year.

Wouldn't you think they'd know by now that you can't burn the flag? Oh, sure, you can burn a flag. But not THE flag.

In my lifetime, Hitler tried to burn THE flag. So did Tojo. They had some early success with a flag. But not with THE flag.

When I was in grade school, we stood up every morning and pledged allegiance to the flag in front of the classroom. I liked that. I thought, while I stood there with my hand over my heart, that I had been blessed by being born in the greatest country on Earth.

I recall my teacher telling us about the "Star-Spangled Banner." It was during the War of 1812 and Francis Scott Key stood on a boat, peering through the fog of gunfire. Then he saw the that the flag was still there. You know the words. It's what we sing at the ball games.

But had his flag been stripped by shell and shot, I don't think the great anthem would have changed. America lives in the hearts of its people.

We have carried that flag through shot and shell. It lives within us. It has, so far, been fireproof.

I had a job once when I had to fold the flag in a neat triangle and present it to a wife or a mother. What they got was much more than just a flag you can buy at Kmart.

They treasured that flag. I hope every congressman treasures that flag, too.

And I hope they protect the flag by voting against protecting it from abuse. If anybody is abusing it, they are. And they can't hide in the flag.

—June 26, 2005

Give "sources" their due—and anonymity

Journalism is not a science. I'm aware they award bachelor of science degrees in journalism. Maybe you can even get a Ph.D. in it.

But journalism is a trade. The best way to learn it is from older guys who know the streets and the dictionary. I had two great teachers. One never got past the seventh grade. The other may or may not have graduated from high school. But they knew their craft and they taught me enough to keep me in business for 40 years.

I meet young people coming up today—people I admire for their skills and education—who like to talk about the immutable rules of journalism. Rules they learned on fancy campi.

"I never interview anybody if he won't go on the record," one of these told me one day. "I set the ground rules straight right up front. If he's not willing to go on the record, I don't want to hear it."

I smiled weakly and wandered away. I thought it was the most preposterous statement I had ever heard. Without off-the-record conversations, the best journalism couldn't exist.

But for those of you not in the trade, let's get one thing clear: We don't have off-the-record conversations with "unnamed sources" and then rush to print what they tell us.

Off-the-record means, "Help me understand this." Then you check out this help with on-the-record sources to see if it stands up.

People aren't going to talk off the record unless they trust you. They have jobs and families and bills to pay. Why would they jeopardize those things for a lousy one-paragraph quote in a story about how their boss was stealing?

I have sometimes offered people "off-the-record" before they've asked for it. I usually follow that up by saying: "Here's the deal. I'll call you back in 24 hours. In the meantime, ask around about me. If you find anybody I've ever burned, don't talk to me."

Journalists and cops (both are trades and closer than they think) have this in common: A good journalist wants to know more than he can write; a good cop wants to know more than he can arrest.

But both rely on trust. You can't sell your source down the river. If you do that, the word gets out and you won't learn anything from anybody.

Forty years ago, two junkies wandered into the *Cleveland Press* city room and offered to show us where to buy heroin.

My pal Al Thompson and I were assigned to them. We never knew their names. They were John Doe. So we called one Big John and the other Little John.

They led us on a tour around the city, from Coventry to the near West Side. We supplied the money and the Johns bought the smack. We sent it over to have it tested to make sure we weren't getting scammed. It was real.

The cops closed about five addresses because of the series we wrote. The heroin went to the Johns. I watched one of them shoot up one night in a tawdry rooming house a block from the old police station. Then we left the Johns and haven't seen them since and hope they are still wandering this Earth.

We broke the law, and the cops weren't crazy about us. They thought we'd shown them up.

There was some talk about sending over a prosecutor to get our "notes" so they could nab the Johns. Or maybe us.

Well, number one, I can hardly read my own notes and, number two, by the time that prosecutor arrived, the notes would have gone missing.

If you haven't guessed, and I'm sure you have, this column was prompted by this week's Supreme Court decision not to protect journalists from revealing their sources.

The case was complicated but the message was clear: Journalists have no federal protection when it comes to confidentiality. And that will surely spook away a lot of sources who may have things to say that you want to hear.

Now we are told we must name names. That harks back to an era I had hoped we would never revisit. Name names or go to jail.

Because of its snub, the high court made it harder on those of us in the trade who need sources to come to us like penitents in a secular confessional, secure in the belief that we will honor their trust.

—July 3, 2005

Requiem

Of dead friends, past jobs, old ways

At a certain age, obituaries stir memories.

The obit page said Max Riddle had died. Max was my colleague at the *Cleveland Press*. He was an expert on pets, mainly dogs, and was internationally known. He was a writer to be taken seriously, but my memory of him makes me smile.

I remember the day in the *Press* city room, when "Irma the Body" walked in. She was a stripper at the old Roxy looking for publicity. She wiggled in with a poodle on a leash and the poodle was dyed pink.

Back then, everybody could walk into a newspaper city room. There were no security guards, no computer ID cards. Fanatics, nuts, bookies came and went as they pleased.

The city editor didn't know what to do with "Irma the Body," but because of the poodle, he sent her to Max's desk. We all peered over at Max interviewing her. If a story resulted, I don't remember it. Stories didn't always result from these incursions.

I don't think we wrote about the time a guy brought Max a device he had invented to teach retrievers how to retrieve. It was a cross-bow-slingshot affair that launched a dummy bird.

Max touched it wrong. The bird zoomed across the vast city room like a cruise missile. It slammed into the window that separated us from the staff artists, narrowly missing a wonderful genius named Bill Roberts.

Our artists were fine craftsmen who did beautiful work. They also spent a lot of time doctoring photos. We were a family newspaper and if a photo arrived showing Liz Taylor with too much cleavage, our artists flat-chested her. They also removed prominent signs of gender from photos of large dogs.

I'm nostalgic for the old newspaper business this week and I know why. For a month, I've been playing the part of a crusty newspaper editor in the Ben Hecht play *The Front Page* at Huntington Playhouse in Bay Village. We close this afternoon.

The play is salty and far from politically correct. In one scene a reporter gets excited when he hears about a love triangle that ended in a homicide. "Was she good-looking?" he asked. "Oh, they were colored, huh? Never mind."

Every time I get too nostalgic over the good old days, I remind myself that there was a lot of bad in them. When I started at the *Press*, we ignored black crime. We also ignored low-income white crime. When the report of a homicide came in, the first question the city editor asked was, "Is it a good-address murder?" Trust me, nobody would ever have heard of the Sheppard murder case if it had happened on West 34th Street.

But for all that was worse back then, some things were better. Journalists did not think of themselves as sages or monks who had taken holy orders. They were not an elite class.

The guys who taught me were blue-collar guys who managed to get a white-collar job—even if the collar was a little grimy. They didn't think their mission in life was to "make a difference."

I hate that notion. A newspaperman's job isn't to make a difference. It's to lay out the facts and trust the reader to make a difference if a difference is called for. That idea has changed astonishingly since I broke in almost 40 years ago. Later this month the newspaper I loved the most will have been dead for 20 years. I'm sure the *Plain Dealer* will graciously run remembrance.

Ben Hecht once said that newspapermen write each other's obits. This column is for Max, and all the rest of them, too. It's an obit for an era that will never come back but will never leave some of us. I'm one.

—June 2, 2002

Hope's big send-off was earned with class

I have to leave a small bouquet near the heaping tributes to Bob Hope and all that he meant to us.

He meant more to us than he ever intended. When the news of his death reached the media on Monday, all other news was shoved to the back burner. CNN and Fox spent most of the day paying homage to him. The newspapers were ready (and had been for years) to print book-length obits. Every copy desk in America knew that when Bob Hope went, there was only one headline to write: "Thanks for the Memories."

The memories go back a long way. They go back to an entirely different era, so foreign to today that it's hard to believe it ever existed.

I turned 65 yesterday. When I was a little kid, Bob Hope was just coming into his prime. There was no television then, just the movies and the radio. I had a small radio next to my bed and was allowed to turn it on before I went to sleep.

"Hi, this is Bob 'To All The Guys And Gals Serving Our Country' Hope. I wanna tell ya we're going to send cartons of cigarettes out to all you great guys in the Norfolk, Va., hospital. And now Frances Langford has a little tune to send you to sleep."

I knew he was from Cleveland. Everybody here did. He bought a piece of the Indians and, when we perennially lost to the Yankees, his writers wrote jokes about it. We felt he was ours, but by the time he died, he belonged to the world. But not this present-day world.

His humor was clean and witty. It didn't depend on four-letter words to pander for a cheap snicker. The old notion of wit fled us suddenly, long years ago, without saying goodbye. These days, if it ain't bleeped, it ain't funny. If it ain't raunchy, it ain't sexy.

Hope was a product of a different culture. When he died, the memory of that former culture died with him. So when we say, "Thanks for the memories," what we're really saying, wistfully, is we'd like to get it back. But we can't.

The great outpouring of love for Bob Hope was partially a lament for the present times. He died without controversy surrounding him. Liberals and conservatives dropped their swords and shook hands and praised him. Bob Hope was a great American, and that was one thing that all the nasty, self-serving, trash-talking, bitterly divided, bruised and ragged Americans could agree about.

He poked fun at every president, starting with FDR. But he wasn't mean-spirited about it. He flew to every U.S. battlefront from World War II to the Persian Gulf. What he thought about the wars, he never said. He was there to support the troops. He risked his life to bring them a bit of the idea of America. And, for my money, he had a better idea of the idea of America than most of our elected officials have.

He was kind to the people who worked for him. He stayed married to the same woman for 60 years. No scandal of any kind ever touched him. And he died in bed with his family around him, having lived a whole century.

Look back at that century. When he was born, there were no airplanes and few cars. There were no movies, no radio, no television and certainly no Internet.

He grew up with all of these devices. Radio made his reputation, airplanes ferried him to far-off battlefields, he was a hit in the movies and later on TV. But he stayed the same Bob Hope all the way. He knew who he was, and he was what he wanted to be. And that is the greatest epitaph anybody can write about anybody.

The day he died, one of my favorite radio announcers said, in a burst of candor: "Kids today don't know who Bob Hope is. Let's face it, most of his fans have passed on."

I won't quarrel with that. Time does march on. But in this era of Jerry Springer and rap music and reality TV, even the kids sense there's something missing. What's missing is class. Bob Hope had that until he left us. And some of us are left thanking our stars for the memory of it.

—July 30, 2003

Listening to pols, and talking to the Wall

Arlington National Cemetery is a very special place. If you've been there, you have heard a great silence broken only by a whisper of breeze. The breeze is a mother's lullaby that rocks and croons over the narrow cradles of the lost generations we have sent off to die in our name.

Next time you are in Washington, D.C., visit the Vietnam War Memorial. On a stone wall, polished like a mirror, you will see the names of thousands of Americans who died merely because they grew up at a certain time in history. The wall will reflect your face and mine. That idea—that reflection—is supposed to remind us that we all shared in the dying. Then we can turn away and walk back to the hotel. They—the 58,000 on the wall—must stay there.

And there they will stay. They will never get a day older than the date carved on their stone. You and I will sensibly and healthfully age. We will live on to hear all the TV commercials about Viagra and Botox and all the drugs that we think will keep us young. Younger than the kids on the wall who died in holes without helpful prescriptions and who we never knew. I've got a friend on the Vietnam Wall. He was a teenager when he was killed. I never got a chance to talk to him before he died. Afterward, I got to know his folks and they told me all about him.

Of course they were biased, this bereft mother and father. He was the sweetest, nicest kid, they said. They showed me a journal he had written. They told me about his hobbies. They loved him and, through them, I got to like him a lot. So, when I went to the wall, I found his name and I touched it. And the cold stone whispered that touching was not enough.

Now I talk to him. I talked to him back in my hotel room that night. I talked to him through all the anti-war protests I covered. I still talk to him, this 19-year-old dead boy. Every time they ship a new body bag back from Iraq, I think about him and I talk to him.

"Why did you go in?" I say.

"To protect the USA," he says. "To keep the Viet Cong from fighting us in San Francisco."

"Did you really think they'd fight us in San Francisco?" I say.

"That's what they told us in boot camp," he says. "But when we got there, it turned out that they didn't want San Francisco at all. They just wanted their country."

"But they were communists," I said. "You were in a war to keep communism from spreading. And you won."

The picture clouds then. The 19-year-old face fades away. And I am left with today's battle and today's 19-year-olds who are fighting it.

The attack on the World Trade Center was the worst attack on our land in American history. We had to retaliate. The dead boy on the wall would have agreed with that.

We all agreed to that. For a couple of weeks, with thousands of our countrymen dead, we were ready to take arms and fight against our aggressors. And we did.

And then it got all confused and we ended up in Iraq. It was as if we'd lost the road map. We all wanted to tear the throats out of the people who attacked the Trade Center. But they, our arch-enemies, melted away in the confusion of the moment. The war on terrorism became a war of politics. And that was the last thing we wanted. Nobody wanted to turn that 9/11 atrocity into partisan politics. But now, that's where the war is. The war is against the suits who will never see war. And now those kids, like the kid on the wall, are out there alone and looking for guidance.

Wars are brutal and brutalizing things. They are not like the Georgetown cocktail parties where they are chatted about and planned. Our kids come back from wars and they are never the same again. Career bureaucrats come back and plan for the next war. Then they send out new kids who will sacrifice anything to win a war. Like their fathers in Vietnam did and their grandfathers in World War II did.

And the wind still sobs across Arlington. It moans extra hard for the kids who died without a plan. The rustling leaves on their gravestones say, "Please, never again." But the suits are too smug to read history. They think they are inventing it.

—October 1, 2003

The news, reported from slightly above it all

Hugh Danaceau signed off last weekend. He was 74.

For nearly half a century, Hugh's voice was the Big Voice of news on various stations in our town. And what a unique voice it was. In an era when the slightest fingernail of news is overhyped, Hugh's news reports were calm, factual and slightly bored. Not boring, but bored.

"Let's not get excited tonight," he seemed to say. "Today's news is nothing that we haven't heard before. So let's stay calm and I'll give you the facts."

In his long career, he delivered the facts on WCLV radio and WVIZ television. He worked for two local commercial TV stations and at least three radio stations. On one station alone, 1100 on the radio dial, he fronted three sets of call letters—KYW, WKYC radio and WWWE. In that period, he survived six different owners. After the owners got bounced, Hugh was still around.

He had a sense of irony. You could hear it in the rich stew of his radio voice. As they say in the business, he had great pipes. He didn't pander the news; he wrote it and read it like some slightly jaded uncle who understands the human failings that make news in the first place.

He knew local politics. His father, Saul, was a respected Common Pleas judge. Hugh grew up in Shaker and he grew up in a political family. His curiosity for politics never left him. To the end, he always wanted to know who was on the inside of the political hustle.

"He had a great social memory," said Bob Conrad, Hugh's last boss at WCLV. "He knew the town, he knew its history. In that regard, he had what a lot of reporters lack."

I had just come back from vacation when I heard he had died. You get to a point in this business (or any business) when your friends start dying on you. When they go, they leave you in charge of their memories.

So when I heard that Hugh had gone, my mind flashed back to a day in 1969. And to a bar in Edgartown, Mass.

Teddy Kennedy had driven a car into a pond, and the woman he was riding with was drowned. Reporters were sent from all over the country to cover this event.

By the time I got there, there were no cars to rent. So I rented a bike and pedaled my way to the pond. Some guy was splashing around in the water.

"Are you a cop?" I yelled.

"Naw," he said. "I'm a reporter for the *Boston Globe*. My editor told me to jump in and see what it felt like."

I helped fish him out and we went back to a bar in Edgartown, where we found Hugh. He had flown in his own plane. The Kennedys managed to postpone any trial. So suddenly there was no story left and a traffic jam of reporters was trying to get out on one single puddle-jumper airline.

"I think I can fly you out," Hugh said.

I wasn't crazy about this offer. I'm not nuts about flying, anyway, and Hugh and I both had a couple of belts in us.

"How much do you weigh?" he asked.

I told him. (I was a lot lighter then.)

He did mysterious calculations on a bar napkin. "I think we can just make it." he said. That wasn't good enough for me. He went and I stayed.

That was 34 years ago. The Hugh in that memory is only 40 years old, and for me he will stay that way. The next 34 years went by so fast that every year seems like yesterday. Last weekend, Hugh left again, and again I stayed. I stayed to write his obit, which is what we in this racket do for each other.

At WCLV they knew there was something wrong. After all those years that rich stew of a voice wasn't sounding right on the air. They tried to cut Hugh's schedule in half. But it didn't work. He was still tired. Finally a colleague persuaded him to see a doctor.

Hugh wasn't a smoker. He was a health nut. He jogged and rode bikes. He was as thin as a rail. But the doctor said lung cancer, and a month later he was dead.

Had he been able to report his own death, this irony would not have escaped him. He would have done a much better job with his obit than I'm doing. It would have been shorter, slightly jaded and somewhat bored. "I'm dead," he might have said. "Haven't you heard of death before?"

So long, Hugh. My imperfect knowledge of science tells me that your voice is still up there somewhere on its way to the stars. But here, over your home town, the thin air suddenly has grown thinner yet.

—October 29, 2003

Remembering those who died fighting for lies

I wonder, every Veterans Day, if the dead vets get the breaking news up in heaven.

If they do, it must lead to some lively conversation up there.

I went through the news wires yesterday and found several headlines that might interest all of the young men and women who have died in our name.

Here's an example:

RUMSFELD MEETS VIETNAMESE DEFENSE MINISTER

The story below this headline said:

"Defense Secretary Donald Rumsfeld welcomed Vietnamese Defense Minister Pham Van Tra to the Pentagon on Monday in the first meeting of U.S. and Vietnamese defense chiefs since the end of the Vietnam War in 1975.

"The agenda included talks about closer military ties and cooperation in regional security in Asia where terrorism is a problem."

Don't you wonder how that story would have played in the part of vet heaven where 58,000 dead young Americans dwell? Their names are on that black granite wall in Washington.

They died, we now know, for empty rhetoric. Their elders, who sent them into war, warned that if we did not fight the North Vietnamese in Asia, we would have to fight them in the streets of San Francisco.

Old men lied and young men died. And now we see it was all a sham. Add one letter to sham and it becomes shame.

The communists rolled into Saigon and stopped there. San Francisco never even flinched. And now our old enemies, without even changing their spots, are greeted as friends. I wonder how that news is greeted in vet heaven. Don't tell me you don't wonder, too.

Vet heaven has freshman occupants.

A story on Veterans Day reported that a soldier from a military police brigade had been killed.

"The soldier was the 37th American to die in Iraq this month and the 153rd killed by hostile action since President Bush declared an end to major combat operations May 1."

We all remember that wonderful photo-op day. The president stood on the flight deck of a carrier in front of a huge banner that read "Mission Accomplished."

Since then, vet heaven has checked in 153 new arrivals. If the banner's message had been true, they would be home now.

But they're in heaven, well past all the lies and posturing. They're up there comparing notes with the Vietnam dead about the perfidious politicians who got them there.

Put a banner on a big boat that says "Mission Accomplished" and Fox news and C-SPAN and CNN take pictures of it, and a free political commercial is flashed around the world as a statement of truth. But it wasn't truth. It was just another lie.

And such a great big lie to tell in two short words. "Mission Accomplished." Nobody is quite sure what the mission is, but whatever it is, it obviously hasn't been accomplished. The banner was a photo-op lie.

We have to tell lies about wars. If we didn't, who would fight them? The most common lie told is this: If we don't get them there, they'll get us here."

That was the lie that opened vet heaven for our dead in Iraq. And I wonder what they thought in vet heaven when the 153rd trooper got there, dispatched on orders from a commander in chief who says he gets his orders straight from God Almighty.

If in vet heaven they get the old news, too, maybe they saw this item on Veteran's Day. Near Ypres, Belgium, an archaeologist excavated human bones and a shoe dating back to the battles of World War I.

There was a clear wire photograph of the shoe. So maybe in vet heaven one of the old-timers came shuffling forth, sock-footed, and said, "Hey, that's mine!"

Who knows? Vet heaven is just a fantasy of mine. But I like to think, as a patriotic American, that I owe such thoughts to the dead who died in my name.

All of the dead in all of the wars are humanity's mistakes.

Vet heaven should follow us every day and teach us wisdom. Otherwise, "Taps" and folded flags notwithstanding, we mock the dead.

—November 12, 2003

If this war ends, we may not realize it

On V-J Day, my mother came into my bedroom and shook me so hard I bumped my head on the maple headboard of my bed.

I guess I sniveled a little bit. But she grabbed me tight and rocked me and said, "The war is over. Dad will be coming home now."

Then she made me put on my little sailor suit. (In those war years, kids owned little sailor suits, Army suits and Marine Corps suits. These costumes arrived, automatically, beneath the Christmas tree in the years 1942–45, along with plastic bugles and toy guns and games that taught us how to bomb the enemy.)

My dad was in the Navy. So my mother jerked me, with uncharacteristic roughness, into my sailor suit and pulled me out into the driveway, where my Aunt Dorothy was waiting. My mother couldn't drive. Dorothy, who had married late, had prenuptially learned to fend for herself. Eventually, she had wed Ziggy, who had been on a military base in Kentucky but then went off to Okinawa, leaving Dorothy the sole motorist in charge of us all.

So, on that V-J Day, Dorothy bundled us into her prewar black Pontiac. I was still sleepy in the back, you understand, and Dorothy and my mother were in high spirits in the front seat.

We drove downtown, which wasn't far because we lived in Cleveland. We parked somewhere near Prospect. There was a solid crowd all around us making noise like I had never heard before. A lot of car horns. A lot of bells. A lot of cheers, especially when somebody in uniform came in sight.

I remember all that.

I was too young to remember Pearl Harbor. It's hard to separate what I recall from what was told to me. I think I recall a hush in the house and my mother saying, "We have to go over to the Yermins," because Franklin Yermin was in the Army in Hawaii. As I remember, we went. As I remember, we sat around listening to the tick of the regulator clock, waiting for the next radio bulletin.

You live long enough, and you pass—ooze, really—slowly through history. The regulator clock keeps ticking the time very well. I remembered the clock this week.

I was a reporter at the *Sandusky Register* and I'd gone to lunch with a wandering English journalist. My friend had had car trouble and he asked me if I'd mind stopping at a car dealership. I sat in the car while he went in. When he came out he said:

"I say, someone has shot your president."

At first, I thought it was a stupid limey gag. But when we got back to the city room, the radio was playing the national anthem and everybody was standing up—even the most cretaceous copy editor.

That was 40 years ago. To me, and to those my age, it seems like last week. But for many of the people who read this, the Kennedy assassination is remote history. No one under 30 can understand the shock it gave our nation.

Now the under-30 crowd has had its own shock. I guess each generation is tattooed with its own catastrophe. People now ask, "Where were you and what were you doing" when the towers fell?

When we lost Kennedy, 40 years ago, we thought we'd lost the whole idea of America. A lot of us think nothing has been the same since Dallas.

Now we know that the world is a grotesque magic show. Since 9/11, we are confronted with an entirely new state of affairs.

I wonder: In this new kind of war, will a mother awaken her son to peace and to car horns and a future? God knows.

Maybe we were better off way back then than we are now. And if we were, how do we get back there?

—November 19, 2003

Parents of dead soldier will get standard lie

The *Plain Dealer* headline said:

U.S. SOLDIER KILLED AT GAS STATION

The *New York Times* bylined story beneath it read:

"Baghdad, Iraq—A U.S. soldier was killed in the northern city of Mosul yesterday while standing guard at one of the long lines of cars that have backed up at filling stations in Iraq."

(The soldier's name was not released as of this writing. So we don't know where he came from or how old he was or whether his parents are still alive. We don't know, we readers of Page A-8, whether he had a wife or a child or children. Here's all we know:)

"The soldier from the 101st Airborne Division was killed when four men in a car opened fire about 50 yards from the gas station. In the last few days, U.S. troops have been called to guard unruly lines of drivers who often wait hours to fill their tanks because of a shortage of gasoline."

(Our U.S. soldier's home town is, for now, Anywhere, USA. Whoever he is, he is temporarily the son of all of us. The photos in the album his parents kept are just like the photos of our kids in our albums. They are always the same kind of shots. A baby on a rug, belly down, looking up. Then a little kid grinning through teeth with a gap in them. And then maybe a graduation picture, the kid awkward in his cap and gown. And maybe then, a wedding photo with the groom looking stiff and formal in a mauve, rented tuxedo, the girls in perfect hairdos. Trying, all of them, so hard to do it right, posing like a rock band.)

The *Times* story goes on to say:

"The Iraqi Oil Ministry said sabotage to pipelines was mainly responsible for the gas shortage. But U.S. officials blamed a recently resolved strike of truck drivers in Turkey, which provides some of Iraq's gasoline."

(The last picture in the photo album might have been our U.S. soldier in uniform. The Army has its own version of *in loco parentis*. After they have trained a kid in the necessary skills of killing and survival, they dress him in his private's suit and take a nice picture to send to the folks back home. To place on the piano, if there is one, or on a table near the TV.)

The *Times* reports:

"As of yesterday, 444 U.S. service members have died since the beginning of military operations in Iraq. The killing yesterday was the 193rd of a U.S. soldier since President Bush declared the end to major hostilities in Iraq on May 1."

"Hostilities" is such a clean word for violent death. Think about it. Hostility is maybe the way you feel about a new boss you don't like. Or the way you feel about the guy in the big SUV who cut you off in traffic. It is far too tame a word for war. Better words for war are "carnage," "brutality," "grief" and "despair."

But those of us who have been spared the experience of war are comfortably cushioned by the words our leaders use to describe it. That cushioning is purposeful. If the right, true and searing adjectives were used, we might think twice about sending our son off to experience war.

By our son, I mean the kid who was killed at the gas station.

What the hell was he doing there?

That's a question too cruel to ask. Too cruel for his family. I can ask it now because he is still just a U.S. soldier in a headline. I don't know his name or where he came from or how his parents got the news of his death.

When I was in the Army, as a junior shavetail, I was stuck for awhile in the role of what was called a "survival assistance officer." That meant I had to visit the parents of dead kids and explain how they died and talk about the insurance benefits that might be coming to them.

I was 35 years younger than I am now. But I knew I would have to fabricate a story that would make the kid live on as a hero to his parents. Because his photograph would be on the table for the rest of their lives. And every time they saw it (which was every day) they would need to believe that their son had died in a noble cause.

By now, somebody will have knocked on the door of "U.S. soldier killed at gas station." Whoever has that sad duty will, I am sure, not credit the kid's death to a Turkish trucker's strike or the kind of hostility that comes when the line for the gas pump is too long.

No. The parents will be told that the kid in the family album died to keep all of us free. That's what I would tell them.

And then, after the door closed behind me, I would look heavenward and say, "Free to do what?"

—December 10, 2003

"A better tomorrow?" Not for Jerry Zovko

"It's going to be a closed casket," said the Willoughby mother. "But I will see my son, whatever is left of him."

From a distant town called Fallujah, the war in Iraq has come home—yet again —to our neighborhood.

When Jerry Zovko died, horribly, the atrocity was captured on cameras and beamed around the world.

In newsrooms, photo editors looked at the pictures and tried to decide how much mayhem they could show.

This is always a tough call for photo editors. They do not wish to allow the terrible truth of war to offend their readers. On the other hand, they wish to tell the truth about war. And war is a bloody mess.

So all the photo editors made their calls. The normally staid *New York Times* ran a picture of charred bodies hanging from a bridge. Other papers showed the bodies being trampled on by militant Iraqis. I think our paper made the best call. Our front-page picture showed a young Iraqi rejoicing, hands thrust into the air, while behind him a red inferno cremated the remains of our neighbor Jerry Zovko.

What ever happened to the notion that we would march into Iraq and be greeted as liberators, having rid that nation of the loathsome Saddam Hussein?

That idea was a fantasy that is fading fast. Saddam is locked up somewhere, getting his three squares a day. But nobody threw roses at Jerry Zovko. They threw bombs instead. And now Jerry Zovko, one of ours, is dead. And his mother has to look into that casket.

According to an interview by my colleague Grant Segall, Jerry's mother, Danica, opposed the war. But her son supported it, thinking "the troops were there to make a better tomorrow."

The young Iraqi on our front page rejoicing in Zovko's death apparently didn't share this view. Zovko was there to liberate him, but he wanted no part of such liberation. So he took a bright, young American boy—one of the best we have to offer the world—and killed him. And desecrated his body.

Now the great question is, how do we respond to this Fallujah massacre? Pundits are full of opinions. Some say raze the town. Some say leave it alone and work for peace.

I say, I haven't got a clue.

People on my side of this argument never wanted to go to Iraq in the first place. We had learned from Vietnam that there is a terrible danger going into a country as an army of occupation. Every time you do it, the same kind of tragedies repeat themselves. It's all there in the history books.

Did the Bushies read history? Is their hubris so jacked up that they feel they can rise above the lessons that history teaches us?

We've come a long way since the president's "mission accomplished" speech. Now it's obvious that no mission has been accomplished at all. Iraq is a quagmire, we need more troops, we have no real endgame in sight and nobody knows what the hell we're doing there.

Those of us of a certain age have seen this kind of adventure before. We never thought we'd repeat it in our lifetime. But now we have.

I raised four kids. I gave them my best advice, but they never took it. The main thing I tried to teach them was cause and effect. "If you want to do this, go ahead and do it," I would say to them, "but if you do, this is liable to happen."

Well, they never paid any attention to me. They went ahead and did what they were going to do. And then, when it all came apart, they came back to me and said, "What do I do now?"

Bush and his cronies are into the "what do I do now?" stage of Iraq. We never should have gone there. We'll never make it work. It was at best dumb, and at worst a swindle.

But we're there. This president has painted us into a corner. A nice guy from Willoughby got caught in the corner the other day and he died.

God bless him and his family, too. How many more?

—April 4, 2004

Vietnam's over, but the lying never ends

There is a place half a world away called Ho Chi Minh City that dozes each day in the Indochina sun. Once it was called Saigon.

Turn the globe. Here are our graveyards where young Americans sleep under the sod. They died to preserve the name of a town. They lost their lives, but they never lost a battle.

They were kids, most of them. If you mingled with them they looked like a Boy Scout troop with rifles slung across their shoulders. They were there to prevent the commies from turning Saigon into Ho Chi Minh City.

The suits in Washington had told them that if they didn't stop Saigon from becoming Ho Chi Minh City, the world would collapse.

San Francisco might become Ho Chi Minh II. So they went and fought and bled and died.

The ones who died eventually got a marvelous memorial in Washington close by where the Congress makes its big decisions. An amazing number of congressmen admit they have never visited the wall.

If you didn't live through Vietnam, you can't understand it. But here's the punch line:

If you did live through Vietnam, you can't understand it, either.

Those of us who lived through it thought we would never see our nation so divided again. But we were wrong.

Vietnam never went away. The discos of the '70s and the sit-coms of the '80s and the stock market of the '90s allowed new generations of draft-free, carefree American youth to enjoy a 24-hour attention span. So Vietnam became quickly yesterday's sports score.

But now, 35 years later, Vietnam has become a central issue in the campaign for president. And, as happened 35 years ago, it is poisoned with lies.

What they ought to teach in high school is how easily the government can lie to us. Vietnam would be a textbook for that. We invaded the country over a trumped-up charge that we had been attacked. And then, for political, face-saving reasons, we couldn't pull out. So the death toll mounted while the politicians ducked.

That's what John Kerry said when he came back from Vietnam. He volunteered to go there, he was wounded, he saw and exchanged shots fired in anger and maybe he even killed somebody, which is harder to do than it looks like on TV.

But, after his taste of it, he thought the war stank. And when he came back, he protested against it.

Well, he was right. Ho Chi Minh City dozes in the Indochina sun. And the commies haven't taken over San Francisco and made it Ho Chi Minh II.

The hardest thing in the world to do is to tell a wife or a mother that her husband or her son died in vain. Everybody shrinks from that task.

And that's why Vietnam is still with us, so virulent and so strong. We got over World War II because it was a "good war." What was Vietnam? What is Iraq?

Many thought they had never seen America as divided as it was during the Vietnam War. But this is worse. Whether you like Kerry or not, he went and he served. He was in combat, and he was decorated for that.

His opposition ducked Vietnam. The vice president got five deferments. The president flew away into the sky and missed the whole show. And yet we've spent the past three weeks examining whether Kerry earned his medals.

Anybody who went to Vietnam earned his medals. The media got off to a slow start, but now the *New York Times* and the *Washington Post* have written stories saying that Kerry earned his.

So what has diverted us for the last three weeks—diverted us away from a discussion of health care and Social Security and outsourcing? Another cleverly crafted lie.

The liars dishonor the dead. They dishonor the soon-to-be dead. They dishonor America. They dishonored Max Cleland, who lost three limbs in Vietnam, by calling him unpatriotic. They dishonored John McCain by smearing him with racist nonsense.

Cleland and McCain and Kerry fought in a war that should never have been fought. But they went. Our contempt should be saved for the guys who sign the order but don't go.

—August 25, 2004

1,000 sons and daughters, each a tragedy

Before we lost a thousand in Iraq, the media were waiting.

It was a neat, round number of dead. It fit a headline or a hurriedly crafted TV special. And so, the day we turned 1,000, the media pounced and trumpeted a milestone.

But by the time you read this, we may have reached 1,011 or 1,012. Those next ones won't make as much press. But to the people who lose 1,011 or 1,012, it won't matter whether their loss is a milestone or not.

Sometime late in the Vietnam War, I traveled downstate with a photographer. We got a tip that they had shipped a dead sergeant home from Vietnam and that the parents were denying the dead boy was their son.

We bunked at a country motel and met the parents. They were plain, simple people who had sent their son, Johnny, over to fight. Johnny got killed and a telegram came home, followed by Johnny. The parents went over to the local funeral parlor to look at him. They took a look and said he wasn't Johnny.

This caused a small stir which rippled out to a minor media story. This was all before DNA testing, and though the graves registration people did the best they could with dental plates and fingerprints, they just couldn't convince the parents that this was their Johnny.

They asked people who knew the boy to look into the casket. Most people said it was Johnny, all right. A couple said they weren't sure. The Army sent somebody out to assure the parents that the identification was correct.

But the parents didn't buy it. And, as the story grew, the whole town kind of voted. Was it Johnny or not?

Eventually, they buried Johnny and then went home and tried to bury their grief.

That's been years and a couple of wars ago. I remember the headline on the story about Johnny. I didn't write it but it was a natural. It's as fresh as tomorrow: "When Johnny Comes Marching Home Again . . ."

I remember the father's face, too. He had such faith that he felt there was no way his son could have been killed in that war. He was so God-trusting that he thought the whole thing must have been a mix-up by God. He thought his son should have beaten the bullets and the odds. And couldn't possibly be in that coffin.

"Look at that nose," he said one night. "Look at that hairline. That can't be Johnny."

But I guess it was. I never heard any more about it.

Journalism is a hit-and-run business. I can't tell you whether the father still wonders if his son is in that coffin. Or if he ever forgave God.

I just remember him as an angry man who did not accept the death of his son. A man whose big farmer's hand rubbed the top of the casket as he said, "Not mine."

That was decades ago. Since then, I have seen a bit of war and covered people who send us to war. It's all pretty much the same. Those who send us don't go. And coffins still find their way back to small cemeteries in towns too tiny to make the news. Little milestones for families in little towns that are not covered by the Weather Channel.

Johnny's war is long over. We are in a new war now, though there's still a lot of talk about the old one.

Johnny comes marching home again and again. Sometimes in a coffin, sometimes hobbling on brand-new legs. Sometimes mentally scarred with nightmarish memories.

Sometimes the people around him hardly recognize him anymore. But you can't blame God or Johnny. Blame the guys who sent him.

—September 12, 2004

Through death's tears, a prayer for peace

My favorite relative was my Aunt Dorothy. After my Uncle Ziggy died, she sat in her living room, despondent. She watched a lot of Lawrence Welk reruns and chain-smoked Chesterfields.

When we visited her, she would show us her Hummel collection. And we would talk about the old days.

I recall those days, during World War II. She drove a car back then and had enough ration cards for gas. That was when Ziggy was in the service and Dorothy had a defense job that could pull some strings.

My Aunt Dorothy was a formidable force. My mother never learned how to drive, so every Monday night after the dishes were done, Dorothy would drive us to the old Shaker Show to see whatever was on. And if we got there late, Dorothy would nudge us and say, "I think this is where we came in." And we'd glide out and leave. Then we'd go to Phillips' drive-in in Maple Heights and have hamburgers.

I can see all this as if it were yesterday. But it wasn't yesterday. It was 50 years ago.

Fifty years is a lot of time. But it's like nothing when tomorrow comes to tuck us in and snuggle us up to the days and years we remember . . .

One night, years later, I was ready to go on live TV when my Aunt Dorothy called me.

"They opened him up," she said. "Ziggy's all cancer."

I looked at my watch. I had 10 minutes to go before the 11 o'clock news. So I read the news.

But she was my favorite aunt and she was calling me.

My aunt was nothing after Ziggy. She smoked her Chesterfields and watched her Lawrence Welk. And one day, trying to get up, she collapsed with a stroke and went into a coma.

They called me again. And I sat there, holding her hand.

I sat there and remembered the Monday night movies and the hamburgers, and Ziggy, too. And the question I had to ask myself was: Is this still Dorothy, or is Dorothy gone?

My vote was to keep her on the tubes. I couldn't bear to let her go. Because if I'd let her go, a part of me would go with her.

So Dorothy slept on for a couple of years in silence. In the course of those years she got infected with bed sores. And pneumonia. That's probably what she died of.

We were grateful when she died.

Thank God we didn't have to play our simple family tragedy in front of the cameras of the news networks.

While Terri Schiavo breathes her last, cameras have gathered outside. Yesterday, Jesse Jackson pulled up near the Schiavo site and addressed the mike.

He's looking for time on the air, as is Randall Terry, the out-of-date basher of abortion clinics, trying to make a comeback.

I recall my Uncle Ziggy's death. It was very private.

I know they gave him drugs to ease him out. I held my aunt's hand until it was over. And then, when it was over, we cried.

These are my private memories. They hurt. But they are part of living. Living hurts. It hurts all the way to the end, and then, at the very end, it hurts some more.

As I write this, I know it soon will be the end for Terri Schiavo. She will die unlike most of us die. She will die surrounded by a circus. And then the tents will fold, the cameras will leave, and the crowd will drift away.

And at last, she will be at peace. As I pray my Aunt Dorothy and Uncle Ziggy are—as I pray all of those who have left us are.

—March 30, 2005

In death, lessons for the living

"In the midst of life we are in death"
—*The Book of Common Prayer*

My mother died the way we all wish to die. One morning, my sister tried to call her and there was no answer. She phoned me and I called the Independence Fire Department.

When the officer called back, his voice was so soft that I knew the story right away. In fact, I felt sorry for him. "Mr. Feagler," he said . . .

"She's dead," I said.

"Yes, sir, she is," he said.

He had broken through the back door and found my mother lying on the couch, Her eyeglasses were on her chest, along with a copy of *TV Guide*. She probably wanted to find out when *Dr. Quinn, Medicine Woman* was on TV. That's how my mother went, at 84, with a heart attack.

The day she died, my father was in Marymount Hospital. We always figured that he'd go first. So, the same day my mother died, my sister and I had to go to my father's bed and break the news that my mother was gone.

I couldn't handle it. I called the Marymount chaplain, Father Joe. It was a reach-out. I'm not Catholic, and Father Joe is. He also happens to be the chaplain of the Cleveland Fire Department.

"My mother died this morning," I told him. "Now we have to break the news to my father. I thought I was a pretty tough guy, but I'm not up for this. Will you go in there with my sister and me?"

He said of course he would. We met him in his apartment in Marymount. A football game was playing on his TV. He had a bottle of fine Scotch. He calmed us down before we took the elevator up to see my father.

"Mom's dead," my sister said. And my father turned his head and cried some tears.

After that day, the care of my father was up to my sister and me. He needed 24-hour care, so we put him in a nursing home and always felt guilty about it. He lived on for some years. His wife, who had always been at his beck and call, was gone. Now we were at his beck and call. And the combination of his frustration and our guilt made his last years awful. My father didn't believe in death. He thought death was an enemy he could outsmart. The mere notion that he was dying infuriated him.

But one day, it did occur to him that he might die. He regarded this revelation as a weakness. And, trying to bargain with it, he said, "Just make me comfortable. Just keep me away from pain."

Then came the afternoon I kissed him on the forehead. And he was dead a couple of hours later. He was 91.

That's the way my parents went. Normally I don't write this kind of column.

But we have been plunged into a week of death. In the midst of life, we are in death. Last week was exceptional—a week where from a hospice in Florida to a square in Rome, we've been forced to confront questions of mortality. Questions we normally duck.

I called Father Joe this week. It had been a long time since he held out a Kleenex to dry my tears. He's still at Marymount and still chaplains the Fire Department.

I wanted his take on the Schiavo case and the pope's illness. I guess I wanted his take on life and death.

"That we pretend that life never comes to an end is merely denial," he said. "We all wish to deny it. But if we do, we deny reality. This week told us we have to be ready for death. And ready to help our loved ones through it."

In the midst of life, we are in life. What we can learn from death is how to live.

—April 3, 2005

Get out the memories and take a long look

Memorial Day.

I remember high school when we read about Woodrow Wilson, who said after World War I, "This is the war to end all wars."

Then he busted his brain to get us to join the League of Nations. But he failed, defeated by an isolationist corps in Congress.

I remember FDR, who, before World War II, said that he had seen war and wanted no part of war. But soon we were in it.

I covered Lyndon Johnson here at Public Hall in 1964, when he said, "I'll never send American boys to fight on Asian soil."

But, pretty soon we were there.

Our weapons are way ahead of our brains. Certainly ahead of our mouths.

On tomorrow's official day to remember things, I'll remember sitting in an ROTC class in 1958, listening to a veteran captain who told us:

"When they invented the crossbow, it was such a lethal weapon that people were predicting that war was dead. And then somebody invented gunpowder. And then eventually, the airplane came along and then bombs with it. Gentlemen, there is no weapon of war so terrible that somebody isn't ready to use it. That's why you're here."

Tomorrow, we remember all wars fought from the crossbow to the Humvee. Was my ROTC captain right? Is war inevitable?

When we buy our hot dogs and potato salad and beer for this three-day Memorial Day vacation, will we even think about the question? Do we care?

Memorial Day is a good day for memories in general. It's a good day to think about where we were yesterday and where we are today. To me and people my age, yesterday is gone and today it is a dry leaf pressed in a book. Yesterday's prom date. Yesterday's prom year. Dry in the book. But not evaporated in the mind.

I remember the oil crisis in the '70s, when we all were supposed to buy compact cars. We pronounced the big gas-guzzler dead forever. Now, the parking lots are full of housewives driving leviathans. On Memorial Day, who remembers the compact car?

I remember the day our grandmothers could sit in the same room with the rest of the family and watch television without being shocked by sex and violence.

I remember when dirty words were banned from TV. I remember when you could have humor without them. Now the F-word gets an automatic laugh.

I remember when the nightly news was only 15 minutes long. But there was news in it. Now it drones on all day and it's filled with Pablum.

I remember when people dressed up to go to church.

I remember when people dressed up to fly on an airliner.

I remember when the airlines gave you a meal and a comfortable seat and were worth dressing up for.

I remember when there were dress codes in school. I remember when teachers enforced them. I remember when teachers could enforce the rules without getting sued.

I remember when the Cleveland schools were among the best in the country. I remember when it made you proud to attend one.

I remember when, before busing, the schools were integrated.

I remember when Euclid Avenue was one of the fanciest streets in the country. I remember the department stores on the Square and the mansions farther east. I remember when we had no state tax or city income tax and still did well here.

I remember a time when we were afraid of the Russians and their bombs, so we all went into the military. I remember seeing my friends home on leave. I remember New Year's Eve parties with everybody dressed in their Class A's and somebody saying, "Hey, we got some nurses at the party."

Looking back, those days seem better than now. But Memorial Day is supposed to make you look back.

Most of my memories on Memorial Day apply only to me. The question is, what kind of memories are we making today for the kids who come after us? It's a cinch we haven't fought the war to end all wars. And we're a far cry from the peace that ends all wars.

My father's generation thought it had given us peace. I guess every new generation feels that way. On Memorial Day, we thank the dead and pray that we can make tomorrow better than today.

—May 29, 2005